PENGUIN

ONE TO ONE

Rosemary Dinnage was brought up in Oxford and in Canada. She has worked in publishing, as a translator, in journalism and as a research psychologist. For eight years she was Research Officer at the National Children's Bureau, where she wrote a series of books on child care. She is now a freelance writer and a frequent contributor to literary journals in Britain and the United States. Her biography *Annie Besant*, in the Penguin series 'Lives of Modern Women', was published in 1986. Rosemary Dinnage lives in London and has two grown-up sons.

Rosemary Dinnage

ONE TO ONE

Experiences of Psychotherapy

PENGUIN BOOKS

PENGUIN BOOKS

Published by the Penguin Group
27 Wrights Lane, London w8 5tz, England
Viking Penguin Inc., 40 West 23rd Street, New York, New York 10010, USA
Penguin Books Australia Ltd, Ringwood, Victoria, Australia
Penguin Books Canada Ltd, 2801 John Street, Markham, Ontario, Canada l3r 1b4
Penguin Books (NZ) Ltd, 182–190 Wairau Road, Auckland 10, New Zealand

Penguin Books Ltd, Registered Offices: Harmondsworth, Middlesex, England

First published by Viking 1988
Published in Penguin Books 1989

Copyright © Rosemary Dinnage, 1988
All rights reserved

Printed and bound in Great Britain by
Richard Clay Ltd, Bungay, Suffolk
Filmset in Lasercomp Ehrhardt

Contents

Acknowledgements

I want to thank everyone who encouraged me in this project and helped me to find people willing to talk about their experiences; in particular, I should like to thank those people themselves for generously exploring thoughts and feelings that were often hard to talk about .

For quotations used in the text, I am indebted to the following:

Carcanet Press Ltd: Hilda Doolittle, *Tribute to Freud*, copyright © Norman Holmes Pearson, 1956, 1974, 1985.

Chatto and Windus: quotation from Sarah Ferguson, *A Guard Within*.

Constable: *The Letters of Vincent Van Gogh* (3rd edn, Fontana, 1970), ed. Mark Roskill.

Karin Obholzer, *The Wolfman: Conversations with Freud's Controversial Patient*, English tranlation copyright © 1982 by the Continuum Publishing Company. Reprinted by permission.

André Deutsch Ltd: John Updike, *Problems and Other Stories*, copyright © John Updike, 1980.

T. S. Eliot, *The Cocktail Party*, Reprinted by permission of Faber and Faber Ltd.

Philip Larkin, 'This be the Verse', reprinted from Philip Larkin, *High Windows*, by permission of Faber and Faber Ltd.

Samuel Beckett, *Waiting for Godot*, reprinted by permission of Faber and Faber Ltd.

T. S. Eliot, *The Cocktail Party* (US edn), copyright 1950 by T. S. Eliot, renewed 1978 by Esmé Valerie Eliot. Reprinted by permission of Harcourt Brace Jovanovich, Inc.

Alfred A. Knopf Inc. Sudkir Kakar, *Shamans, Mystics and Doctors: A Psychological Inquiry into India and its Healing Traditions* by Sudkir Kakar, copyright © Sudkir Kakar, 1982.

Macmillan Publishers Ltd: Rilke, *Selected Letters 1902–1926* copyright © 1947 by Rainer Maria Rilke.

Hilda Doolittle, *Tribute to Freud* (US edn), copyright © 1956, 1974 by Norman Holmes Pearson. Reprinted by permission of New Directions Publishing Corp.

Pan Books Ltd: Maria Cardinal, *The Words To Say It*, copyright © Marie Cardinal, 1983.

===== Acknowledgements =====

Pan Books Ltd: Maria Cardinal, *The Words To Say It*, copyright © Marie Cardinal, 1983.
Søren Kierkegaard, *The Concept of Dread*, trans. Walter Lowrie. Copyright 1944 by Princeton University Press. Copyright © 1972 by Princeton University Press. Unwin Hyman: Sudhir Kakar, *Shamans, Mystics and Doctors*.
Urizen Books: Tilmann Moser, *Years of Apprenticeship on the Couch*, copyright © Tilmann Moser, 1977.
Van Vactor and Goodheart: Marie Cardinal, *The Words to Say It* (US edn), copyright © Marie Cardinal, 1983.

Introduction

Unless disabled from communicating, people in mental distress have always, naturally enough, turned to others for support, and talked about what ailed them. Nevertheless the idea of a 'talking cure' proposed by Breuer and Freud in the 1890s did have something new in it – chiefly a new kind of listening. Patients had talked, and doctors and others had listened, after their fashion; but it had not occurred to the doctors to eschew tonics, diets, water cures, electrical cures, hypnosis and the rest, and arrange a time every day for the patient just to be listened to. The talking method was combined with another simple but radical idea: that what was in the unconscious level of the mind had got there because of its *unacceptability*, and that this was what caused the nervous symptoms. Bring back as much as possible into consciousness, and the tension would subside.

It would be ridiculous to say that Freud discovered the unconscious. For at least fifty years before he began to write philosophers and psychologists – Janet, Taine, von Hartmann, Myers, Dessoir, Ribot, Carus and Sully among others – had been obsessed with the multiplicity of the self and the fact that most of it lay outside the bounds of awareness. In the unconscious, said Taine, 'innumerable currents incessantly meander without our being conscious thereof'. 'If the activity of peripheral soul-life is not connected with that of the central soul-life,' Carus wrote, 'the central soul can know nothing about the processes that take place in the peripheral regions of our mind. Accordingly we call them *unconscious*.' And about dreams, he continued: 'An association is produced, and the whole chain of the dream-memories or a great part of them can be hauled up, as it were, to the surface of conscious recollection.'

Two things in particular had shaken the conception of a simple and single soul by this time – the phenomenon of hypnosis and the existence of multiple personalities and hysterias. Even earlier, the Romantic writers in England and Germany had focused on the self and its multiplicity. And during the nineteenth century the number of words beginning in 'self' proliferated; Bain's textbook of 1868 devotes a chapter to 'The Emotions of Self', among them self-esteem, self-gratulation, self-complacency, self-conceit, self-respect, self-abasement and self-reproach. Freud grew up intellectually in a world fascinated by the various strata of consciousness and the self's contemplation of itself.

What was missing, though, was a working model of the multiple self that would also link it with mental functioning, with illness and health. What Freud essentially supplied was the idea of *defence*, of a vulnerable self that defended itself by pushing painful things out of reach. Where defence worked badly, mental unease resulted and could best be helped by fishing for what had been repressed. Halfway between conscious and unconscious was the area of dreams, fantasies and muddled speech or actions, all of which now could be seen to have meaning in the schema and could profitably be studied. However much has changed in the theory and practice of psychotherapy since Freud's time – and no doubt he would be astonished by some of the material in this book – this was, and remains, the rationale of the talking cure. (Whether it is a cure and whether it has chiefly to do with talking remains to be discussed, however.)

In the ninety years since the idea of the talking cure appeared a vast literature on the subject has been produced, almost all by practitioners for practitioners. Modern theories and therapies now bear about as much resemblance to the prototype as a television set does to an early radio receiver (not an exact analogy when it implies that the former is better than the latter, for the early cases seem sometimes to have been rather successful). In all this literature, much of which describes individuals' case-histories as seen by the therapist, there has been very little written by patients describing how it felt to *them*. I thought, therefore, that it was time they were heard.

There is no way that such a small-scale project could claim to *prove* anything or to be typical of psychotherapy* as a whole. A scientific study depends on choosing an absolutely representative sample of people to be interviewed, and of course this was not possible. The voices you listen to here are those of people found by a quite unscientific method; simply, I tracked down everyone heard of who was, or had been, in individual therapy (I excluded group therapies of any kind, though several interviewees mention them). Only three people declined to be interviewed. I conducted about forty interviews, and chose twenty – the most vivid and fluent. Women outnumber men, as it seems they do in therapeutic practice; it was much more difficult to find men who were prepared to speak freely. I have made no attempt to subdivide the stories, to take up points or analyse them. Each person's story seemed so much of a piece that I felt it would be a pity to interrupt it. Names and identifying details have, of course, been changed.

How 'true' are these stories likely to be? Some psychotherapists, I am sure, would object that therapy is such an emotional experience that patients cannot describe it with any kind of objectivity, especially those who are still undergoing it. The pseudonymous analyst Aaron Green in Janet Malcolm's *Psychoanalysis: The Impossible Profession*, for example, compares the analysis to something happening almost under an anaesthetic:

---

* The use of 'psychotherapy' and 'psychoanalysis' is confusing. Strictly speaking, psychotherapy is any kind of therapy for the mind, including psychoanalysis. The term is also used more specifically, however, to mean a less intensive form of treatment than psychoanalysis; usually fewer sessions, a chair instead of a couch, more focusing on day-to-day life than on unconscious meanings. There is no cut-and-dried distinction; some analysts do 'psychoanalytic psychotherapy' once a week, some therapists see patients as often as analysts. To make it more complicated, the main schools of psychoanalysis are subdivided; different trainings, different emphases; some lay analysts, some doctors. Then there is the psychiatrist, who in Britain, but not in the United States, is a doctor working in a psychiatric hospital and not usually doing psychotherapy; the clinical psychologist, chiefly doing tests and assessments; and the counsellor, often working specifically with marriage problems or bereavement. Some of the people interviewed knew exactly what type of therapy (in the word's broad sense) they were getting; some had no idea. I have left out all references to specific schools of thought and types of therapy, as they are immensely confusing, and asked interviewees simply to describe their experience. In this introduction I shall call the whole field 'psychotherapy'.

'At the end of *A Midsummer Night's Dream*, the human characters wake up and rub their eyes and aren't sure what has happened to them. They have the feeling that a great deal has occurred – that things have somehow changed for the better, but they don't know what caused the change. Analysis is like that for many patients.'

I think this underestimates patients' awareness. The individuals whose interviews I chose to include were, I felt, being as honest as imperfect mortals can be; the imperfect bits are for the reader to make up his or her mind about – but psychotherapy does, after all, make people very expert in talking about their feelings and experiences. The few interviews that did seem really guarded or defensive were not chosen.

It is also true that a patient's emotions about his or her therapist are often very intense; can these possibly be described as they are? They can be described as they *feel*, and again I think a lot of people were able to explore them honestly – sometimes with indignation, surprise or amusement. The therapists' side of the story might be very different of course, but no more valid.

The one big question raised by these interviews is: does psychotherapy work? No complicated answer will be attempted here. It is not unlike asking whether marriage works or education works, and the short answer is obviously 'sometimes'. One-third of marriages end in divorce, perhaps another third are highly successful, and the rest somewhere between. Out of the twenty interviews here, a few speakers are disappointed or angry, a few deeply impressed and grateful, and the rest are a mixed category. They had a bad experience of therapy and then found a better one; or they are in the thick of their treatment and don't know the outcome; or they feel that something was gained, though less than they hoped; or that it was gained at more expense of time and money than they would have liked. And the question arises, who is to judge success, the patient or the onlooker? If someone spends half a lifetime in psychoanalysis with modest results but does not regret it, is this success? There is the point that, unlike dentistry or appendectomy, the treatment is interesting in itself; that, indeed, the travelling is sometimes so hopeful that arrival is shunned.

Is there, in fact, a final arrival point? Although we started with the term 'talking cure', the word 'cure' now seems to be taboo among therapists (one of the interviewees not included said she could always get a rise out of her analyst by mentioning it). In her interview Ruth asks what there is to cure, after all; depressions, Patrick might answer, or panic attacks, David could say. The patients here have started from very different points: some from symptoms that were quite disabling, others from a sense of incompleteness or loneliness or failure. A few had a fairly well-functioning life but wanted something better. Some knew exactly what they wanted, some just hoped for relief from misery, some found that they wanted different things than they had thought.

The patients that Freud and Breuer saw in the 1880s and 1890s were much more likely to come with something that did ask for a cure, a paralysis or a tic or a non-organic pain; but now that everyone knows that a stomach-ache is what you get when you are nervous, a cold when you are miserable, high blood pressure when you are overstressed, it takes some naïvety to reproduce those early hysterias. End-points as well as starting-points differ greatly, therefore, and make criteria of success and failure that much more difficult.

Some of the interviewees talked about how things would have been if they had *not* undertaken therapy. I would like to take two potential patients from pre-Freudian days and speculate on how they might have fared if they had had therapy: James Boswell and Alice James. We know a lot about them because, of course, both kept diaries.

Boswell was the son of a strict and disapproving father and a retiring mother about whom we know little. One of his brothers was kept in custody for supposed insanity. James Boswell's symptoms were severe depressions, alcoholism (later in life, as a result of the depression) and compulsive whoring, though he was quite happily married.

Alice James was the sister of the writer Henry and the psychologist William, and of two other brothers. Both of the latter had fairly disastrous lives, and William had a long period of neurasthenia and breakdown. Family pressures were subtly confusing and depressing, and Alice as the only girl was the most affected by them. She was not pretty or gentle, and was offered no chance to marry. Until her death from breast cancer at 44, she became gradually more and more of an invalid with unspecified pains, which her doctors ascribed to nerves.

Would Boswell and Alice James have fared any better in the age of psychoanalysis? Both, like most diarists, knew a great deal about themselves. Boswell was very aware of the deadly relationship with his father, but seldom spoke about his mother. His psychotherapy would perhaps have focused on his relationship with her and with the other women in his life, and on the causes of his anxiety. Let us guess that it would not have been very successful – depression and alcoholism are both hard nuts to crack – but that he would have revelled in it, changed his analysts frequently over a twenty-year stretch, entertained them mostly but bored them every time he got the pox. His wife would have been relieved to have him with the analyst rather than the whores. His diary would have been slightly less interesting.

Let us imagine a better outcome for Alice James. Her dominant emotion being rage rather than anxiety, with a competent therapist she would have had a chance to vent her intermittent hatred of her family. She would have lost her physical symptoms but become very sad; she would have wept at not being able to find a life companion. When this passed, she would perhaps have become a feminist, like Freud's patient Bertha Pappenheim, and a strong-minded, successful social worker. She would have continued to love her brother Henry, but firmly rejected the patronizing advances of William.

And then again it might have gone the other way: Boswell might have stopped drinking and damned his father, and Alice James might have stayed permanently crippled by bitterness.

Lurking behind these imaginary case-histories is the question of free will. Sergei Pankeyev, the 'Wolf-Man' of Freud's 1918 paper, who was interviewed in his extreme old age, pointed out the fallacy in Freud's statement that psychoanalysis gives one a ticket to get well that one can *choose* to use or not:

Freud said that when one has gone through psychoanalysis, one can become well. But one must also want to become well. It's like a ticket one buys. The ticket gives one the possibility to travel. But I am not obliged to travel. It depends on me, on my decision.

That point of view meant that he recognized free will, doesn't it? . . . According to Freud, one really would have to say that once everything has been cleared up, the person should have to become well. And not that he is free to decide for health or not. But that idea with the ticket invalidates that.

As Pankeyev implies, what, after all, lies behind the refusal to use the ticket? Damage to optimism, to generosity, that was not repaired by the analysis? Psychotherapists in general try to eschew the notion of blame, but here Freud is, in effect, distinguishing between 'good' and 'bad' patients. Evidently the problem of free will is no more soluble in the matter of therapy than anywhere else.

What, according to these interviewees, makes for success, what makes for failure in therapy? The factors involved must be so many, so tightly knit that it is doubtful if they could ever be really unravelled. Those who practise psychotherapy will be able, I hope, to scrutinize carefully what these patients have to tell them (and to remember that the point is that this is what it *felt* like). There are a few pointers. 'He [or she] liked me!' was the astonished discovery of several patients, who linked it with the beginning of liking themselves. Philip, Elizabeth and Véronique raise the issue of forgiveness of people who have damaged one; but not, Carmel says, before the expression of anger. Helen, Jeffrey and others talk of acquiring a sort of internal helper who stays around for life. 'I felt safe', Sarah says, and others imply the same. 'We shared jokes and found out things and a weight fell off my shoulders', Andrew says. It was the therapist's personality, say several: 'Strong, healthy, rock-like', 'real enough to make me feel it's worth being real', 'He never hid or pretended to be what he wasn't.' Acknowledgement: 'The more you start owning things, the more the emptiness and the sense of self fills up.' Survival: 'I survived it. It was as if whatever negative thing came, I was in the end able to cope with it.' Foundations built, say Hugh and Jeffrey.

Jeffrey adds: 'There's a mysterious element in there . . . What catalyses all those elements into healing someone, I don't know.'

What goes wrong? Never did he say anything encouraging, according to Elizabeth; and she describes how her analyst decided to stop saying 'Good morning' because it was too communicative. 'He didn't feel safe', Helen says; Sarah says, 'She was afraid of me.' Antoinette: 'You do have a capacity to see yourself, and they override it, they undermine it. My sense of myself is tremendously important to me, and if I'm enclosed somewhere with someone and no verification, then I'm at this person's mercy.' Véronique: It was 'a terrible caricature of what it should be . . . a misunderstanding of what the whole business is about.' Philip and Alexander both talk of difficulties that went too deep for their analysts to handle: 'My problem is that my need is so great that I can't be satisfied. There's an insatiability, there's the unbearable quality of becoming aware of the frustration of the need.' 'My difficulties went very deep, very deep indeed, and psychiatrists in general have only had limited experiences in analysis themselves and so they don't really know what you're talking about.'

So the talking cure is not always a cure and not always to do with talking – laughs and sobs and silences are often spoken about here. It has something in it of medicine, religion, love-affair, addiction, education; the latter in particular – Alexander says he feels when he is with other people as though he can see an extra dimension that they miss. Unsuccessful so often as treatment, perhaps it could be compared to learning to read, with the blessings and drawbacks of literacy. The venture itself and the seeing of the extra dimension (which, of course, does not come necessarily or only from therapy) are, at any rate, certain special twentieth-century phenomena – phenomena that have been approaching for two hundred years of increasing self-consciousness.

'I have two or three, perhaps four friends, but I am forced to be a different man with each of them', wrote Delacroix in his journal. 'It is one of the saddest things in life that we can never be completely known and understood by any one man.' Whether that *is* possible or not, people have wanted it. And when Amiel wrote this, also in a journal, Freud was a schoolboy of 15:

Introduction

It is indeed very interesting to have an immediate consciousness of the complication of one's organism and the play of one's machinery. It is as if my joints were loosening and parting just enough for me to have a glimpse of the way I am put together and and a distinct feeling of my fragility. This makes personal existence an astonishment and a curiosity. Instead of seeing only the surrounding world, one analyses oneself. Instead of being a single block, one becomes legion, multitude, vortex, one is a *cosmos*. Instead of living on the surface, one takes possession of one's inwardness.

Helen

There may be a great fire in our soul, but no one ever comes to warm himself at it, and the passers-by see only a little bit of smoke coming through the chimney, and pass on their way. Now, look here, what must be done, one must tend that inward fire, have salt in oneself, wait patiently yet with how much impatience for the hour when somebody will come and sit down near it – to stay there maybe?

Vincent Van Gogh: *Letters*

Helen is beautiful and animated, the opposite of her own view of herself. While she talks she uses her hands as eloquently as an actress. Thank heavens, she says, this pretty north London flat is so cheap; she is chronically without money.

———————

I'll do my best to give you as coherent a picture as I possibly can. But I've got to say now that I'm still befuddled about the whole thing so it'll inevitably come across as a mess and a muddle.

Don't worry if I burst into tears – I'll try not to, but I'm extremely prone to tears.

You see, I had reached one God-awful, three-dimensional full-stop. It was a black hole that I fell into, and it went on and on and down and down. Though in a way I think I was destined to have psychotherapy from the moment I was taken from the womb. It's like being born with a bank overdraft: all the time you're going on and on drawing overdraft after overdraft until the time comes when you just say, dear God in heaven, where do I go from here? It's not worth taking another breath. And you just *sit*. You might as well be a little lump of protoplasm.

As far as I'm concerned, my parents are the worst thing that ever happened to me. I love them dearly, but Jesus Christ they were more than bad news to me! They had every good intention, but they themselves were damaged people. They'd been damaged by their parents; you know that awful phrase that I believe the psychologists use – cycles of deprivation. And I'm quite sure that with me the buck rests. I don't want to have children of my own, because I feel that I'd bring up somebody who is perhaps – horror of horrors – even worse than me and has even more of a hell of a life trying to cope. There's a marvellous Philip Larkin poem – I think about it over and over again; I recite it to myself when I'm doing the washing-up. It starts:

> They fuck you up, your Mum and Dad,
> They may not mean to but they do.

It's the last verse I like:

> Man hands misery on to man;
> It deepens like a coastal shelf.
> Get out as quickly as you can,
> And don't have any kids yourself.

Now, that – it's very short, it's not terribly deep or esoteric, but it says it all. Really that sums it up.

I've got to get over my parents, you see, that's why I've been such a bad patient. One's supposed to find out what's gone wrong and – in the therapists' parlance – mourn it, and then move on. I've never got past that bloody stage of mourning it so that I could move on. I can't seem to leave it behind. There's obviously something in that misery, in the muddle, that I'm still feeding on – getting something out of it.

In my family the academic was immensely important. My father was a doctor, and I think he probably did have a good brain – he passed all his exams with flying colours. He was very much a science-based man and felt that that was the only way to think. I was the first-born. Like a lot of first-born children, there were very high hopes for me. To quote my father, they expected me to be Einstein and Isaac Newton rolled into one. First of all, I was a girl, and I don't think that was quite what they'd wanted.

They hadn't worked out what they wanted, but when they got a girl, they thought, gosh, what is this? Especially my father.

It became obvious fairly quickly, I think, that my brain wasn't going to work in the way that was the approved way. I have one of these woolly arty-farty brains (again my father's sort of language) that doesn't think in a scientific, intensely logical way, just sticking to the facts. I was always trying to deal with the emotions – struggling to get at them. There were no emotions in our family. Never anything acknowledged. If you got angry in our family, you could only tell it by the quiet. People got more and more quiet until . . . The only exit line for getting quieter and quieter is to leave the room, which is what always happened. There were never any slanging matches, it was always tense and quiet. It was: well if you really feel like that about it, then there is nothing more that we can discuss.

And then days of silence. It was my father's *anger*. It held the whole house in thrall. And if he was angry with you, he was angry with everybody and he wouldn't speak. So everybody was sucked into this vortex, and it was *terrifying*. It was literally like walking on eggshells; you knew that if you did anything that irritated him you would unleash this, this . . . He never physically hit us, that was probably what was worst. It was just this dreadful potential for anger that he always seemed to have with him. It was like a nuclear pile threatening to go critical all the time. You know, we all used to go round silently and my mother's face would be set in *granite*, as though she was going through a long dreadful illness, and we'd all feel terrified and feel guilty – oh! too awful for words.

Anyway, I've struggled with all that and in particular with the academic problem, because all the time I was trying to force myself into the sort of daughter he wanted and please him in the academic field, which was the only way he wanted. And just completely failing, utterly. Because I always thought in the wrong way, in a way that was unacceptable, I just stopped thinking. To this day I go into a panic if somebody says to me, 'Well, Helen, this is a book we're thinking about publishing – what do you think?' My mind wipes clean; it's the same old panic, the same old fears. And I *cannot* learn, I can't walk into an examination room, I can't take a driving test.

Anyway, to try and sort of keep my end up within the family, so to speak, I chose to be busy – one always had to be seen to be busy and occupied and have a product at the end of it. So my thing was cooking; you know, it was non-committal, and it was feeding the family. And they said, 'What do you want to do? You like cooking, don't you?' I was a really sullen lump of a teenager, just sitting there and shrugging; I must have been dreadful. I have a tremendous sympathy with them, coping with somebody like that. I didn't come up with a suggestion of my own, because I'd *erased* myself. I couldn't. I bent over backwards to be the creature *they* wanted, and I'd wiped out Helen a long, long time back. So it was to be cooking.

Actually, I think I surprised everybody, including myself – I managed to get eight O-levels. I worked for three weeks in my entire school career, that is the three weeks before the GCE, and I managed to pull that off. I hated school. I hadn't a clue to what I was doing there, none of it made any sense. I was dreadful in a crowd, and it was a huge comprehensive. I didn't have to do an 11-plus, which my father maintained was the luckiest thing that happened to me because I'd never have passed. I suppose he was right. I was in a huge class, never turned up, never did anything – nobody ever missed you! So I couldn't wait to leave, and I came to London to do a course in Home Economics. And of course, not surprisingly, it was a repetition of my school career. I hadn't a clue what I was really doing, and all these – horror of horrors – exams! But somehow I struggled through.

So I started cooking food for photography. I was always extremely bad at earning a living; I never had any confidence whatsoever. But for the fact that fairly early on I met a photographer and lived with him, I wouldn't have survived financially. It was just the pooling of our very meagre resources that enabled us both to struggle on. So I went on till I was about thirty, doing all sorts of things in the food world, trying a little bit of this (but I'm no good at it), a little bit of something else (not much good at that either) until I got to the stage where I was heartily sick of food. I'd had it up to here; I'd had enough.

I got myself accepted with a grant to do speech therapy. I'd always thought I wanted to do medicine, be my father's daughter, please Daddy – I'm still at it – but of course it was far too late and with the qualifications I hadn't got it was laughable. So I looked around for something that was peripheral to that, and speech therapy seemed to be something I might be able to do. My father thought it was a waste of time. You know – what the hell use is a bloody speech therapist? What do *they* do to get patients out of hospital? – all that sort of thing. I thought perhaps I'd be able to cope, but actually it was worse than it had ever been before. I would sit in the lecture thinking, I'm never going to be able to do this, I'm not going to be able to remember this. And I'd turn round to look at somebody else's notes and then think, Jesus Christ, I've missed a bit and I don't understand what she's saying now. And it was a sort of spiral and by the end of the day I'd come home and just sit and shake. And I got to the stage where I started crying in the lectures, I just couldn't stop myself. I remember the final day I was just in floods of tears – there was a lecture on phonetics – and I had to leave the room. I walked out of the building and it took me about three hours to get home. I couldn't cross the road, I couldn't remember where I was going. I had just sort of blown up and scattered my parts to the wind.

And I came home and I realized that this was the end and I could not go on. It took me the whole weekend to pluck up the courage to phone my parents and say 'I can't go on'. My poor mother had to come down on the train and collect me and take me home. And I stayed there for about two months and I don't think I ever stopped crying for more than five minutes – I don't think that's an exaggeration.

My father was in practice with another doctor, who'd known me all my life. He saw me first of all, and I realize now, looking back, that he was a very depressed person himself. I remember him sitting in our drawing-room and saying 'Life is a very lonely business.' He just really talked about how he felt about his own life. It seems to be a very common thing when you're in a deep depression, people come and tell you how much of a struggle their life is. It's very, very few people who listen. I realized soon after I got home that it was the worst place on God's earth that I could have been, that these people were the last people who could help me, because this was where it had all started.

Then I was shunted along to the hospital to see the consultant psychiatrist there. He was the most inhuman person I ever encountered in the whole of my time. I just had the overwhelming impression that I was a silly little girl who'd reached a stage in her life where she didn't know what to do next, and if she'd just settle down and get married and have children she wouldn't have time for this self-indulgence. It was – 'Well, I have to oblige a colleague in this instance but otherwise you wouldn't catch me sitting here listening to this sort of rubbish.' Probably he did have far more important things to do with his time than sit and listen to someone like me.

In the end they allowed me to come back to London. I had a lovely GP, a woman doctor. I went along to see her. I was a shambles; I couldn't speak I was crying so much. She said, 'Well, we have a couple of options here. We can either prop you up with pills when you go badly down or we can try to get to the bottom of this.' She said, 'As far as I'm concerned there really is no choice. We've got to try to find out what this is all about and help you to cope with it without medication.'

Then I had to see a social worker, and then I was referred to a lady called Mrs Smith, who acted as a sort of clearing-house for patients to be referred to psychotherapists – patients who were unable to pay the full fees but would agree to go to a trainee psychotherapist. She was so worried about me that she saw me for about eight or ten sessions at a reduced fee to keep me going till I could find a home, so to speak, with a psychotherapist. I do remember she said, 'Have you any idea of what you are looking for in therapy? Anything at all?' And, of course, I hadn't. The only thing I came up with was that I would like a woman therapist. And then the available person came up and it was a man, but I wasn't in a position to argue, so I went to him as a trainee patient for three years, three times a week.

It's difficult to explain what went wrong. We just met and locked horns, head on, the whole time. No ground was gained on either side; you know, we would just shunt backwards and forwards. I've got this mental picture, literally, of two deer fighting with locked horns. You know, you go along as a dreadful shambling shapeless mess, and what you need more than anything else, I now realize, is a sort of strong container. Now, the therapist needs to be sure of himself to provide that container, and perhaps it's expecting a lot of somebody who's in training. This is where I think some of it went wrong. I felt he was . . . wobbly. He said I used to home in and find these Achilles' heels of his. I expect he was right; all I can say is that at the time I was totally unaware of this. I would find myself up to my neck in a strange situation where he suddenly *rounded* on me and would just lash me in the same way that my father used to do, with just one cutting sentence – and I just went down like a ton of bricks. I was a moral pulp.

Maybe I was too susceptible to that sort of attack because it was what my father used to do. But he, the therapist I mean, would turn round so suddenly and make an acid comment, and I'd be lying there on the couch and I'd think, what have I said? Looking back on it, it used to be to do with remarks which in any way were connected with class and status. He seemed to have a real hang-up somehow about his own status and upbringing. I remember on one occasion I said something about Rapunzel, Rapunzel, let down your hair. He said, 'Sorry?' And I said, 'The fairy tale, you know, you must have had all those read to you as a child.' And he said, 'No, I didn't have the benefit of a middle-class upbringing.' Anything like that, he'd sort of come out of his corner with his fists up.

I think from the moment I met him I felt an antipathy towards him. And I always had the feeling that he really did not like me. I know it's not necessary, I've read books where it says that it's not necessary for the patient and therapist to enjoy some sort of mutual liking, that, in fact, it could get in the way . . . But I don't know. Sometimes he used to go out of his way to say, 'Look, I'm sure you're a marvellous person' – I just never believed it. With Mrs Smith, in those few sessions, she never had to say anything like that but I felt – how can I describe it? – she liked me! This awful dreadful mess that walked in through the door! She never said so, but I felt she was 100 per cent for me and I couldn't believe it, I'd never had this in my life before. I was bowled over by it.

When you go into therapy you have no idea what it's all about. You struggle along in this strange sea, in this boat which hasn't got a rudder or a sail; you've got no compass, no land in sight and you think, where the hell am I? Well, these particular seas were very storm-tossed and still were after about a year and a half, by which time I should have settled. And I went back to Mrs Smith. I rang her up and said, 'Please can I come round and talk to you?' I said, 'Look, I don't know what's happening but I just feel that this isn't going right.' And she at that time said, 'Well, you've undertaken to be a trainee patient – if you pull out it means that this man has got to start all over again. You did give a verbal undertaking that you would stay the two years.' She sent me back to him; you know – come on, try again. So I carried on for, in total, three years. Until I'd reached the stage where I thought, I cannot go on.

I tried to talk to him about it. I would say, 'Look, please, I think there is something going wrong here and I don't know what it is. Can we talk about it? Because I feel I am just not getting anywhere at all; we are locked in this impossible struggle, I am making *no progress* here.' He would sort of sit back and say, 'Well it all depends on what you mean by progress!' And I would say something like, 'I am still in the same awful job, I'm not earning much money, I can't face going to any gathering, parties of any kind, I can't go into the pub, I can't pick up the phone and talk to people' – a whole catalogue of things. And my relationship with my parents was dreadful, absolutely dreadful beyond measure. All the time I was struggling to keep on working while going through this searing psychotherapy. I was in a terrible state, just crawling along.

At the end of the three years I went back to Mrs Smith again and said, 'Look, here I am three years later. I look and sound exactly the same as when I first came to you. What is wrong? Is it me; am I an unsuitable case for treatment? Is it my psychotherapist? Is it the combination of us two? What do I do now? What's your opinion of this shambles?' And she was very good; she sat and listened to me for about three hours on end. At the end of it she said, 'Yes, I agree with you, something *has* gone wrong here. I think originally I was at fault in sending you to a man. Perhaps time will make it a little bit more plain just what has gone wrong.' And she said, 'I have a feeling now that the damage you are suffering from happened very early on in your life. The earlier on it happens, the harder it is to undo. With you I think it started the moment you were born, and whether or not that can be undone I have my doubts.'

So I said, 'Well, where does that leave me? I can't go on like this.' Because I was unemployed and had ground to a complete halt again. She said, 'Would you like to see me? But I'm afraid I'll have to charge you a lot more than Dr Black. I can see you for £10 a session.' That's very modest indeed for a woman like her. And I still had some savings at that stage, about £2,000. She said, 'It's quite a decision spending the money on this sort of thing.' No, never would I ask my parents for money, never. My mother does give out lump sums to the three of us from time to time; mine goes on therapy and always has done. I think I've always been regarded as the family's sort of Pandora's box. They're horrified to think that the little box might be opened and something might come out that would reflect on them. They'd rather not know – I don't blame them. They've never asked me about my psychotherapy.

So I'm with Mrs Smith now and we battle on. It's about three years, I think. There are things now that I've got to come to terms with. Things that won't change. I won't marry. I can't form relationships – I couldn't form a relationship with a dog or cat. I'm hopeless at it. I have no conception of my own sexuality, none whatsoever. The fact that I have a name that is female and that I menstruate is about all I have to tell me that I am female. Since I parted from the photographer all those years ago I've had sex with about four different men on a one-off basis and found it so off-putting, so difficult to cope with . . . I found that I just retreated and retreated and retreated, and that way I got worse. I have no conception of falling in love at all. I don't understand it. No. I'm 38 now and I don't want to marry and have children but I do wish I could have got involved in a relationship, that I could have that progress in the shape of a person. I have no idea whether that person would be male or female, even now – none whatsoever.

Men in particular I treat just like gelignite or a bomb, something I don't know anything about but which I know is going to go off. So I just tiptoe around, hoping to God I'm not in the blast area when it goes off. I never know how to be with them; I have no idea. I just try to be what they seem to want me to be. I completely erase myself . . . and then go away feeling really . . . yuk! Because if one of them said, 'Why don't I take you out to dinner,' or something like that, I'd just think, oh he's fallen for the old cardboard cut-out that I wheel out, that's what he wants. And then there's the sheer social aspect of it: by now the pond is fished out and the people who are left behind are people like me! And I don't want another one like me. I've completely rejected the idea of married men. I did go through a stage when I thought that might be the answer, since I want to keep a certain distance built in. But, of course, that was terribly naïve of me.

I can't get involved with other people because I'm frightened of them – men or women – just any remark could hurt. I wait for the remarks, you know, like kids waiting at the bottom of a conker tree. I even shake up the tree sometimes like kids do. Even friends I've known for a long time and have a great regard for just occasionally come up with something . . . And I *crawl* away, trying to keep the pieces together. I try to go into this in therapy, still tending to sort of skirt it because it's a real minefield – it's like a huge hill and we tunnel in from that way and I get stuck in the centre, and we tunnel in from the other way and get stuck in the centre again. Every way I try to attack the problem, I come up against the complete barrier of my own psychology.

Fundamentally I find Mrs Smith to be absolutely rock steady. I trust her, which I don't think I can say of any other human being in my life. If there's progress, I think it's not recognized much by the people around me, though they're a very useful sounding-board. I can now face the fact that I won't marry, that there won't be that sort of back-up, comfort, reassurance, mutuality of any kind, that there'll be just me. That's quite frightening, especially as my earning power is so little. I have nothing really except my typewriter and a bicycle – and I'm knocking on 40 now. With the cost of therapy, I don't think I'll ever be able to buy a flat. I don't think that's ever going to be possible. I wouldn't be able to save enough, let alone pay a mortgage. So you're left thinking, how on earth am I going to keep body and soul together? I've got no sort of expectations from my family; there's not much money there. It's going to be a long, lonely haul.

The trouble is that I feel everything I do work-wise is just crap. I work for a cookery writer, a very nice lady indeed; gosh, she's been solid gold, she and her husband, to me. She'll ask me to research an article for her, and after a bit of work I can just sit down at the typewriter and do it for her. But if a magazine editor came to me and said, 'Do us an article, off you go, anything you like' – I'd sit there and not be able to type a word. Because it would be *my* name up front. I find that's the only way I can operate, behind somebody else.

Mrs Smith has brought me round, I think, to accepting limitations. OK, I'm going to be on my own, there's only me to look after me. Right, what's positive about being on my own? I can sit down and think, I'm totally free, I haven't got encumbrances of any sort – except monetary, I suppose – so what do I want to do? Well, one of the things I've always wanted to make myself do is to travel. I get terrified travelling on my own, absolutely terrified – but I am getting better. So I've thought, right, that is one thing that I might be able to get going with a bit more.

And I suppose I am a bit less unhappy. I don't think I quite get to the bit *underneath* the barrel, I just sort of hit the bottom of the barrel. I don't go down quite as low. But last year I went home for Christmas for the first time in about five years – very misguidedly, but I think I wanted to test myself. I went home and it was dreadful. *Awful.* I came back from there and my sessions had been cut down to two because the summer before Mrs Smith had said, 'You're really going along quite well, how do you feel about cutting down your sessions?' And I'd said, 'Marvellous'; it was like, you know, going up a form at school. I came back from Christmas and it was January, February and I was very frightened. I'd never been frightened before about suicide; I'd found the thought a consolation. But I began to have dreams like I'd never had before in my life. They're very difficult to describe. They really bore very little relationship to anything. They were just total chaos dreams: people sort of with their faces distorted, like a Francis Bacon painting and then they would lean forward and seemingly smile and then their heads would come off like a lump of hot mozzarella; and all the while there was a movement backwards and forwards with noise and colours altering; total chaos. The first time it happened I woke up and thought, that's the first time, Jesus! I didn't mention it to Mrs Smith. And it happened the second time and I thought, I am getting bad, I am getting quite bad; and for the first time I feared for my sanity. After that second dream I tried to explain it to her, and she said, 'Yes, I think things are not going well and we ought to go back to three sessions a week.' So you see, there wasn't the black depression, but there was this instead. So I'm not really sure about less unhappy.

In some ways there's progress. I do have friends; not people that I ring up and say, 'Will you go to the pictures with me?' Because I never do that. If they were to say, 'All right', I'd think, they don't really want to come. I'm a very bad friend, they have to ring me. But I'm fortunate enough to have people who put up with that and will phone me – 'How are you? Come on, meet me for a drink.' And that counts for a lot, because it requires a lot from somebody to keep on being outward-going, being giving to somebody, when they're getting nothing back. I do find now, particularly just recently, quite a lot of friends have been ringing me and I think, well this is extraordinary – more social contact than I've ever had in my life. Because I am difficult, I'm a dreadful strain on people. I have this dreadful compulsion to tell people I'm depressed, because if you offer them the false front you go away feeling like shit.

Another thing is recently I have been wondering, just wondering, about trying to get a different job. I got some brochures about training courses last week. Oh and, believe it or not, it occurred to me this summer that I might in some extraordinary way reach a stage with Mrs Smith where I could go back to Dr Black and get that right. With the work I've done with Mrs Smith, perhaps the two of us could get it right. Funnily enough, he's cropped up in my dreams; nothing bad, I would be laughing with him. I woke up and thought, well, that's a turn-up for the book. Funny. Nothing changes with my parents, no. I still come off the phone after ringing home and I think, now I'm not going to cry, and I put the phone down and I just bawl. I . . . *burst* . . . into floods of tears. So there's a long way to go.

Of course I see myself going on with the therapy for quite a time. It keeps me alive. Though a lot of the time I feel . . . it's terribly uncomplimentary . . . but when I was doing part-time work in the London Hospital, trying to get back on my feet again, and I was in the intensive therapy unit, I used to see people who were literally just lumps of meat attached to a ventilator which did the breathing for them; and especially this year, when I did such a dive, I felt just like one of those patients. For ventilator, see psychotherapist. I've just felt that that was all that I was doing, just living and having my being, but at such a low level that it was barely worthwhile.

Sometimes, though, I find that I've got to the stage where I can do a bit of my own psychotherapy. I know I'm as bats as they come. I'm a totally batty woman and I shall become battier as I get older; you see, I just sit and talk out loud to myself. I usually sit in that kitchen, which is the furthest point from the house, and I have the washing machine going on top, so nobody can really hear. And I have this very intelligent conversation – sometimes I really surprise myself with what I come out with. It's like a game of chess, but I'm playing chess with myself and I am patient and psychotherapist.

I look back to the time when the doctor offered me pills or psychotherapy. I don't really consider the pill option worth while but I do look at the quality of my life and the potential that is there, and think, is it worth it, was it worth it, to arrive at this, to go through all that? and I never come up with an answer, because it's perilously near to being evenly balanced. I have to be honest about that.

Alexander

> Some of the fragments were hardly as big as a grain of sand and whenever they flew into someone's eye they got stuck there and made things seem distorted, so that the person saw only the bad side of things. Some fragments even got into the hearts of a few people and then a terrible thing happened – these hearts turned into a block of ice . . . There are still lots of these fragments flying about in the air.
>
> Hans Andersen: *The Snow Queen*

Alexander and his flat give off contradictory messages. He describes himself as a lonely man, and this is reinforced by the tidy, bleak flat, the huge moribund houseplant, the empty fireplace. Alexander himself, though, in rich Glaswegian accent, finds himself, and life, a good joke. He is fun to talk to and punctuates his interview with squeaks of laughter.

I think it may possibly be a record. I started analysis in January 1956 – in fact, it will be thirty-one years tomorrow!

I was a young doctor when I started, working in a psychiatric unit. No, I didn't go into analysis as part of my job and I certainly never wanted to train as a psychoanalyst myself; I wouldn't have had a clue, I wouldn't have had the commitment to the patients. I've stayed in hospital work. In fact, I really drifted into psychiatry – drifting's the story of my life – probably because I had two close friends who qualified at the same time as me and they both went into psychiatry. I just kind of followed. Frankly, I was – and remain to a significant extent, alas – a butterfly; my only aim in life was to avoid responsibility and amuse myself.

The honest truth is that I'd so little capacity for introspection in that phase of my life that I really didn't know why I opted to

31

go into analysis. I think at some level I was aware that there was something very wrong with my life. I had a sense of aimlessness, feelings of futility. I suppose I knew that there was a future waiting for me which I wasn't going to be able to accommodate to. I mean, if you think in terms of Freud's standards of success in living – loving and working – at the superficial level I gave the impression of not doing too badly, but really it was a case of all my goods being in the shop window, there was nothing in the store. So it was living a kind of 'as if' existence, and successfully bluffing my way through life.

I had a kind of Don Juan complex. My sexual relationships were really disastrous in the sense that as soon as I'd made a conquest I started losing interest. I always blamed the girls – oh, they weren't interesting enough, they weren't sexually attractive enough or what have you; but you begin to run out of excuses, the law of diminishing returns operates . . . I haven't married because I haven't been able to. I still haven't reached the level of emotional maturity in which marriage or even living with a woman becomes possible. I feel trapped in relationships. And I'm sure that any marriage that I'd entered into would have been an unmitigated disaster.

So these were the general reasons . . . Although, as I say, I hadn't formulated them at all, I kind of drifted into analysis; and, you know, I honestly think that in its intitial phase analysis was just another game for me. It wasn't to help deal with my patients – not at all, not at all. I've been, I think, a reasonably effective psychiatrist, but I've been a good psychiatrist in order to get rid of my patients. My patients by and large are devoted to me but I'm playing a kind of game all the while.

Anyway . . . I went into analysis. It's rather an absurd story. I was finding sex increasingly unsatisfactory and I'd developed the idea that something adverse was happening to my potency, and I'd read a book by a chap who was head of one of the psychiatric departments so I consulted him. He said, 'I wouldn't advise you to go into analysis, but if you're determined to, I recommend Dr X.' Actually, I don't think he knew much about psychoanalysis, but Dr X was a friend of his, a traditional sort of analyst. And I went to him for two or three years, my first analyst.

I don't think it meant much to me. It was only like taking up a new hobby. Oh, I went along for my sessions, four times a week. I didn't miss the money particularly – I was living in hospital, I had a kind of moderate private income of sorts, it was pocket money. I don't think I ever liked or trusted the analyst much. You see, I have this problem that I don't really get emotionally involved with analysts except in negative terms. There's always been this barrier of my lack of capacity, really, for empathy.

After about two or three years in analysis with him I became friendly with a doctor who'd grown up in Glasgow with me and he said I was wasting my time with this chap and he persuaded me to change. And so I've been with my second analyst ever since. And there's still the barrier. Of course, I feel gratitude to her in a way, a certain degree of warmth, but – you know, she's an old lady now – if I arrived at the door and her housekeeper told me that she'd died in the night, I wouldn't *really* feel it. Do you know the Hans Andersen story, is it *The Snow Queen*? You know, the boy has a splinter of ice in his heart. It's like that.

I know I don't give that impression, I'm very much aware of that. People like me, they always have, they're fond of me. But that's because I'm operating to some extent on a false basis. I've developed quite an impressive persona. It's not that it's false, perhaps, but I feel it's very superficial. I'm able to be warm as long as I don't have to be involved with the other person. I have friends – I like them, I enjoy their company, but I'm aware of the fact that I don't really feel anything like as warmly for them as they apparently do for me. I mean, my closest friend died tragically just under a year ago, and . . . I don't really feel it.

Of course it goes back to childhood, of course it does. Well, my parents separated before I was born, while my mother was actually pregnant with me. So for the first four years of my life I lived with just my mother and older brother and my mother's parents. Then apparently my father wrote to my mother saying that if she didn't agree to a reconciliation, he'd divorce her, so we went back to live with my father in a flat in the Gorbals. Actually we weren't poor – we had two maids! You see, the Gorbals was originally an upper-class area, but the wealthy people moved out to the suburbs.

The street I lived in retained a few last traces of gentility; as well as my parents there was another doctor and a dentist living there.

My mother – well, she was genteel, a 'lady'. I think she was the first woman in Glasgow to qualify as a doctor, though when she was young she'd lived in a much poorer area of the Gorbals. I think she was always motivated more by duty than by any kind of spontaneous warmth, though she was basically a kind person, but rather undemonstrative and cold. I think she suffered quite a lot from depression – she would retire to her bed for a few days and although ostensibly it was with a stomach upset, I now know these were kind of depressive equivalents.

My father was a strange man. He was highly intelligent, but emotionally quite disturbed – he was a rather sort of chaotic man, he had odd ideas, he was extremely stubborn, he was detached, wasn't capable of showing much affection – although again I think the warmth was there somewhere. We always had a cat and I would occasionally find him clumsily stroking this cat! When he did, I used to feel sorry him, because he did it so ineptly – he just didn't know how to do it.

Yes, they were both Jewish. Psychoanalysis is a Jewish racket! Arthur Koestler said that the Jews were the same as everybody else, only more so; and that applies to neuroticism! When my father first came over from Russia he was a Talmudic scholar and a cantor, but he gave this up when he became a freethinker and then a doctor. He was a disappointed man. He felt he should have been a lawyer or a surgeon or something instead of a family doctor with a slum practice. Then there was the enormous problem of his pathological miserliness. If he came in and someone had just put some coal on the fire, he'd go mad, he'd start plucking pieces out of the fire. He had no emotional control at all, he was quite a kind of primitive person – I mean, he'd fly into constant friction between himself and my mother, seemingly because she wanted to spend more money. Not in a kind of extravagant way. But he couldn't stand this. One of the most vivid memories of my life is a terrible quarrel between my father and my mother. He raised his fists to her and she retreated from the dining-room into the hall, and I rushed out screaming – I thought he was going to kill her! If he went into a rage, he went completely out of control. He just became kind of insensate.

The analogy that I'd give about our family structure or atmosphere is, imagine a number of people working in a workshop, each is getting on with his job and they relate insofar as it's necessary in terms of the work they're doing, but they're not really relating to each other. My brother was very affected by it: in his second year of medicine he just ground to a halt and really became a kind of semi-invalid; he became tremendously hypochondriacal about his blood pressure . . . He was admitted to a rather superior kind of psychiatric hospital and was there for some time. Then he went back into medicine and got through and became quite successful – as a psychiatrist, actually. He's just retired. I reacted in an entirely different way. I became a kind of butterfly, I lived for the moment – like a kind of eternal child. I could always charm people and so I got away with it – people liked me, they forgave me!

It's possible my analyst – I mean the second one, the one I've been with all these years – isn't quite the right personality for me. I mean, she's like a very dry, subtle white wine, whereas I might do better with a full, fruity Burgundy. I don't think I know what we *have* talked about all this time. My parents; but only very, very rarely indeed would she make a comment which seemed to me cogent. She's talked a lot about . . . oh, the fact that I operate on a false basis, that there's this little child hidden away which is real. Again and again I would say, 'But this is old-hat, I know this backwards.' I don't know that talking about it helps; I think you can talk about it till the last trump.

I do not believe – and I'm pretty sure that she would agree with me – that anything can be done about a very basic split in the personality. I think the people who benefit from therapy are those who got through the early stage of development reasonably well. My mother must have been very depressed while she was carrying me. I mean, who knows, they're thinking in terms of pre-natal influences now. Do you know this thing that's come out recently about women singing to their children? There are primitive tribes where the women sing to the baby in the womb. They've discovered that if the mother sings the same song to the child after it's born, the child goes wild with delight, whereas if she sings another song, it doesn't respond. My mother didn't sing to me . . . not before or after birth!

I remember a friend saying to me once, 'You are your own mother' – which I thought hit the nail on the head. I kind of gave up my mother as a lost cause and learned to be my own mother. Does it work? It depends what you mean by work; how do you define working? It works in the sense that I get by – I've never broken down, I've been able to have a reasonably successful career and go through the motions successfully. Happy? Not . . . particularly. No. But not particularly unhappy either. Well, as a young man I went through – I suppose many young men do – a phase of despair and so on, *Weltschmerz*. But – oh no, I *can* be very happy.

I just don't think it's possible for my analyst to be a mother to me herself. Not at all. Perhaps some analysts can, with some patients; I don't know. I find it difficult to believe that any other analyst would have been more successful with me, anyway. Let me give you an analogy. I was a member of an encounter group for two years and I got a hell of a lot out of it and had a lot of very, very significant experiences, but within weeks of finishing I was back to . . . It was just a kind of ego graft, you became a member of a group and got a lot of support and it raised your self-esteem a bit. But I went back to square one.

Anyway, I suppose in some sense my analyst has in fact become a kind of maternal influence, in fantasy terms. But, as she's often said, my problem is that my need is so great that I can't be satisfied. There's an insatiability, there's the unbearable quality of becoming aware of the frustration of the need. So all that the person can do with the need is completely repress it, deny its existence – it's not there and therefore I'm not suffering.

Oh, I know patients *can* get better. I used to do some therapy at the hospital and my patients did get better, oh yes. But I think it's for those people whose early development went reasonably satisfactorily. Yes, of course that means that an awful lot of analysts are wasting their time! It's hard to say why my analyst has agreed to keep me on for so long. I think her attitude is, as long as there's any hope of her being able to modify any of my neurotic behaviour patterns, she's prepared to struggle on. She's often threatened to let me go! But then I cling on again, you see. She's aware that there's a concealed feeling I have for her. And if she died, I'm sure I would be a bit sad, though not to the degree many analysands would be. It would be as though fate had decided the issue for me of whether to carry on, because I've been very ambivalent about it for a fair number of those twenty-eight years. But, in fact, I haven't left, because it's easier . . . I am not a person who acts, but *reacts*. I'm very passive. I will never initiate any new development in my Unit, for instance. I only became a doctor because I just followed in the family footsteps. And then, in purely practical terms, analysis has played a part in my life in that I'm rather underemployed, I don't work very long hours, so going to analysis has helped me get through the day – yes, it's been quite an important aspect. You could say, yes, that it's been a kind of surrogate marriage to a certain extent.

Then there was, of course, a period when I mightn't have managed without analysis. At that time I was actually in a rather demanding job and I felt overwhelmed and I had a kind of odd depression that lasted for several years. It may well be that then without the analyst's support I wouldn't have got through, because although I was suffering dreadfully I didn't miss a day's work. It was a sort of breakdown, almost.

Of course, there's an incongruity between my coldness of heart and the fact that I've stuck to her all these years. And presumably it's the real bit of me that wants to carry on. I mean, I know that these feelings for her are there and I can feel them – I mean, I'm feeling right now a very slight feeling of . . . warmth, gratitude, devotion to her. It's not very strong, but it is there. Talking about her, I suppose, is stirring the pot a bit; I'm aware of some feeling coming through. But it's not anything like as strong as it should be, and would have been if my analysis had been able to break through this kind of false-self barrier.

Oh, I have felt angry at times that I've invested in something that didn't work, yes. I've said that to her, she acknowledges it.

Yes, I suppose so, in the past. There *is* an angry part of me. I was in a store yesterday, for instance, and a woman who really was behind me cut in front of me and I was seething with anger, which I felt was quite inappropriate – what difference does a minute or two make? I think the reason was that I've a thing about feeling disregarded. I can't stand being short-changed, for example – the fact that I'm being taken advantage of, even if it's just a few coppers, I'm tremendously resentful of that. But I don't think anger comes up in analysis much now. I don't think I've had very high expectations of it – especially after the first twenty-odd years! I mean, hope springs eternal, but not *that* eternal!

It's a bit sad, yes. But then I'm used to being the person I am; it's a case of the devil you know, so to speak. I would like to have changed – obviously that's the reason why I went into analysis in the first place, at least I think so – but I've had an awfully long time to adapt myself to the idea. Then you have to bear in mind that I went through that very, very bad phase in about 1960 for several years, when she kept me going, so that, I think, has become my baseline. Anything better than that, you know, is a plus and 'I'm only too grateful for small mercies' sort of thing. When I think back to what I went through then, I think I feel almost complacent.

I was struck many years ago by something that a senior analyst said. 'You know,' he said, 'analysis can do very little, but just occasionally that little is enough.' And I think that's it in a nutshell. The difference between getting 49 and 50 in an exam; in quantitative terms it's very little, but in qualitative terms it's the difference between a fail and a pass. If you stay at 49 that's too bad, but if you can get up to 50 you can just scrape along. There's an awfully big difference.

Funnily enough, I had a very vivid dream last night about my childhood. Not that I think I ever really understand dreams, it's like crosswords or chess problems. The entire dream somehow took place in the street outside my grandparents' house, where I lived for the first four years of my life. I saw that directly opposite the house was an Underground station – you know Glasgow's the only city in Britain other than London that has an Underground system, I'm very proud of that – but it was a peculiar round structure like the tomb of Alaric in Ravenna; he was the leader of the Goths who sacked Rome. Also I saw to my surprise that the house had many more storeys (there's a pun for you!) than I thought it had. Actually it was a two-storey house, but in this dream it had six storeys – and do you know what that reminds me of? I'm reading that book there about the Industrial Revolution by Hobsbawm, and he says that one of the tragic effects of the Industrial Revolution was shunting the urban working-class population into appalling slums, whereas before – and this surprised me – they lived in the same houses as the wealthy but on the *upper* floors; in Paris, for instance. So there were the top storeys in my dream and the Underground in my dream. And you've only told me now that you're going to Paris and Ravenna! I don't know . . .

The big question is whether it's all been worth while. It's terribly difficult to answer. I think I would say that the odds are in favour, taking the rough with the smooth – no, I don't regret . . . I mean, I'm aware of a feeling like God knows what might have happened to me if I hadn't had analysis, so its benefits may have been more negative than positive. I'll never be a good swimmer, but without analysis I may well have drowned, whereas I've just about succeeded in keeping my head above water. So I think in relative terms that probably has been an achievement and it's been something worth investing in. I don't think I'd have married if I'd stopped analysis earlier – not at all. There would never have been any question . . . No, I'd have had a bit more money, that's all. And I think it's better that I did carry on for so long because it's only in the past few years or so that I've acquired some insight. I couldn't have said this to you ten years ago. But what is the result of analysis and what just of living – how can one know?

I do think psychoanalysis can be something of a religion or an ethical discipline, definitely. A book's been written dealing with the influence of Talmudic thinking on Freud, you know. It's not entirely a Jewish thing, though; know thyself, the Socratic creed.

It is in a way a whole new life. I do want to say that whether or not analysis has done what I would have hoped it would, I've no regrets about it. In fact, if I'm with acquaintances who haven't had analysis, I'm very much aware of feeling that there's an extra dimension to my perception of reality and relationships and so on – it's as if I feel that they're blind and they're not aware of things that they're doing or that are being done to them that are so patently obvious to me. I'm not saying that I'm happier than these people, not necessarily; but there's no way back, you can't un-scramble an omelette. Because maybe the aim of life is not . . . I remember once saying to a friend, 'All I want is to be happy', and he just roared with laughter at this naïvety. That was twenty years ago, I'd like to say; it's an indication of how childish I was. I mean, what *is* the purpose of life? To experience it as fully as possible? Psychoanalysis can help one to do that.

And I told you all I had to say about it would take about two minutes! There you are. But I always do feel I'm empty. When I'm called on for an after-dinner speech, for instance, I'm abso-lutely panic-stricken and yet I'm a most talkative and opinionated person.

Oh, I remember something else. I was in – what's that city with waterways, not Venice – I was in Bruges, and I was walking along the edge of the canal and I saw this cat stranded on a little sort of island in the water. And I straight away threw off my coat and went in and brought the cat back. I rescued it! And yet . . . But it was myself, the cat.

Carmel

I let the images come, and the ideas; one image led to
another and I tried to express them without sorting
them through, without choosing what was flattering,
intelligent, pretty or funny rather than mediocre, base,
ugly or stupid . . . Some slipped through and disappeared like sand between the fingers. We felt them
very near, ready to appear, and yet, the second we
thought we had grasped them, they had vanished into
the unconscious which they frequented . . . Just by
asking, 'And that? What does that make you think
of?' he could transform everything, provided I said
what the 'that' in fact was.

Marie Cardinal: *The Words to Say It*

Carmel is small, pretty, large-eyed and has a broken accent.
We meet in a characterless room borrowed for the occasion;
her home, she says, is so noisy. She talks intently and with passion.

————————

It was the Day of Atonement and I was staying at home, and I
decided I was so desperate that I was suicidal. I didn't know
why. There on the surface I had a lovely house, lovely husband,
lovely children, there were my studies, I was having more and
more of what I thought I wanted – and I was more and more
desperate. And I didn't know why, I'd no idea. The pain all came
from inside. And in despair I called this psychiatrist friend of ours
and I said, 'I really want to die. I don't know what it is, but I'm
just desperate. I've no idea what's going on.'

At the time I was about 30 years old, I was married about ten
years, I had two young children; and from my culture, the background I came from in Israel, it was expected that the woman
once married was going to remain a housewife. My husband is
Jewish but not Israeli. We came from different cultures and we

had some personal problems, each one individually, and the marriage itself – it was moving to another phase as the children were growing up. I did some studies at the university – history of art – and I enjoyed it – it was very satisfying emotionally and for developing mentally – but somehow I felt that there was a very deep core . . . that whatever I do I will never be satisfied unless – unless I do something about myself. I knew nothing about psychology, absolutely nothing. I think you have to be really naïve for this experience. And the other thing is that you have to be quite desperate.

I only did three years in analysis, five times a week – a relatively short time. It was a terribly painful three years. I remember it was like a raw wound, continuous pain. I cried for hours every day for three years. My eyes became all sore . . . It was just – it was a nightmare. But it was a kind of a pain that I knew if I'd only survive that I'd survive anything.

I thought I had the normal conflicts of childhood, it's only when I went into analysis . . . I remember saying, 'My mother is a lovely person, and my father . . .' I said, 'All my problems have nothing to do with anyone, not my husband either. Oh yes, father used to beat me once in a while, but that's no reason for me to be unhappy.' But then, when I went deep into associations and memories, I actually realized that I had had a very, very painful childhood. Which I totally denied. I created actually a myth that I came from a very warm, affectionate and loving home. Even the beatings – I came from a home where my father used to beat me terribly, physically, with the collusion of my mother – even that meant that I was really beaten because I was loved; you know, a kind of biblical thing, spare the rod . . . if you love your child you show it by caring and beating. And it was very painful to break the myth.

I realize that my husband, my husband who came from supposedly a very aristocratic English family, we had a kind of competition – that his family was superior because of money and class et cetera, but *mine* had warmth and the heart . . . But in fact we were very, very similar – that emerged from the analysis.

My analyst was also a person who was trained as a family and group analyst. About two years after I'd started, my husband was feeling very threatened – I'd started changing, I started demanding, asserting myself – so we went to marital therapy together. I must say that if I would have gone only to individual therapy I would have divorced my husband, our marriage would have ended.

It's very hard on the partner, you know, he feels an outsider, regressed, Mummy and Daddy are talking together. By the second year I realized I was alienating myself from my husband, and part of me knew and believed – and still does – in the family, and part of me knew that I loved my husband and I cared enough to try and do something. He too, he realized . . . He objected, of course. He felt very rejected, he felt angry, but he felt the fear of losing me. And we had a choice of either making a go of it . . . And he knew one thing, that he didn't want to lose me and he didn't want to divorce and neither did I.

But at the beginning . . . Well, immediately, within one week, I developed this strong feeling for my analyst. It was like the time was so ripe; immediately I developed a transference and all those things I didn't know about. I think it was more than that: there was a mind outside that was inquiring into my mind and asking me questions that I never dared, that I thought of and never dared to ask them loudly. So it was almost like a part of me out there that was voicing for me things that were allowed to be named and allowed to be voiced. It was magic for me that somebody knew exactly what kind of questions to ask; that made me feel immediately that there was something beginning to move . . .

It was an understanding quite different from anything that came before. I remember after about a week I woke up with a dream that somehow I was not afraid any more. I had the feeling that I *was* afraid, but that the quality of my fear had changed. Before, it had been like facing a mountain of the unknown. I knew that I had to climb this mountain, but I didn't know how to do it, I didn't know if I should do it or what was going on.

My life had been a thick layer of pretences, never sharing with anyone my unhappiness – I wasn't even *aware* that I was depressed. I would say that I was almost manic in the sense that I had the false concept that I was superhuman: I would be a house-wife, I would study, I would have guests for dinner, I would have people from all over the world staying in my house; I could do anything and everything for everybody. Except I didn't want to live. I didn't realize that I was mothering everybody else because *I* needed mothering. So I was like an empty person that allowed everyone to fill my space.

My marriage, too – it was based on roles. We'd learned from our parents the role of being a good husband or wife, the role of being a civilized couple – we don't fight, we don't shout – and you know, all this had to change. I was always helpful, and nice, and in a good mood but there was a very, very depressed true self. The real lost child inside me was totally depressed, suicidal, morbid.

I come from what you call the Sephardic Jews – they're the Oriental Jews, who are very traditional, close, they've an Oriental view of women. And apart from going into the army, I lived with my parents until I was twenty years old, so I came from a world that was very rigid and settled in its views, in its attitudes. I met my husband – it was only about two weeks after we met that we decided to get married. Well, twenty-five years later we are still around! But my parents did not let me grow through the different developmental phases that a normal child would. They didn't want me to grow at all but to remain a little girl they could control, they could manipulate; they projected onto me all their fears, their anxieties. There I was, a person but not in my own right, an object, filled with fears and anxieties that I didn't know what was mine and what was theirs. And basically when I met my husband – since he just came to Israel for a short visit from England – he was like a ticket to run away. I just wanted to escape, to run away, and at that time in Israel you couldn't go to university and share a flat with a friend; you just moved from a home to a home. Even in the army, on the surface it sounds very free, but it was a puritanical society. I'd wanted to be an actress, but my parents saw it as a whorish profession.

So when I met my husband it was a ticket for freedom; I wanted him to save me. And so not going through the process of the natural separation from parents – I jumped from the saucepan to the fire! When I got married I actually expected my poor husband to solve all my problems! To make me happy! Yes. And he expected the same from me. And as time passed by we became more and more depressed – I was incapable of solving his problems and saving him, and so was he for me. I think there was a deep sadness in it. It wasn't bitterness, but sadness, that we did marry out of attraction, love, whatever, that there was something that attracted us to each other and at the same time realizing that no, the other person can't do it for you.

If there had been no analysis, it would have been a mess. A mess. Knowing myself now – I would have acted out, I would have run away with another man, found lovers. Really, expected other people to make me happy. I would have divorced and been miserable and repeated the same experience. But I think at the end, maybe ten, fifteen years later I would have gone to therapy – I would have done *something*. I was desperate, yes. I'd have done something eventually, you know, to find responsibility and to own it myself for my life.

Of course I had resistances, of course I fought against analysis. But I also knew . . . There are two parts of oneself that go to analysis. There *is* the adult part. I was intelligent, I was bright enough to realize . . . I mean, I'd be driving there early in the morning, thinking, bloody hell, you know, I hate this thing, here I drive one hour, get up at six o'clock in the morning, pay so much money, and what for? For another person to tell me I'm lying!

But at the same time there was the other part of me . . . well, you know that you're avoiding something and you know that today something will be found out . . . A part of you reflects all the time on what it is that you're feeling. So there are two beings really, and one part of you is mature, allies with the therapist whatever happens, knows that these are the rules and that you're going to abide by them – that it's part of the process of growing up.

My first commitment in life, my analysis. Yes, more than my marriage or my children – absolutely! It was a commitment to myself and I could not run away from it. At times, yes, I wanted to run away. But I never thought of breaking it off. Never. No, no. By nine o'clock in the morning I felt drained, exhausted, totally squeezed out, and I just wanted to cry all the time. But I went to the college and I did my studies and I coped with the children. Underneath there was a terrible depression, my tears rolling, but I knew that I was becoming stronger and stronger.

Perhaps I was on the verge of breakdown, but somehow by the fact that someone was there I felt I didn't need to have a breakdown. I think that some people have a breakdown when they don't feel there is *anyone* around who can actually contain them. And I had a sort of anchor at home – a context, a very realistic context, where I had to continue. Yes. And I must say that my children were a tremendous help to me. I did tell them. I didn't explain much, I said very little, and I explained as the questions came from them eventually. My daughter was very young, she was only about 5 years old; my son was 9. They knew that I was going to see someone and that I was very unhappy. But, as I was regressing, I was almost their own age, sometimes even younger. And they were a tremendous comfort, just to be with them. I was like a little girl – there was part of me that was the little girl who enjoyed playing games, you know, with the dolls of my daughter and being with her. I could really understand them – not only as a mother but as a child, with them, knowing what they were going through. Today my children are grateful that in many, many ways I accept *them* as not being completely strong. No, I didn't give them any lectures and I didn't hide it from them. It came about naturally, their growing up and asking me certain questions – 'What is it like?' – as they developed and got interested in a different way about my analysis.

I had parents who were very aggressive, who gave double messages all the time. They didn't give me the kind of love I needed. But the analyst contained whatever I put out – it's a whole process, you know, asserting, voicing your needs. Finding them, your fantasies, your inner world of needs, of anxieties, of fears, and realizing that your parents did not fulfil it. They interfered, they impinged, they disturbed, they oppressed, whatever. You come with a certain association – like, I was very naughty at school and one day I threw my schoolbag from the balcony at school and the teacher said, 'Go and call your mother' – it was a story that went on and on for years – but my mother always said, 'I'm busy, I don't have time', and she used to send either her sister or my grandfather or neighbours but never went herself and accepted responsibility that she is my mother and that she is going to do something to stop me from being naughty.

Now I come with this association in therapy and at first I felt I was bad all the time, but then I thought, why did I do it? I wanted my mother to acknowledge some responsibility for me. I wanted to *do* something so that I would see that I make a difference in her life – that she cared, that she was angry . . . But she was totally absorbed with her mother and her sister and her father, and cooking, cleaning. So through analysis I separate between what I did, *why* I did it, the need to do it, the *despair* of acting out so that my mother would acknowledge me in some way, show me that she was angry, she was sad; not just, 'I don't have the time', and somebody else goes. You see yourself differently, you discover your needs – for love, for a real contact with the mother, for acknowledgement as a daughter – you discover a whole complexity of them and the more you start owning things, the more the emptiness and the sense of self fills up.

I got so angry, you see! There I was in England, ten years after I'd left home . . . During these years I'd been a *perfect* daughter; I had a lot of money and I would send them tickets, take them to Switzerland on trips. I tried everything for them to say, you are a wonderful daughter! Whatever I did was always . . . 'Oh, but Switzerland is awful and look at Lugano, and Venice is dirty . . .' I could never please them, whatever I did. So I got very angry; and I felt *wonderful* when I got angry, I felt really good, I said, 'I'm right, I'm right'; because I'd always emptied myself, trying to satisfy them all the time. Instead of thinking about *my* family, it was always: where shall I take my parents next year and how will I organize for them to be happy; no, they will not like that and they will not like that – living completely for them. I was *furious* – and I was so happy to be furious! That I had the right to be furious!

The usual ritual had been that I would call them about once a fortnight, and I just stopped calling them and they were worried about me. So they would call and then I would be very angry and scream and shout, and I'd write them very nasty letters and not invite them. They didn't come for about four years – I just insisted I didn't want to see them. So that was wonderful, because I actually asserted myself. And they did change. We have quite a nice relationship now. Something changed in them after my fights: they realized that I am not to be taken for granted, I am a separate human being and I'm not going to carry for them any of their bullshit.

It's a terrible sadness, too, to realize you will never be a child any more. That was it. My parents would never satisfy . . . I don't want them to satisfy it now – you know, it's redundant. Whatever they do now – and they do a lot – it can't undo things. To say I was depressed and now I'm happy – that's a lie. There is a kind of undercurrent, it's like a deep wound that became a scar. But my scars are me, they're part of me. In that sense I learned to accept my parents as part of me; the more I accept myself, I can accept their ignorance – I don't know what I would have done in their place at that time, Second World War, Independence War. So – really I let go of them.

Because it's when parents are *never* satisfying that the children will dote on them. They still need their parents to say, 'OK, you're grown-up, you're separate and God bless you – go on your way.' Yes, I did rebel, but it was a kind of false rebellion. It was on one hand saying, 'I'm independent, I'm speaking my mind' – and yet there I am, clinging . . . I was saying some things, but I was doing things to contradict it. Like to my father I was saying, 'It's not nice, you are beating me, nobody beats his children' – and yet I stayed at home and . . . there I was.

It's a mixture of a hundred things that makes you grow better. You find someone who can contain whatever you are going to say . . . The setting itself, that you go at a fixed time and the time is yours; you learn about time and space. You give yourself time and space internally – I think it's very important – and in that time and space someone is containing whatever you are bringing. Then the transference, through which we see our needs and fantasies, our ambivalence, our confusions, whatever – our emotional, internal, mental world.

Certainly I did get angry with my analyst in the transference. The other thing was I realized how much I loved and depended on that man. And I realized, my God, if I'm that dependent on a total stranger who I see for only five hours a week, how can I deny my dependence on my family, I lived with them; that's when you see the magnitude of your dependence on your parents. Eventually, by the last six months, I could sit by myself and ask myself and talk to myself – I internalized him, asked *myself* why am I saying that, why do I feel that, what's going on, and he didn't have to ask so much as before, his role changed. It was very painful, I mean the end, when I knew I was going to leave. Both of us decided that I could leave within six months and then it was within three months, and I think that it takes even a year or two after that to get over the mourning. But the parting can be a positive experience if the goodbye is done properly. I thought I needed him, like a crutch, but then to discover that he is there inside me, I'd know what he would say . . . Even being able to look back and maybe criticize him. The experience was only wonderful because I *used* it; it was a vehicle for me, I learned how to use it fully for my own benefit.

I had been so self-destructive before, totally denying myself. I didn't allow myself even to admit that I was sad. Self-destructiveness is expressed in many different ways and for me it was a total denial of my true self. Until the point that . . . that I found I was suicidal. And I was terribly greedy, spending a lot of money. But I realized how it was a substitute for emptiness and a sense of hunger and evasion; my greed was expressed by just going to shops and wanting to empty them; really it's an expression of deprivation, a sense of emptiness, a sense of envy, and once you deal with it you can contain your envy and destructiveness – you don't feel like doing that any more.

Of course therapy is not the only way to help people. Understanding from a friend . . . I do think therapists can take the place of rabbis, priests, good friends, uncles, aunts. In fact, many times therapy can harm people. If the analyst doesn't fully understand himself and takes up a patient that creates terribly negative feelings, it can be very harmful. Or if a person has to leave the treatment and isn't ready. I think that patients should shop around at the beginning. If the therapist *hits* somewhere here, then you know that this is your therapist. Something has to move inside you.

I remember the week when I experienced being born – and the sense of coldness, the sense of depression and helplessness. I felt like that all through the week. I remember I had an interview in the Courtauld Institute, I was applying to do my MA. You know, there is a small square facing the Courtauld and I arrived there quite early . . . I was sitting there . . . My skin felt totally raw and like a newborn baby. And at the same time there was part of me that contained it, said it's all right, it's not ridiculous, it's not terrible, that felt compassionate. I remember sitting in that interview, and there was an inner image, an internal image I had of a mother who is sitting in this interview – you know, it's a very academic place, very intellectual – and I remember sitting there and whatever I was answering it was fine, you know, and at the same time there was part of me that saw this mother with a little tiny baby, just holding that baby all the time. And I was holding myself. And I felt very sad and compassionate . . . It was OK.

My analyst wasn't cold and remote. I felt his personality all the time and he was a very passionate human being. Caring, angry, demanding, observant. He asked very analytic questions, but the tone of his voice, his reaction . . . I knew when I was entertaining him, I knew when I made him angry, I knew when he thought, 'stupid bitch, absolutely hopeless'. It was projection, but also it was real. Yes, he was a real person. And I remember at the last session he asked me, 'What do you think made the difference?' and I said, 'You. You came across as a really human being. And you were real enough to make me feel that it's worth while being real. That's all.'

I do . . . I do love my analyst as a person, someone who helped me, as someone who, yes, went through the deepest experience of my life. He was a midwife. He gave birth to me.

June

'Look at his left side', Mataji said. 'It is weak. See
that block?' There was an answering chorus of 'Yes!
Yes!' 'It is because he is a Freudian', she continued.
'Freud approached the psyche through the left,
forbidden side. The only mantra against Freud is
"Om Sakshat Mokshadaini Sakshat Nirmala Devi!
[Om, verily the giver of moksha, verily Nirmala
Devi.]"' The devotees began to chant the mantra as
they exorcised Freud.

Sudhir Kakar: *Shamans, Mystics and Doctors*

June's flat, impersonal in a huge 1930s block, is full of the scent
of the incense that she uses for meditation. She sits cross-
legged for the interview and speaks with brisk authority.

I'm 42, I'm divorced and I'm a psychic counsellor. I take
patients, yes, I have done for the past year. I don't meditate or
anything, I don't need to. I can give you a reading by just sitting
here and talking to you. I get pictures from anywhere and everywhere, I hear things – and I'm not screwy, by the way. I do
sometimes use cards for divination – they're not Tarot cards. I
stopped using those because people would say, 'Oh, I know what
that means', and I'd say, 'Oh no you don't!' – for six different
people it'll be different each time. Psychics are born this way, you
know. I'd many times been told over the years that I was. Now
my teacher recommends people to me; she sent me three today.
She's a woman, yes – in this lifetime. People recommend other
people, it's quite amazing the way it's all taken off.

The Freudian way really isn't the way. I had three years of
therapy – that was ten, twelve years ago. I don't think it's very
much in use any more. There's no two-way stuff, you get no

feedback. I know many, many people who found it very frustrating, people who wanted to help themselves, not people who were blocking or anything like that. What they use nowadays is transpersonal psychology, Gestalt, things like that. They're very helpful to get all the angles.

Rather than just let a person go on about their dreams, or maybe they've crossed the road and seen an orange balloon and what does it mean, it's much more useful if, for instance, someone is sitting cross-legged like I am now and you say, 'Now, why are you sitting like that? Why are you scratching your head? Think about it, get into it' – it's much more useful that way because you get your answers like *that*. There have been tremendous advances made, tremendous. People do terribly well now with three months, six months; it doesn't have to go on for ever.

Who's got the money? Who could lay on a couch for fifty minutes – and then, never mind what you're saying, when the fifty minutes is up, you are *out*, kiddo, that is it. Mind you, I used to be very much a Freudian until about two or three years ago, but I've talked to a lot of people, I've listened and I've read and I've taken very careful note, and I don't think it works any more.

In my case I started off with a guy who was a psychotherapist – he'd been fully trained – but because we got keen on each other he sent me to his own guy, who was a psychiatrist. We both fell for each other, yes, we had a relationship for quite a long time. So I went on to his own psychiatrist instead.

I went into therapy because I felt that I was screwed up. My parents had died, my marriage broke up because I went into it for all the wrong reasons, I wasn't having very satisfactory relationships and I just felt that I could do with some sorting out. And I went to my doctor and I said, 'I want to go and see a shrink', and he said, 'Oh nonsense, anybody who says they want to see a shrink doesn't need them.' Which I thought was a load of absolute rubbish, because I had realized that I wasn't as together as I wanted to be. I didn't have any experience of it at all, I just didn't feel together. And in the finish I nagged him, so he recommended me to this chap he knew, who was the one you know, we became interested in each other and then he recommended me on to his own psychiatrist.

In retrospect . . . well, at the time I thought it was useful. It explained a lot of things intellectually, but it never got to *here*. Inside. It helped me to intellectualize about things, it helped me to understand people; it didn't help me to live with things particularly well. He was one of the top people I think, very much trained in the traditional school; he died two or three years ago.

With so many of them the answer to everything is, 'What do *you* think is the problem?' OK, fine, we do have our own ideas – we may be right, we may not – but if we don't get feedback and we don't actually get led, which one doesn't with that kind of therapy, then we just don't know where the hell we are. You have these weird dreams and you have to hang on to them for a week, and then you might pick on the wrong dream because it's the one you happen to remember first . . . You see, the way I help people is very, very different. I certainly wouldn't go about it in that way. We discuss their problems together and I plant little seeds that take root and people seem to feel a lot more helped than by months or years of going to a shrink.

I went once a week, sometimes twice I think. Then I stopped seeing him eventually because he told me that I'd gone as far as I could and that there wasn't any more I needed to do. I knew that there was. That was after about three years. I didn't actually get very much out of these things being related to sex. I remember when I was getting . . . when I wanted to get to the bottom of everything, I said, 'Look, why can't we use some hypnosis? I really want to get to all this, get to the root of it, then we can talk about it after.' And he said, 'No, I am not going to use hypnosis; you unconsciously want me to fuck you.' And this is what the Freudians believe!

What *I* knew was that I couldn't afford twenty quid an hour for ever. Of course I wasn't working as a psychic counsellor then, I wasn't working at all, and that was a lot of money. I don't know, it's a bit like a farce, isn't it? They plonk themselves down on a chair or whatever, there's a clock on the desk, then – time's up, next please; it's a bit like a sort of cartoon, isn't it?

I don't think I can remember what we talked about – gosh, it's quite a long time ago. I'm not sure I ever really got to the bottom of everything. Then there's the question of, we are what many lifetimes have made us and how much do we want to get rid of? I do believe though that a little insight into themselves is something that everybody could do with. I don't know about digging and delving very deep – I think it depends how strong you are, because some people can't cope with it. Truthfully, now, looking back . . . it did seem to help at the time . . . but I didn't know, you see, that you were supposed to get in touch with your emotions. Later on I tried the sort of Californian type therapy groups and I think that helped. Mind you, I didn't realize that the guy who ran the encounter group was actually quite a freak himself – the group was one of the means by which he'd meet women who he'd later take to bed and screw.

The trouble with ordinary therapy is that they won't tell you what to do – no, no, no, they don't, they don't tell you anything at all. They don't explain, and the average person who is in a mess who goes along, not knowing how it operates, can be really thrown. If somebody says to you, 'Look, you do this and you do that, we will do so-and-so and so-and-so, right now let's get on with it' – that's fine. But you can't go in like that, and sit there like that and talk to a complete stranger about all sorts of intimate things without having established some kind of rapport. I don't think so at the beginning, anyway.

I never felt I got at my *feelings* in the three years; I got in touch with my thoughts. And we discussed why this and why that and my father and my mother and my brothers and relationships, but it never got further down than *this*. The funny thing was that he didn't look unlike my father in certain ways. Which had I realized at the time, not having got on well with my father, I would have changed immediately. It's not a good basis to start a therapy. I think really it's terribly haphazard the way people go on about finding somebody for help. I wish there were a more efficient way of finding the right person. At the time I went to therapy there wasn't anybody to talk to about it and I didn't know how I should be thinking, how I should be feeling – how do you know if you can't compare? And then if you're not getting on with the particular person, he might say you're – what's the word? – resisting. I can never remember that word – I resist the word resisting!

I never ever burst into tears there. Not that I can recall – there might have been the occasional sob from within that didn't come without. I always felt in awe of him. I didn't feel that I could walk in there and relax or be however I wanted to be – which let's face it, paying x pounds per hour for someone under those circumstances, you should be able to. I always felt I had to be in control – a totally wrong kind of thinking. The fact that his physical appearance was a bit like my father's didn't help. He was very big and very broad and very seemingly together – I didn't find out until he died that he was really quite screwed up at home; he was a good therapist, psychiatrist, but he was screwed up at home. But, then, that's the same as me and my clients; we've all got problems. I can help anybody, but when it comes to me, I have to think about it that much more carefully.

One thing that really used to get to me was that he had nice little knick-knacks and ornaments around the place, and on occasion I thought, that's nice, I haven't seen that before, and he'd say, 'That was a present from a patient.' So that for some reason I used to feel, God, he expects presents from me. OK, it was my problem that I felt inadequate, but I didn't know at all, I didn't know, I felt I needed guidelines. Why I thought I needed guidelines, I honestly don't know. Because one ought to have been able to go in there and just behave however.

We would either sit facing each other or sometimes he would sit behind me and I would be on a sort of chaise with a blanket over me and the lights dimmed. He tried a little bit of . . . not hypnosis as such, but sort of, 'Look at the light over there and relax', that sort of thing. But I didn't ever really relax with him. He called me by my first name – not Christian name, if you don't mind. We all say a lot of things without thinking; I don't have Christian, Jewish or Buddhist names. I called him – well, at the beginning I was too much in awe to call him anything, then I used to call him by his first name. He wouldn't let me smoke, and as an inveterate smoker I found that quite disconcerting, so therefore I wasn't relaxed . . . It was, 'Why do you need a cigarette?', you know, oral satisfaction and all that kind of stuff. 'Oh,' he would say, 'well, you can have *one*.'

No, of course, I didn't discuss my analysis with the first therapist while we were having a relationship. He would say that any problems that you've got, you must talk to so-and-so. Which was quite right, because he wasn't going to interfere or put his own stuff in. I remember that he gave a Christmas party one year, the one I was having a relationship with; and the other one and his wife were invited because he'd finished the therapy with him. It was very nice meeting him outside, very pleasant, but very . . . well, a bit stand-offish, which is how it should have been. I liked him socially – he was nice, he was great socially, had a terrific sense of humour – but I didn't particularly go overboard about him in the consulting room.

I remember sort of enthusing for quite a long time after the analysis, and yet in retrospect I realize that it wasn't that great. Things have changed so much for me in the last two or three years. I suppose at the time it was something to hang on to . . . I remember when he was ill or on holiday I used to get frantic, everybody does. I mean, I have clients doing it to me, they'll phone me up two or three times a day.

I used to write things down between the sessions because I am a great writer-down; and then I was told, 'No, don't write down, just say whatever comes into your head whenever you come again.' So then you wonder, well is it what I should be remembering, am I resisting, am I this, am I that? Because all the time I was being told, 'You're resisting this, you're resisting that.' I think that is a very handy answer to a lot of things – I'm not saying that I wasn't resisting, but I do think it's a very handy answer.

You've got to remember something that probably doesn't get told – you will always get to see the therapist who has got similar sorts of problems to you. All of a sudden, for instance, I start having a batch of clients who will have something that will come up in my own life; therapists always attract people with their own problems always. That's the way it works. It's psychic, of course

– I don't think, I *know*. I've discussed it with several people who do that sort of work and they all say the same thing.

I suppose at the time it heped me to understand as much as I was able. I am, for instance, about *here* at the moment, while in those days I was right down *there*. But my relationships with men, it never helped with those. Only recently I've managed to choose the right sort of men for me, whereas in the past I'd always chosen men who I called rats. My father, I would say, was that kind of man. I was just copying what I knew, what I was comfortable with in a sense. You know, I was used to being rejected, so what did I choose? Comfortable rejection stuff. I don't now.

I left the therapy when he told me that I didn't need any more. I didn't feel that that was actually the situation, but I thought, well, he knows what he's talking about. I went to see him on the odd occasion after that, the very odd occasion, perhaps two or three times a year if I had a problem – which nowadays I go and talk to a friend, because I don't think he was that helpful actually. And then, I suppose, between then and these last few years, there was probably a kind of limbo state. I was just doing secretarial work and I met a man who conned me for a whole lot of money – oh yes, I didn't know it at the time, a very clever con man who had done it to many people. I was very vulnerable, very emotional, very much on my own, like a rotten apple ready to fall into the hands of somebody who was seemingly kind and caring and stuff. I mean, can you imagine believing such a load of rubbish? It seems very unlike me now, doesn't it? Nowadays I think I'm quite a shrewd cookie. In the old days I was the least thing like a shrewd cookie that you can imagine, but one changes, fortunately. All the changes have been in the last few years.

I suppose I started to become aware, psychically, spiritually, in those sorts of ways, about four years ago and it sort of built up. I've met all sorts of people who have helped. My life has expanded, I have expanded, I understand a great deal more; it's to do with the spiritual development, that's what actually helped. I'd started questioning at the age of about 24 what is life all about, this can't be all there is to it, and that was actually when I started to see the shrink – I thought he would help me find some of the answers, which he didn't. But I started to meet people who seemed a little bit more aware of the other side, the higher stuff if you like.

I found that the path I followed was a pretty convoluted one. The people who at that time I really looked up to and thought, my goodness, you know a tremendous amount about the higher world – well, they weren't quite the teachers I thought they were. I became more and more aware and I started to listen to my own inner ideas, which at one stage I used to disregard and say, 'Oh, it's your imagination' – that kind of thing. I found myself voraciously going to the library and reading everything I could lay my hands on about spiritual unfoldment. I did go into the spiritualist side of things, but it's not for me.

Then, not terribly long ago I met the person who became my teacher, my master, whatever you like to call it; who when I walked in said, 'And what are you doing with your psychic ability, young lady?' And I felt, here's somebody who can help me, train me! It's an amalgam of things that I've learnt, philosophy, psychic development, cosmology. It's what this person has found has worked over the last 6,500 years, it's what has worked for *me* over the last 6,500 years and for all the people in the group surrounding this person for 6,500 years. Oh, I don't believe in reincarnation; I *know*. You don't honestly think that this life is all there is to it, do you?

My answer to things didn't come through psychotherapy, though it helped me to understand intellectually a bit. Two years after it I met the guy who conned me, so I don't think I'd learned much. I still had a very negative self-image. What really helped me was meeting these people, learning these things . . . I didn't realize at the time that there's always a reason why you meet who you do when you do, the right people at the right time.

You see, a friend had rung me from abroad and I'd tuned in and been able to tell her all sorts of stuff; and my teacher said, 'Well, if you're able to do it at that distance, you can start taking clients whenever you like.' That was what *really* helped my self-confidence. People ask me how long have I been doing this for and I generally say, 'Many lifetimes'. They say, 'Oh, but that's very expensive for an hour' – but you're not paying for an hour,

you're paying for developing all my life and many other lifetimes.
I always wanted to help people and now I do. I was interested in
this kind of thing even when I was in therapy, but the shrink was
inclined to pooh-pooh things, you know, and say, 'On no, no,
people who see things and hear voices, they're in funny farms.'
Which, of course, isn't the case. Over the years I'd been told,
'You're very psychic, you're very psychic'; and then I met this
person who said, 'Right, I'd like to teach you.' It was just what I'd
always wanted. And it sort of snowballed.

I don't use psychoanalysis in my own work, no, not at all. My
confidence has come from proving that I had an inherent ability
that was trained and developed, that I can use, that I can help
people with. I know what my role in life is now. But it hasn't
anything to do with going to see that guy. Unfortunately. All that
money spent! In a way I think it might have been the guy
who conned me who taught me something, because I remember
him saying, 'You can say anything to anybody providing you say it
right.'

Margery

I wanted to sit in the outer breast pocket of his suit, sticking my head out and eyeballing the world from that safe vantage point. Once I dreamt that I had, Jonah-like, entered the inner space of his body and wandered about in it . . .

Tilmann Moser: *Years of Apprenticeship on the Couch*

Margery's cottage is at the end of a dark mews, forlorn and isolated like its owner. Up above the garages everything is in miniature – tiny kitchen, tinier bathroom, sitting-room with two chairs facing each other; it's the shipshape world of her sailor father. She sleeps on the sitting-room couch and won't go back into the bedroom she shared with her husband.

===

I was 70 when my husband died. At first I thought I was going to be all right; I got through everything for the first few days. Then I found I was shaking when I woke up in the morning. When I was in the street, I thought my legs were going to give way. I can't describe what it was like. No, I'm sorry, I don't know how to describe it. Something very dark and bitter, if you know what I mean. It was a dreadful time. No, I didn't have friends to turn to; my husband wasn't a sociable person, he didn't believe in my making friends. Of course my doctor sent me to the hospital and I got given pills for depression – they made me *ill*! My tongue swelled right up and I was staggering even worse in the street. I stopped them; I said, 'No, thanks'. So it was on the Health Service when I first started seeing Dr Grey. Once a week at the hospital.

I remember the first time that was just to assess me, whether I was to be a patient. But the second time! Of course I went in expecting him to say more than good morning – and he was silent.

I just went in and he said, 'Good morning', and then he said, 'Sit down'. We were both sitting in chairs, he was to the left of me. Not a very nice room; it seemed like someone else's office. And there was silence! And . . . I waited for something to be said. And there was nothing. And I hadn't the faintest idea what I was supposed to say. I'd already explained to him my situation, how it had come about, but what more could I say? And this went on for practically the whole of the session. I did say a few things, I can't remember what now; but I went out of the room very concerned, very disturbed.

I couldn't just say, 'What's going on, why don't you talk to me?' – well, I just couldn't. I mean, here's somebody who's a psychiatrist; you think he knows what's happening, he knows what we should be doing. But surely, when it's a new patient who's never been in therapy before and hasn't the faintest idea what it's all about – somebody at least ought to say, 'Well, look, don't be surprised if I don't speak to you, I'm just waiting for you to say the first thing that comes into your head.' Because it just makes your brain seize up and you can't think of anything, not a thing!

I was secretary to a psychiatrist way back in the Fifties and he used to do this quite differently. He used to talk about questioning the patients, taking them back over all the events of their lives, till they came to the point when the trauma had occurred. And if they got stuck because the trauma was too deep, he would give them pentothal, and question them under pentothal until he could hit at the trauma. So I absolutely expected to be asked questions, and when I wasn't asked questions, I didn't know what on earth I was supposed to talk about.

Well then, the second time I went I did try to say something and I said it was very, very difficult to feel there was nobody in the world who loved you. So he said, 'Yes, but I'll love you.' Yes. Wasn't it strange to say that? That's what he said: 'Within the context of this relationship I love you and I care for you.' And yet, of course, the first time I'd seen him I hadn't liked the look of him at all! I'd felt this is just exactly the type of man I can't stand. Small, slim; and mostly the men I'd met who were small and slim were madly self-opinionated. I had an uncle who was like that and he was totally unbearable. So at the beginning I'd thought, what can I do, I must go back to the doctor who'd recommended me and say, 'Please can I have another psychiatrist'! But then by the third time I went to see him I was completely hooked. Completely. It was like falling in love, you know, looking across a crowded room and seeing somebody and oomph! you're overboard. I think it must be some kind of influence, rather like ESP in a way, I suppose. It was a sort of feeling: right, I'm on the other end of an umbilical cord.

I was still so worried and I thought, well here I am, I have the opportunity to have this therapy and I don't know how to do it. I told him various things and we began to get a little bit somewhere, but still I wasn't really feeling that I was doing the right thing. And I was feeling so bereft, I felt that all I wanted was for somebody to be terribly kind to me, to take my hand and put their arm around me and then that would melt me inside – because by now I was a screwed-up ball inside, you see, and that was bloody painful. You see, with this silent technique . . . unless somebody speaks to me, primes the pump if you like, I just can't start saying anything. And this was, of course, the great problem.

He did sometimes say, 'What are you thinking about now?' – but then my mind went such a blank! It was rather like if you're trying to go to sleep and you can't and your brain either thinks silly things or seizes up. I just went absolutely inarticulate. But yes, I did feel someone was caring for me and looking after me; and the other thing was that as far as I was concerned, if there's nobody in this world I can love, I'm lost. So I suppose he was . . .

And yet I thought he'd not really shown much interest and sympathy, in a way. Because the second time I went to him I'd discovered before I went that I'd locked myself out of my own front door – I was so flustered. So when I got there I told him I'd locked myself out; he didn't say *anything*! And when I went back the next week I thought he would surely say to me, 'How did you manage about getting into the house when you got back?' He didn't say a word! And then the trouble was that this began to have the effect on me that I was confused the whole of the time. I went about everywhere just trying to think, how was I supposed to deal with this – what should I say and what should I be doing? Sometimes he said to me, 'That's not up to me, that's up to you. Say anything you like, say the first thing that comes into your head.' And yet I do remember one time when I was feeling terribly distressed – and this happened more than once – and I said exactly what I was thinking, and he just answered, 'I don't know why you're telling me this – I can't see what relevance it has at all.'

Yes, of course I was dreadfully upset by that, but I'd had it drilled into me by my mother that people like doctors and schoolteachers, you didn't argue with them. So I didn't turn round and say, 'Well, you just told me to say what came into my head and I've done it and you've told me it is the wrong thing.' I couldn't do that, ever. No, I didn't seem to be angry, it's just that I was thinking all the time, I'm doing this all wrong, what's the matter with me? – if only someone would explain it to me. I wondered if it was like a wife who stayed with her husband even though he beat her. But no, he's not like that . . .

I used to have dreadful pains in my inside when I had to go to the session – terrible! And my mind was continuously on what I was supposed to do. I did the daftest things. I got into Tube trains going in the wrong direction. When I tried to do the bookkeeping in my voluntary job, it was murder, I simply couldn't do it. There was only one thing going on in my mind all day and all night: that if I go on like this and can't do it properly, then he'll get rid of me – and I couldn't possibly do without him.

No, I can't really remember what we talked about. I just remember the feeling of being a sort of prisoner in interrogation – you know, whether he's guilty or not he eventually shouts, 'I did it, I did it!' Of course, we did talk about my parents and my childhood, my father being away at sea so much of the time, how awful my mother was, all that. Whenever I said something about being depressed, that I didn't know what to do and all the rest of it, he always said, 'I can't help feeling that this is all to do with your relationship with me.' And that annoyed me and I thought, well I'm not talking about my relationship with you, I'm talking about *other* things in my life. But, you see, I couldn't get annoyed with him even though he said I should. I thought that if I ever did say to him, 'I don't believe what you're saying', he'd say, 'Well, all right, if you think I don't know what I'm doing just get out of here and don't come back.' But it *is* different now, yes; we've been talking about it only this week.

All this first eighteen months was on the Health Service. Then he said if he was asked to take another Health Service patient, one of his present patients would have to go and that would be me. And so I said would he take me as a private patient? I think really he was a bit worried that this would be something I couldn't afford, but everything got muddled and mixed up and I thought he really wasn't going to take me. And I had exactly the same feeling, *exactly* the same, as I had when the doctor at St Mary's said, 'Your husband died an hour ago.' And I just thought, now he's going to get rid of me, he's been waiting to get rid of me . . . Well, then, of course, it all got worked out and he did say that it was the cost that had worried him, and could I afford it? I thought about it all a lot and I said to him, 'What would you have done if I couldn't have afforded it?' He just said, 'Oh, I would have referred you back to your G P.' And I said, '*That* would have been a lot of good!' Well, of course, I've never told him yet how much that upset me. It sounded so offhand . . .

When I could go to him privately I felt much easier with him than at the hospital. We started out sitting next to one another and I said, 'Look, it's no use. I can't communicate with you sitting on this chair alongside you.' So he said, 'Would you like to go on the couch?' I said yes. At that time I was still having those dreadful pains in my inside. I looked forward to the session all week and yet each time I came away frustrated; there still seemed to be a barrier between us that I couldn't get over. He said to me, 'This seems to me very much like the situation you have described as regards your father; that you wanted comfort from him and his support against your mother, and being away at sea he wasn't there to do it.' And I said, 'Yes, that's right. That's the situation we keep coming back to.' And he's said to me once or twice, 'You must be angry with me, you must be thinking, here's this man, I'm paying him and we're not getting anywhere!'

But I can't be angry with him. I'm angry with myself. I remember this psychiatrist I used to work for said unless the person is intelligent enough to understand the therapy, it's no use taking them as a patient. And I thought, my goodness, I must be an idiot, I don't seem to understand what's going on. I get angry with myself, though he's always telling me I should be angry with *him*. I don't get the pains inside any more, though. I think they were caused by my always thinking, is this doing me any good? Am I ever going to get any better? Am I going on for ever not knowing the right thing to say and not getting the right answers? Sometimes I get pains when I come away still because I've asked him questions and not got any answers, or when I say something and he always brings it back to my relationship with him – that I'm worried about a break or I'd like to see him more than once a week. Sometimes it doesn't seem to me so, but I say to myself, well, he knows better than I do.

One thing right from the beginning that was very strange was that I had awful sexual feelings. I don't know whether they were about him, but I was just roused . . . It went on for weeks! I went through absolute hell! I did tell him to some extent, but not completely. But he knew it . . . At one time I said to him, 'All I want is physical contact, not absolutely sexual contact, but my hand held, you know.' 'But that's no good,' he said; anything like that – putting his arm round me, holding my hand, saying sympathetic things – that would only be a palliative and we had to get to the bottom of things. But, of course, I would have loosened up and not been so tight inside if I could have had that response. So later on he did hold my hand, and then one time he let me stroke him all through the session. Yes. But after a while he withdrew and sat further away from me. He said, 'The time when it was a purely sexual feeling and you wanted the physical contact and to touch me, that's over now.' But I don't know . . . I said to him, 'I want to crawl inside you; crawl up that umbilical cord and inside you.'

Last week when I got back to the flat I found a mark on the

ceiling where some water had come in. And I kept ringing and ringing the builders and couldn't get any reply and then they said they'd pass the message on and nobody phoned. What with coming back from holiday, which is always awful, and then seeing the patch on the ceiling and thinking the whole thing would collapse – well, it's a feeling like a nightmare I can hardly describe. It's as though I'm pressed in, I'm totally isolated; inside me there's despair, bereavement. And there's also 'I hate everybody' and everywhere I go is grey and grim, and wherever I am I want to be somewhere else. He said, 'The grey, that's the suppression of all your anger which ought to come out.' And he said, 'What you have to do is grow up.' I told him again how I *couldn't* really get angry, I was afraid he'd say, 'Are you suggesting I don't know what I'm doing?' He told me, 'You've *got* to get it into your mind that you can say anything you like to me, it doesn't matter what it is, and I shall not think any the less of you and I shall certainly not tell you to go away and not come back again.'

I told him I felt like I did when I was about fifteen or sixteen. My mother was treading on all my sore points and getting enraged with me and it was all absolutely horrible, so I wrote to my father, whom of course I only saw when he was on leave from the sea, and told him about this. And he wrote and told my mother. And instead of taking it sensibly, she said I was trying to alienate herself from my father and I shouldn't write to him like that, and went on and on. I felt my father had completely failed me. And when he'd retired – I was about twenty-two – I remember so clearly saying to him, 'Why don't you and I go and leave my mother and live together?' He said we couldn't, we mustn't upset her like that; and, of course, that to me was a blow. He had failed me again. So I felt like that sometimes with Dr Grey – you know, 'I asked for bread and thou gavest me a stone'.

Oh, I don't mean he hasn't given me bread. You know how much better I am these days. I did gradually begin to see more what he was getting at and to see that some of the things that in my mind I had rejected were, in fact, right. And that made me able to sort out exactly what we were talking about, and always getting to this point where definitely he is my father and I'm the daughter wanting consolation and help from a situation which is unbearable. But the whole thing isn't yet resolved because, of course, it doesn't take much to send me over the top again. And I've been coming once a week for nearly four years now! But I am better, yes.

I think it's because you come to understand more. You don't think as you go through life. You take what happens to you for granted to some extent, you don't analyse what it's doing to you. Particularly when it comes to relationships with parents. In my day, sixty or seventy years ago, you had no rights with your parents — if they said black was white, black was white. I know I've got right to this situation which is absolutely a replica of my feelings about my father in relation to my mother — the fact that I wanted from him consolation and help to get rid of the awful thing that was happening to me, of the way my mother was. And he didn't give it. I say to Dr Grey, 'Look, you haven't got rid of all this', and he says, 'Well, no, you've got to get all this anger out of your system and *I'm* the person you have to get it out of your system with!'

I say, 'Yes, but it's so difficult.' He says, 'I know, you're frightened I'll reject you.' And then I've said, 'The trouble is, you're the professional, so to speak, and why should I question what you're doing?' 'Well,' he said, 'you've every right to question what I'm doing. You're paying for it!' He said that to me several times, you know — 'What do you think you're paying for?' Actually, I did tell him about several times when I'd thoroughly disagreed with him and it had upset me, and he said, 'Now you're beginning to be angry with me, aren't you? You're telling me now, aren't you?' But I do still throw it all back on myself. And when I think it's me that's wrong, then, of course, I get the feeling that I'm somebody not worth bothering about and *he* won't bother if I can't get angry in the way he says I should.

There's a funny thing too, and I'm going to tell him this — he's got three different faces. Well, first there's the one that he didn't use so much when we were in the hospital — but you know when you're on the couch and they sort of sit looking like this, as though they're asleep, very withdrawn; that's rather off-putting. Then there's another face he has – I'm telling him something and he looks as though to say what on earth am I telling him this for. And then there's another one, when we're talking and his face changes entirely and he looks like a quite different person – nice, yes, very nice.

He's said sometimes that he didn't remember saying such dismissive things. He says, 'Well I'm very sorry but I didn't mean it that way'; but they don't realize . . . I think he's just beginning to understand how easily I can be thrown off balance and how something quite ordinary will, in my mind, start all sorts of trends of thought that to me are very upsetting. But I hate it. Nobody should be like I am.

I don't think it's just my parents. It was also that time when I first went to school and the whole class bullied me. My mother knew how desperately miserable I was at that school; I had all sorts of illnesses just to stop having to go to school. I was the odd one out all the time, not just among the children but among the nuns as well. They picked on me for everything, even if I hadn't done it. I'm sure that had a tremendous effect on me, because although my mother had been so difficult, at least I'd been sheltered. I'd always been among adults. Children recognize an outcast like animals do.

I told you, didn't I, how my mother never really wanted children but that she decided to have me to resolve her problems – but, of course, having a baby doesn't resolve anybody's problems. She'd had to look after my youngest aunt and didn't want to have to wash any more nappies or baby clothes. And, of course, I used to hear about how I used to cry and keep her awake at night, and how difficult it was when we went to see my father on board ship and she had to do my washing on the ship, and how awful all this was and what a nuisance. When she went ashore with my father – I remember it, though I must have been very small indeed – she left me with the bosun. A cross-eyed bosun! And she said I screamed like mad because although it was time for me to be fed, I didn't want to leave the bosun. The sailors used to make a tremendous fuss of me when they were doing jobs like polishing or scrubbing the decks – they used to play with me for hours. Oh, she made it quite clear to me that I'd been a dreadful nuisance.

But it was a self-inflicted wound, wasn't it? I mean anybody who thinks that having a baby is going to solve their problems is doing a great deal to that poor child.

Oh, he has helped me to get a lot better. I have more confidence now, you see. I never felt I could manage if anything went wrong in the house. I've often said to people, 'Please, show me how.' And then it's: 'Oh, you'll never do it, it's no use you trying.' When I had this leak in the lavatory, I didn't realize that there was a tap you could turn off, so there was water running all over the place. So easily I just seem to turn into a little helpless person who doesn't know what to do. But I realize that everything that's gone wrong in the house since my husband died I have managed to cope with. And also when I go out on various excursions or holidays I can talk to people now without any problem. I simply couldn't communicate before, but now I even find people saying, 'Oh, that's very interesting.' When we were talking, Dr Grey used a very old-fashioned expression. I was saying how in spite of this feeling that I was useless, I always managed to get things done in the end, and he said, 'Yes, you're no slouch, are you!'

I suppose when you have to finish the treatment you are debriefed so that your feelings are reversed. Because if you weren't debriefed, you'd never be able to leave him. I said to him, 'I can't possibly see myself going out of this room and never seeing you again.' He said, 'You don't have to – when you come to the end, you can ring up and see me any time you want to; the only thing that worries me is what it's costing you.' But what else would I be doing with that money? I've got nobody to leave it to. Mind you, he did say once very curtly, 'You know, you've got to come to an end of it some time.' But I didn't remind him of that.

In a way I'd rather not have had this whole experience; on the other hand, of course, it is something extraordinary, a very weird relationship. Suppose I had met my analyst socially, I mightn't even have liked him, as I didn't when I first saw him. If I were to meet him socially now outside, it would be very disturbing – I don't know if I'd ever be able to get back to the relationship again. I did meet him just coming into the door once. It was a shock! He just smiled at me.

I said to him once, 'You know, if I'd been younger, I'd have done my very best to seduce you.' Because, you see, I used to be able to do this very easily – I'm not boasting, because I didn't want them, never did it on purpose, but I was fighting men off! And the number who wanted to haul me off to bed with them is nobody's business. I really didn't want to go out and meet people sometimes because I got so sick of them wanting me to go to bed with them. I found it very easy and I didn't even try! So he said, 'What would you have done if you'd succeeded? Think of what it would have done to me! What about my wife?' I said, 'You haven't got one – as far as I'm concerned you have *no* wife and no family!'

I said, 'You'd have invited me to your flat to dinner and you'd have put some nice music on the record-player and we would have had drinks. You would have cooked the dinner and put it in the oven, and then while we waited for it to cook we would go to bed. Then we wouldn't get dressed, we would just get up and have our dinner and then after we had had dinner we'd go back to bed again.' He just kept saying, 'But what about my wife?' 'No, you haven't got a wife,' I said. I didn't allow him one. And he'd sometimes mention all this – but I notice now he never ever mentions it any more.

And I do come back all the time to the other thing, this feeling of being a depressing person, the feeling that because you're old you're just rubbish, not worth bothering about. I say to him that I'm like a motor car that someone's had for years and years and keeps on taking back to the garage because they can't bear to let it go to the junkyard, and then one day the garage man says, 'Look, mate, I can't do any more with this, you've got to let it go.' I feel I'm wasting his time. I'm a depreciating asset. I feel, well, after all at my age . . . but then I don't *feel* my age; why shouldn't I be having him? I can't have things like I used to have when my life was interesting and stimulating, all that's gone and there's no way I can get it back.

Last year there was a time when suddenly I felt very much better, it was in the summer – I suddenly felt, my goodness, I'm getting back to normal. I was lying on the couch and I suddenly had a vision of myself as I used to be. I told him about it the next week. 'Well, then,' he said before the summer break, 'maybe we should start thinking next year about phasing the sessions out.' That did it! That really did it! So you see I'm not ready. He said after the break, 'We were talking about phasing it out, weren't we?' – and of course that sent me oomph! down into the depths. So I just said, 'I'm terribly sorry but I'm afraid *not*. No.' So I'm going to go on for as long as he can carry the burden. Definitely.

Véronique

But often in the world's most crowded streets,
But often, in the din of strife,
There rises an unspeakable desire
After the knowledge of our buried life,
A thirst to spend our fire and restless force
In tracking out our true, original course . . .

Matthew Arnold: *The Buried Life*

Véronique's long drawing-room looks out onto a pale stone bust at the end of the garden, ivy-overgrown. 'There's my bit of France in the suburbs', she says. Polished woods and gilt and marquetry – heirlooms – shine in firelight. She threads her elegantly tangled hair as she talks.

———————

I was 10 when my mother died. She'd been ill from the time I was 5 or 6, I think with high blood pressure and other things. My father was quite a disturbed sort of personality, very immature, narcissistic; an officer in the navy, always out to get reassurance through adventures and excitement. He saw himself as being very charming – and he did have a lot of charm – but his sense of commitment as a father and to the family was really rather lacking.

Going into psychoanalysis was always connected with the intention of training to be an analyst myself, but it was firmly coupled with a clear knowledge that I needed an awful lot sorting out in my personal life. It started . . . well, I suppose it started with my Catholic upbringing in a very aristocratic French family with a strong Catholic tradition, growing up and questioning all these things – the nonsense of aristocracy and the unanswerable questions that come up when one looks into religion and religious beliefs. And so, really, in my teens I started wanting to get rid of all this, to find something more satisfactory.

There was a lot of pathology in my family – I suppose there is in most families, some more, some less. I've always felt that my family lived about fifty to a hundred years behind the times. Families with traditions that they cling to are more or less closed to change, so that might have contributed to the atmosphere. My family felt to me . . . it felt as though I couldn't have an ordinary life like my peers because there were these pressures to behave according to all these codes. And my sister – well, I'm one of three children, my older brother, myself and my younger sister – my sister I always perceived as very vulnerable, very much in need of protection. I think unconsciously the whole family treated her that way. She was very talented, very beautiful, very artistic; she could paint beautifully and from the time she could put two words together she would make little poems. She gradually became a very good writer and continued painting as well; so she was quite gifted, and yet emotionally very frail and she had breakdown after breakdown from the age of 21 onwards.

I sort of became the obvious mother substitute – my brother too was always difficult and I was the one who was trying to be sensible and grown-up. That had its compensations, in the sense that I always felt competent and managing in many ways . . . but on the other hand it is very burdensome and doesn't really allow one to live spontaneously. I was aware that although I was considered so very sensible, reliable, all these things, my personal development had suffered very much. I was always in some dim way aware that there was a lot of me that hadn't had a chance of growing and developing. I couldn't have been able to say it as clearly as I say it now, but I think I have always known what I wanted, this sort of basic orientation has been there all the time and I've always been very determined that if there was something really important, I would relentlessly go for it.

While my mother was alive we lived in Paris. My father always wanted to live above what we could financially afford and I think that caused my mother a great deal of anxiety, although things like money wouldn't be discussed. On the one hand we had a very grandiose set-up, with an apartment on the rue de Rivoli and a cook and servants and batman and all that, and on the other hand my mother would say one day, we are not going to have jam for breakfast, or it was jam and no butter; it was incongruous, difficult to make sense of, when everything else was so out of character.

My mother's death was devastating, it was really devastating. We went to live in Lyons with my father, who left the navy and decided to look after us, not really having a clue on how to deal with children. So it was very traumatic for him, I think, and for us. We were very afraid of my father and we knew him very little. He was very given to temper tantrums, and if things weren't just so – if his silk shirts weren't ironed without a tiny crease – the house would come tumbling down. Idiotic things like that . . . I was expected suddenly to be mini-house-keeper – you know, we'd had a nanny looking after us and I had never had any idea of housekeeping or anything like that. And also my father quarrelled with all of my mother's family, so that meant that we not only lost mother, but the whole of the network – my grandmother used to live with us, and aunts and uncles, and they quarrelled until we kind of went into isolation in Lyons with this frightening father.

There were lots of disturbing, upsetting things like that. Then it came time to go to the university and again my father wanted me to be at home and run the home for him. In the old days I suppose I would have been doomed to be the unmarried daughter living at home and looking after father, and as I guessed that that was his plan, I rebelled with all my might and refused, though there was nothing I could do because legally he could keep me in his house till I was, I think, 21. So till 21 I would have had to stay whether I liked it or not. When I realized that I think I cried the whole summer, and my father in disgust cast me off and said go. I went and lived with my aunt, and went to university and studied. Even that was a very disturbing thing for me, that final un-satisfactory break from home. I see now that there was break after break, a sort of spiralling repetition, starting right from the time when I was weaned as a baby. But then I learned, I think, to break the vicious spiral gradually, to get more in charge of it, later on; that's what happens if you can go over and over the experience in a more bearable way.

So you see, there was a lot that I knew had upset me enormously. I was longing to sort out all kinds of confusions and muddles in my head. While I was living with my aunt I started to read Jung, on the advice of a friend of hers. I thought it was fantastic and I read avidly most of his books, though half of the time I only dimly understood them. This was the kind of reading that leaves room for magical fantasies and also for not facing facts, or for interpreting things as you like or idealizations – all sorts of things, as I found out later.

This was while I was at the Sorbonne; I was reading languages, not because I wanted to but because it was my only choice, given that my father had decided my course of study without asking me what I wanted. That was one of the other horrors, you know. I would come back from holidays and find that he had put my name down for a school or something without even asking me – so in the end I did foreign languages and literature. And there must have been some faint idea that I could get away, travel somewhere with languages. I went for lessons of English from a young Englishman who was working for one of these schools of English, and eventually he is the one that I married and therefore came to this country when he decided not to stay in France. He was a lawyer who had temporarily got fed up with law and decided to have a year or two abroad, so he came back to return to his law and I came to this country with him. And I had a child straight away.

He was Scottish, and we went to live in Scotland, in the country. Yes, it's a lovely part of the world, but I was utterly miserable there – wanting to train as an analyst still, I felt really cut off; it's one thing to go there on holiday when you choose, but to live there all your life is a very limiting and limited sort of situation for someone who has my interests. There were mainly retired people there, retired army people or landowners, people interested in farming, a handful of solicitors and doctors, and that was it. I felt really very much a fish out of water. I couldn't really find anyone who understood my ideas – they thought I was very intense! Eventually I made a very good friend and we still remain great friends – she's a farmer, but a very unusual farmer and very widely read, you know, an interested and interesting woman. In all sorts of walks of life you can find very interesting people in spite of whatever upbringing or background they may have had.

But those were years of isolation and study. I survived just through reading like mad for five years, but in the end I just couldn't stand it and I had to come to London to do my training as a therapist, which was what I'd always wanted. First of all I did a course of social study as a preparation. The very reason why I live in this house is because there used to be a college here where I could do this course. I didn't want to have long distances to travel and I could be there for my son when he came home from school and all that. So he started his primary school here and I started my social work studies course, and then I looked for a placement in a clinic where I could have relevant experience, working with children and families. And I worked there for a year before I started my analysis in order to save enough money to buy a car to travel to and fro. Then I started my analysis. But really I wouldn't like to call it an analysis; it would be more appropriate to call it supportive therapy.

I began to realize with this therapy that I was acting things out instead of really learning to understand them. When it's a question of getting in touch with early childhood, it needs to be interpreted and understood and contained, otherwise you just act it out again. Gradually, as I listened to friends who were working with their analysts in this way, I began to have great doubts. It was a very painful, long-drawn-out realization that this wasn't good enough. I was dissatisfied with my parenting experience as a child and I had gone with the intention of finding some good experience that would sort things out for me, and I found myself repeating so many of the negative patterns in which I was the one who was carrying the parents, instead of being the child cared for.

I wasn't, for instance, allowed to be depressed; if I felt de-pressed the analyst would think of ways of cheering me up, so there was no opportunity of working through the problem. One of the worst things was that I was reinforced in my deep conviction that I knew better than the people I was supposed to be depending on. So I felt I was the only truly marvellous one, in love with myself – I didn't start to know how to love other people. This whole muddle made me angry and despairing, and I wanted to hurt, to get my revenge.

Of course it depends what people are looking for in therapy. I was very clear in my mind that I was looking for something deep, thorough and fundamental. I wasn't looking for a little patching-up business over this or that little thing that needed sorting out. If somebody is not too dissatisfied with their personality and maybe wants only some minor area touched on, then maybe, I don't know . . . But I really wanted to go back to Adam and Eve and have a thorough rethinking and revisioning, and have things clarified and confusions and muddles sorted out – that's what I wanted. And I wouldn't have been satisfied with a little patching up, because I felt there were some very fundamental things that hadn't been attended to in my life.

I think it appeared from the second analysis I subsequently had that there was a very traumatic time in my life connected with weaning and the birth of my sister, when I had no father to turn to. I know that there was the war, that my mother was extremely anxious about my father, who was on a convoy and always in danger of being bombed or sunk by – what is it in English? – torpedoes, yes. My mother was sort of trying to reach my father in any place where he stopped for a bit. I don't know whether we were bundled up and taken here and there with her. I think I must have from then on turned into this precocious mini-mother-helper, and been very sensible and very good and really denying and setting on one side all my real self. I mean people would say in amazement, '*You* are needing an analysis?' – because I always managed to function; but a lot of my more primitive and in-stinctive early emotions had to lie completely dormant, weren't allowed to be experienced and lived through and integrated. So there was only a very partial me there.

The problem with my first analysis was partly that I was in the position every patient is in – I wanted to change, but didn't want to have my nose rubbed into what was no good in me. I did want change, but without coming down from a sort of pinnacle of superiority that I'd got used to over the years, what with my family background and precocious pseudo-adult role. But that kind of supportive therapy doesn't aim at restructuring the personality, more at strengthening the good parts of it. I needed to *do away* with that pseudo-adult person altogether. I needed to be as dependent as a child and then eventually emerge as a real adult.

So I was caught in that first therapy with a conflict of needs and wishes until I couldn't ignore any longer that you can't have your cake and eat it. Of course, at the time I wouldn't have been able to describe it as clearly as I'm doing for you now. I think my saving grace was that I'd had some good early mothering – I had some notion of what I lost too soon and wanted to go back to, just enough of a good start to give an idea of what I had lost. I had a sense of what was imitation and what was the real thing.

At first, you see, after those years in Scotland and a broken or breaking marriage, I was glad to feel supported, I thought, ah, here is somebody nice who is encouraging and supporting me. But gradually that didn't seem enough, I was looking for something more meaty to get my teeth into, to do some hard work – and that didn't come. And so I was getting this despairing sense that it couldn't be done, that what I'd hoped for could never be found. I wasn't able to put it into words, you know, but I started thinking that perhaps this deep change isn't possible; I always felt so sure it was and then after all it isn't.

There was no kind of heart-searching in the analysis itself, nothing disturbing. And I'd specialized in never having quarrels and tears – you remember I grew up as the one who could always sort out problems and was always sensible and never lost her temper. I was comparing notes with friends who were in analysis too and seeing that they had upsetting times, while for me it was just plain sailing. To me it began to seem just a terrible caricature of what it should be; not even a caricature, it was really a misunderstanding of what the whole business is about.

The worst of it was my fury. I was angry at what had happened. Very angry, by the end. At first I'd felt it must be me who was an absolute mess and disaster, and then when I realized that really it wasn't my fault, that was when I was furious. At the time I really wanted revenge. It was an absolute devastation.

I had by now done three-quarters of my training, I was towards the end. But I actually dared break off my analysis, my supervision, everything, a few months before I was due to complete. They allowed me to change my analyst and take more time over the course. So then I was lucky, thank goodness; I changed to another analyst – and he could read me through and through, he wasn't fooled by any false charming front I put up.

By this time I thought, now no one is going to give me the wrong analyst, even if God in person recommends! I did my homework; I chose very carefully. But at first I didn't trust him an inch, in fact I didn't trust anyone very much any more. For the first three months of that second analysis I made notes, I supervised his work with me on the quiet! By that time I knew what I was expecting and looking for. I wrote down in detail every session and sat there deciding whether I approved of the way he worked, for about three months. He was on trial! I wasn't going to have another catastrophe. And he has been really an excellent analyst; I'm completing my work with him in a few months. It's been over seven years.

It was very reassuring from the first, though also a bit persecuting, a bit harsh. But I could tell I was with someone who knew what he was doing. There was a tremendous sense of relief and a real sort of clarity. Because when things get in such a muddle, there is a sense of fuzziness in the head, so that even proper intellectual thinking is hampered by it. I found my capacity to think things through clearly was coming back; it had been like a fog. The part that was very painful was all the depression, tons of depression to be worked through, and through it there was also my sister's illness. She came to live in London to be near me and she never would allow me to get her any help, proper help. She just went from breakdown to suicide attempt, to suicide attempt to breakdown, till eventually she did kill herself.

There was so much guilt and anxiety . . . I've always had a vivid fantasy dream life – my dreams have always felt as if they were real, as if I'd done this or that. It was in my dreams that I experienced myself doing this or that cruel thing, destructive thing. So because I had a good analyst who could understand the dreams and interpret them, I led a kind of restrained, boring, dull life from outside – just home and work and tears on end in my analysis; but actually I was recognizing all these fragmented parts, aspects of myself that I could never experience in real life as a child. Because he was so good, it was contained within the fantasy level and didn't break through in anything destructive. Except that when my sister died I felt . . . not a breakdown, but a sense of being too distressed to want to function, an extreme depression, and I did wonder then whether I would ever be able to recover from it.

At the beginning and for a long time I was rather fearful of him, as if he would for ever catch me out or belittle me or hurt my pride. But this didn't last. The disturbed emotions and feelings about him were what came in the dreams. There were times when thanks to his understanding I experienced almost a physical healing – it was emotional, but it felt almost physical. A sense of physical well-being, following a period of working through one problem or another. But the bulk of the work was . . . well, I haven't come across anyone who has cried as much in the analytical work as I have. Because of all the tears that I never cried in my childhood and adolescence. People who have known me closely have said they found it very painful to see me sort of so depressed for so long. I could set it aside enough to concentrate on work; in fact, being able to focus on something that wasn't *my* problem, helping other people, that was good for me, took me away from myself.

It was good that I had the possibility of being so very deeply depressed, with no one saying, 'enough', or 'no, you can't cry any more.' What I was crying about – well, it's hard exactly to say. I think it was to do with feelings of exclusion or isolation, not being allowed to live, not feeling there was anyone for me . . . And usually it was attached to some small details of a daily occurrence that acted as a trigger. I mean, I knew in my conscious mind perfectly well that it wasn't that little small event – a friend who didn't have a kind word, something that in ordinary life you don't think about twice and you carry on. But with it all sorts of things came up, fantasies, dreams, connecting with events in my childhood.

It was like being in an operating theatre: you are open and very sensitive to everything. The thing that goes together with that was that I wasn't active in my personal life in any way. For years, you know, weekends were just times of suffering in which I was lost and alone and didn't know what to do with myself. I wasn't consciously longing for the analyst – I would have been furious as an adult to think that there I was waiting for him on a Monday, but that's what it amounted to. It was really feeling completely forlorn and lost and unable even to arrange to go to the cinema; not that I didn't have friends, but my life was just waiting. Until Monday, and then it would start again.

I knew intellectually what the theories said, but there is always this gap between theory and the feeling that it is absolutely bloody ridiculous as an adult to be longing for another adult with whom you have only a very particular kind of relationship. There is a jump to make, you have to say you are longing for your analyst, who is the mother who is looking after you – although he's not a woman even, he's a man, who isn't tucking you in, who's not doing any practical thing for you. It's a kind of musical ear you have to have, to be able to tune in, to make this jump from what rationally seems so ludicrous. It took me years before I could fully feel it.

He was able to put to rest this hurt, then this other hurt, then this other one – so, that's gone, and that's gone. And if you ask me what they were, I find it difficult to remember what each hurt was . . . because they are gone and they no longer belong to me and I wouldn't be able to remember. It was as if they had just fallen away. It is like people say, giving birth is such an ordeal, but then somehow afterwards you forget. If you don't bear any grudge, if you can make your peace with whatever it is that hurt you, then it no longer is. This is where the best of religion has got some of these things right – really to be able to forgive. And also I was very anxious that my anger had been destructive towards my mother, who died so young, or my sister, who was so ill; I had sort of cut off from those feelings.

So it has been really a bit at a time, becoming in touch with these feelings, with someone who understood, was clear, took the time that I needed, was always active – and that is one thing that I think is wonderful, he has not been one of those analysts who sit back and say nothing, but always full of intelligent, imaginative ways of understanding things, which has been so refreshing and restoring. He has been a very lively, strong, healthy, sort of rock-like person. Someone who can be active like that is someone who has hope and can give a new understanding of things. There was only the odd day when I felt like getting up, couldn't stand lying there hearing him say one more word, wanted to get up and go; only a very few times in seven years, and when it was so, I could say so and then he would look at what it was he had said or done that had caused it. There was a time when I was struck in a *marais* – what is it? a marsh, bog or depression – and yet his attitude was always alert, not saying, 'Oh, this is so boring, I have run out of all ideas of how to interpret it.' But every time he looked at it in a slightly different way, he showed me that there was a difference from the time before. You know, this is really taking you by the hand, being resolved to move on through whatever bog you are in. That I admired most of all, that he had the patience to do that and not to go to sleep or just be silent because he couldn't think of anything more to say.

I've been accused at times of being a bit of a masochist, because I always wanted to *know*, even though every new piece of truth feels like a piece of persecution at first. But always I would rather know, whatever it costs. But, then, in my family, not knowing went as far as madness, so I found out that your life depends on accepting reality. Not everybody wants to restructure his or her life in any fundamental way, as I wanted. I knew what a good experience should be about and so I looked for it. But for other people there may be different needs that can be met in different ways. I can only speak of my own experience.

The greatest and best thing analysis has done for me is to have enabled me to have a most rewarding deep relationship with a man, when I never felt I would have been able to. I think I would always have remained aloof, not allowed anybody to get really close. I think without my analysis I would have been always a nice and sensible person, who could be useful, who could carry on my role in society, but it would always have been in shadow, there would have been always a part of me . . . cut off from me. Other people would not have suffered from me, but it would have been a poor life, an impoverished one.

David

A segment has been cut out of the back of his head.
The sun, and the whole world with it, peep in. It
makes him nervous, it distracts him from his work,
and moreover it irritates him that just he should be
the one to be debarred from the spectacle.

Franz Kafka: *Diaries*

'I'll come to your house. I'm still living at home. I'm not sure
why!' David apologizes for being inarticulate, but through his
tentative, ruminative manner his feelings and ideas emerge more
distinctly than he realizes. Over the ridiculousness of his more
disastrous moments he gives a small nervous laugh.

———————————

To begin with, I failed my second year music exams at . . . well,
Oxbridge, and they wouldn't allow me to continue. Well,
yes, it was a shock. I just hadn't been working very much, I think,
and I obviously wasn't up to the level they required. And apparently I made my teachers angry. I don't know how, that was what
I was told. Perhaps I'd been warned and just hadn't taken notice
of the signs. I really didn't do very much work. I mean, I did a lot
of other things, like running a magazine and conducting, and I
had a girlfriend at the time and was using that as a way out of
doing the work.

After that I was lucky enough to get into – I'll call it East
Anglia. And it was in the summer before my finals there that it
started. I was living in a little barn somewhere at the time and
doing some work as a super at the opera, and one day I suddenly
had these symptoms – I thought it was a heart attack or something.
I phoned the university doctor and made an immediate appointment and was told that it might be pleurisy, and then went to

84

another doctor who didn't agree. I came back to London and stayed with my parents and had medical tests, and it turned out that it wasn't anything at all. I mean that it was just that I was very tense and it was something psychological. I went to have an interview at a private psychiatric home, but I didn't want to go in there.

There were lots of things – mainly the exams coming up and then I was living with a girlfriend who was planning to leave, and I'd had a car crash – I wasn't hurt but there was the shock. And the fact that I'd failed my exams at Oxbridge made it more . . . I wasn't aware of all these things, it was all unconscious, but I was having these . . . anxiety attacks. I obviously wasn't in full control of my emotions or whatever. So I was recommended to see a psychiatrist at the university health centre who specialized in students in this sort of stage – going out into the big wide world. Apparently these sorts of symptoms were fairly common.

I'd quite reformed myself at East Anglia: I'd done an incredible amount, I'd got very good grades, I was very friendly with the tutors. So it wasn't them that were failing me; it was me – I was failing myself. It came out later in therapy that there were reasons, like I was afraid of success and also afraid of failure for different reasons. There were reasons why I'd failed at Oxbridge.

I wasn't one of the people who got panicky over exams at school, I remember people who were much worse. I'd enjoyed exams really, I'd enjoyed the academic side and I'd done lots of other things when I was at school, like conducting, and I wasn't really just a bookworm type of person. But I think there was a sense in which the teachers and the whole environment said, 'You must do well, because how could you possibly not do well, especially with your sort of upbringing, in which everything is there to make you do well.' I mean, if I hadn't got into Oxbridge it would have been a terrible blow because I wouldn't have been as good as my parents and my friends or whatever. And so there was a lot of pressure. My sisters didn't have this because they were girls – I mean, that's stupid.

There's this Jewish joke, you know, about 'my son the doctor'. That's quite an interesting thing because what it means is that if *you're* the doctor, people are all looking at you. These jokes are quite true to a certain extent. If you happen to be the one who the joke is about, you get this feeling that people are looking at you, that you are performing, so that whatever you do becomes something for other people to talk about. You know, if it's an exam, or getting a job, or playing the piano, or having a girlfriend or whatever. Or having a breakdown. Whatever it is, I mean, you are doing it for an audience. But that takes away the feeling that you are doing something because you want to do it.

There can be a sort of adolescent rebellion, which I never had. My sisters did; some people do. And they get out all the anger against the parents and the system and all that sort of thing. I never actually did that really. You sort of toe the line and do things well and then you get envied because you do things well – when you should really be fighting and battering up people. So you miss the rebellion. You go to university and then again you do well. And then you suddenly realize that after university it's society and everything, and you're going to go and miss your chance to rebel, to sort of say anything and be yourself. So something's got to happen.

It can be a smooth thing where there is a certain amount of rebellion and then you assert your independence and then you realize things for yourself. Or else it's sudden, you realize you're on your own and there hasn't been that gradual process. You haven't emotionally gone through it, only intellectually. You feel sort of a pawn. You think of all the patterns you've been used to and you suddenly realize there are different ones in the world . . . It's very difficult to explain. There's a sudden freedom, but the transition is the difficult thing. This is the sort of thing that someone goes through when they're about 16 or 17, but I was 22.

It did upset me about failing at Oxbridge. I think I still haven't got over it. There was a feeling there of being pushed along in a certain direction. I think my rebellion was that I didn't go along with it and I didn't play the game and I failed. I had to tell everybody I'd failed, which was like . . . like jumping off a bridge or something. For my family it was a very shocking thing. I was making a statement really and sort of saying, 'You out there, I'm not going to do what you want.'

But, of course, at the time I didn't realize any of this. At the time, on the conscious level, I was just trying to do well, to make up at East Anglia for the Oxbridge thing. I'd work all through the night. I did very well, I also put on operas and did all sorts of things – I mean, I was considered the top guy musician.

But there was this sort of avenging angel, as the psychiatrist put it. That every time I did something for myself, this angel came and struck me down for doing something positive. The more sort of elemental forces came from much earlier on in childhood. Things like grandmothers and family . . . being very young and performing at the piano, and doing things in a sort of public context in order to get approval, and only having that way forward and the fear of what happens if you don't . . . if you don't perform. And never having tried that out, tested it, until the first failure. Actually, I had had one previous failure, I failed my German O-level. German's my mother's native tongue! I never wanted to learn it.

I was quite a normal kid in some ways. But on one level my role was – it still is – my role was to perform. I started when I was 4. I think I was very spoiled. I wasn't actually . . . I mean, there are real prodigies, I was never that. I was more spoiled than my sisters because I was a boy. I don't think I was at all an unhappy child, but there was this performing thing. There were a lot of women in the family and I suppose I got extra attention. The women were the ones who sort of decided things, there was a lot of feeling that it was women who were powerful.

I was given quite a lot of independence, but there are certain realms where you do just obey and so there is a sort of domination. The problem comes when that domination falls away and you have to be the one that dominates and tells yourself things. It's fair enough to want to perform to impress your grandmother so that she hugs and kisses you and gives you strawberries. But if you do that a lot, then you get into a pattern. You think that if you play well, everyone will hug and kiss you and give you strawberries. And you suddenly realize that the world isn't like that. And you don't want the strawberries anyway, you probably want other things; and if you're not sure of what you want, you won't know what to do and that sort of thing.

It was strange about my failing at Oxbridge. What you have to do is go and look for your results, and if you're not on the list, you've failed. And my name just wasn't there. What was ridiculous was that I felt *pleased*. I had this wonderful feeling, now I can go and do what I really want, go to a conservatoire, do something, get a job, I don't know what. I had this fantastic feeling of elation – you know, at last it's clear. I don't have to go on sort of faltering my way through and not know why I'm doing it. I had no sense of reality! I don't think I was at all into the world. It was almost like, you, the Oxbridge system, are stopping me from doing what I want to do, and by pretending I don't exist on that list you've actually fooled yourself – because now I can do really what I want. Childish!

And then, of course, I had to discuss it with my parents and the practical reality was that it was very difficult to actually carry on. Then I was very lucky, I got into East Anglia and had to do my first year again, which was good.

I think I wanted the rejection. Of course I didn't know this at the time. I wanted a real rejection so that I could feel, will you still accept me even if I'm a failure? And then there was revenge. I mean, the worst thing that a nice Jewish boy from a middle-class background with everything going for him, the worst thing he can do is fail his exams at Oxbridge.

But how can you get that statement across to this family? I mean, they never listen. This is part of the problem. You may want to say, 'Look, I'm fed up, I want to assert myself', but you can't ever make that statement. The other side of it is that you can never be too good. Let's say I got the best triple starred first and then got accepted for a wonderful job somewhere. I still wouldn't match up to my grandmother talking about some brilliant professor; I would never be good enough for my grandmother.

Then, my mother is a very powerful dominating woman and an achiever, and you have to keep up. You don't get any sense of you're OK if you don't achieve, there isn't that element of human warmth as a very important value. It means that when I get into my own relationships with women there is this need for a dominating woman, and then you're wanting to be rejected, because of the need to be rejected before by the mother – which never happened. It could be just that when you get to a stage of being accepted, which was dangerously near happening at East Anglia – that was the real danger, somehow there's a threat in it. And then my mother did have ambitions to be a pianist and there was a sort of rivalry, a competitive element. So, you know, I start being good at it and I get better than my mother. There was a decisive point where my technique was definitely better – we were both aware of it, it was quite fun. I mean, it could have been an unconscious thing, that I was actually doing this because she wanted me to fulfil her own ambitions. But then what happens when I get to the point where I suddenly *am* successful? Help!

Then there must have been a lot of anger in the situation. There's naturally going to be a lot of anger in a situation where you have to do something against your will. Or it could be a hangover from childhood, and you don't allow yourself to express the feelings early on, but sort of suppress them, not because anybody says you must, but when people don't express certain feelings you will copy that pattern. What was happening at the time of the breakdown was that I was getting completely bottled up, everything got overloaded. It was just a big sort of crisis. If it had been one thing, I would have coped, but it was everything at once. Of course, I didn't realize anything at the time.

I went to the official psychiatrist at the health centre; you know, free service to students. I went once a week right up until my finals. But there were times – it was a health centre, on the campus, and I was living nearby – occasionally I went in for two or three days and stayed there. We concentrated on behavioural things like . . . well, I had these panic attacks, and I had to do certain things – I would stop myself and start asking myself certain questions like, what am I afraid of? what's in the situation? what are my feelings? I mean, once I was buying a cup of tea in the cafeteria and I suddenly realized I was asking for something from a woman . . . I managed to cope with these panic things. And I sometimes had to write down the things that were in my mind and talk about it in the session. And we actually progressed quite far to the basic issues – things like music, religion, women, the family, work. I was getting much more aware of what I was doing and my relationships with people changed.

At the same time I was feeling extremely low, I was realizing that the feelings that had caused the physical symptoms were more important than the symptoms themselves. It was a depressing discovery. First of all, I didn't expect myself to have so much . . . to be one of those people who . . . There was a guy, a mature student of 28 – I thought that was incredibly old! – he had attempted suicide, he was incredibly depressed, and I would never have gone that far. But at times I couldn't go anywhere, I couldn't sit in the library or be with the people I was living with. I couldn't be with student friends because they would be talking about this and that and I couldn't say, 'I'm feeling terrible', you know.

I did the papers that I was supposed to do, I went to classes, I carried on with music, preparing recitals and all that sort of thing. And I wrote all this poetry, I was very introspective suddenly. And I was very religious in a funny sort of way. There were some people I could speak to for the first time, adults, you know, non-students. I'd been *répétiteur*, I'd been very active, I'd got to know a lot of people who weren't students, and suddenly I was able to talk to these people because they often had similar problems, anxiety, stress. My supervisor knew a bit about what was going on and he was concerned that I should find some way to cope. But, in general, I kept it all very much to myself and got the work done.

There was once when I got into an ambulance and was taken to some place because I sort of couldn't walk any further or something. There were a few dramatic moments – I had a panic attack in the bank, I lay on the floor! But I mean I was a student and you're not expected . . . you don't have to be normal! But it was OK, I did my exams. I got a First.

After that I went to America. In spite of all these problems and things I was offered a place to do my Master's degree there. Before I went over, there was this sort of religious thing, I went to a very ultra-religious Hassidic sect and got very involved with them. I had a phase of thinking that what I should really do was get back into the religious side of things. But I realized I was doing something escapist, some part of me realized it was a bit mad. So I went over to the States.

I'd only been there a little while, then one evening I was very nervous and I took some Valium and I had some pot and some other drug that somebody had given me and some alcohol. And I went completely round the bend. I had a sort of horrible thing, people said something to me, and then they'd say it again and again and again. It was almost like I wasn't moving forward in time. It was incredibly frightening. Somebody actually fetched . . . the men in white coats came and put me on a stretcher and took me to the university hospital! I stayed there for only about an hour.

So then I decided that, well, this wasn't the right time for me to do this Master's course. I had to do analysis or something a bit intensive and get myself sorted out. I'd been all geared up to, you know, get on with my work and be successful, but as soon as it got to me on my own, I wasn't ready for it, I got out of control, whatever. So I decided to chuck it and come back.

And that was a really awful year, when I came back, because there was nothing. You know, I'd given up everything. I did have my First. I went to see the university psychiatrist again and we sort of discussed what had happened and what I ought to do. I almost went into hospital, I actually wanted to go into a home, because I was driving everybody bonkers. But I got there and suddenly realized that I didn't really want to go into this home, because, you know, I'm not really mad. I thought, what the hell am I doing here? I wrote to the doctor I'd seen and said I'd decided to do something else; I gave some excuse. So I was eventually recommended to the person I actually saw. I was with him for about four and a half years; mostly three times a week.

It did help an enormous amount. I wasn't doing a thing when I started; I was in an almost catatonic state. First, I did manage to go out and get various little jobs, my parents told me I had to – I played the piano in a hotel at night. I was living at home. I was still totally unrealistic – because I'd got my First I thought I could

go and do this and do that and go and live on my own. The
trouble was I was finding it difficult even getting around, going
on the Underground even. I had sort of feelings of being dragged
from place to place, and I wasn't thinking straight, almost. Because
of, probably, all this emotion, or something, being bottled up. I
don't know exactly what. Whatever it was, it came out. And from
not being able to even get around, from those years in analysis I
was able to get my Master's, to get qualifications to teach, and get
back into music – you know, just get going. And I had a relationship with a girl.

So it was quite successful. At another level, I didn't do it
properly – I went late to sessions, and I'm still getting some
symptoms – so it wasn't entirely satisfactory. We did have a good
relationship and I found out all these things about myself. The
point was that I wanted to do it, it was *me* who actually got in
touch with him. It was always in my mind that I was doing it for
myself, that however confused the ambitions had been, the analysis itself was something I'd chosen to do.

I had a lot of aggression obviously and I remember there were
rules, like, you know, I wasn't allowed to go and kick in the
window or bash up his things. The couch – well, all the way
through I never had a simple thing about the couch. There was
either lying on the couch or sitting on a low chair opposite him,
and I never felt really comfortable on the couch, but I did actually
use it for certain times, and that was when I was really doing the
analysis properly. But a lot of the time I was just sitting on a low
chair and talking, talking face-to-face. I would come and tell my
dreams and he would interpret, we'd both interpret, and we'd see
how it connected up with things. Dreams are . . . you suddenly
realize that you're living in this other world.

We talked about all these things I've been saying, the family,
the pressures, why I was doing things – and the parents, of
course, that's a very big topic! He'd actually gone 4,000 miles
away from his own parents and he admitted once that, you know,
he'd had to get away, a long way away. One of the reasons I liked
going to him was the fact that even if I was living at home, I was
being told there was some sort of separation . . . Actually, now

I'm realizing that parents really don't want you still around. My problem was that I was too attached, *am* too attached, because I'm still living at home. My parents don't want me to be so attached, even then they didn't. I was driving people crazy – I wasn't doing it on purpose. What we came out with was that I was acting out these feelings at home and that was very unpleasant and unconscious, and I should be acting them out in the psychoanalytic situation. I had to try to express, go through feelings . . . There were times when I got to the point where I was feeling very powerful feelings in the analysis.

I think it was quite rare that I actually treated him as a person. He wasn't aloof, no, he wasn't aloof in terms of not saying anything – actually he talked a lot, and joked; we laughed a lot! I'd come in with all this about what I'd been doing, and I'd suddenly realize I was the guiltiest person in the world and that was what was really bothering me.

But at some point . . . you see, he was a bit anti-academic. He thought academia was all dry and boring, but it wasn't to me. He'd done his own PhD and then gone on to something else. He was trying to get me to feel. You know, he was always saying that I'd never been allowed to be a child or feel, I'd always been having to think and intellectualize, and that was my problem, basically. He was playing devil's advocate all the time, so that there wouldn't be any excuse, it would have to be my own choice that I was going on with my work. I argued an incredible amount!

In fact, I think one of the reasons I did eventually leave was that I didn't think there was a positive support for carrying on my academic work. But the good thing was, you know, I'd talk about how I'd been sitting opposite somebody on the train and felt really nervous – what does this person think I'm doing? where shall I put my arms and how should I cross my legs? – such a waste of energy that was going on inside me. So he would say something like, 'You're projecting. You're projecting onto him the fact that he's ashamed of you or angry – it's *you* that's angry or ashamed or nervous.' It took me a long time to actually feel this. It was all inside me, myself.

There would be a pattern of having a family dinner on Friday nights. So what do I do? The family comes, so I have to act, get an act together – that became incredibly tense. So he'd say things like, 'Just be yourself! Forget about all this crap that's going on.' And he gave me a point from which to be able to stand objectively a bit and look at the situation. I feel that that was a very useful thing, because it was, again, saying, what do *you* want? Because my family and friends were getting on with things, my sisters having their own families and households – and I'm just having difficulty walking down the street! I thought that when I was with everybody I had to be what was expected of me. I looked with dread on these Friday nights.

It was a sort of double life that I was leading. I mean, when I was in America there was somebody there, the first day I met him, he said, 'Oh, I can't see you at three because I've got to go to my analyst.' I just was never like that; I hardly told anybody. I was trying to take the threads up again, get back into things at quite a high level, because, in fact, the course was now much harder. But I'd started something and I wanted to finish it. I was getting more realistic, too, aware of what the situation is with jobs. There was a lot of change, I think. I was able to do much more and sort of think differently and unclog and be a bit more just myself. I was more interested in other people too.

I was trying to get myself centred, because I'd been completely knocked off balance. Going there was sort of like recovering the centre and trying to fit in the bits. In fact, a very significant dream I had right at the beginning was that I was on a sort of sea and there were lots of little rafts all over and I was on one raft; and that was supposed to be me, everything was split into little fragments and everything was floating around in different places and there wasn't a way to sort of get them together. And now the disparate parts of it – family and people and inner self and outer self and public image and private and all this sort of thing – they much more hang together, they're much more coherent.

All the same . . . I was actually resisting the analysis the whole time. First of all, I didn't believe in it. So that he also said, 'Well, I don't believe in it either' – we were both sort of saying we don't really believe in all this! I think we both agreed that apart from the theory there was this unknown factor, the actual therapy; that however much you wanted to go into all these theories and so on, they weren't necessarily the answer. I'd still always arrive late – that was just pure resistance. And somewhere along the line I didn't really want to talk about certain things – my girlfriend, for instance. But I think wherever there was something I didn't want to talk about, that was where the problem was!

It was a constant topic from the beginning, being independent and giving up analysis. And he would say, 'Why not stop talking about it and get on with the analysis.' It all sort of dried up at a certain time and this was what made me think, well, this really is the time for the analysis to stop. And he would say, 'No, this is the time for it to carry on!' I'd say, 'All I want to know is, am I getting better?' He'd say, 'What do you mean by getting better? This isn't a cure, there's nothing magical about it.' Yet I knew there was this enormous benefit. Anyway – I went to talk to a consultant and she said, 'Well, it sounds like you could give up.'

But the idea of just stopping analysis was totally inconceivable. I was afraid of what would happen – I'd start acting out the symptoms, everything would all spill out. With analysis there, things could function, but without it I was afraid everything would grind to a halt. I haven't yet developed my strength and my own internal analyst to the point where I can do things. Or maybe I have, I don't know exactly. So I've started seeing somebody else – two weeks ago. There are a lot of things that have come up that I didn't get out with the other analyst and which I feel are bubbling up again. And also it's a question of just getting through to this summer, getting my PhD and getting a job. At this point the stakes are much higher, the failures get worse. Whether or not I like the new analyst I really don't know. That's one of my problems, being indecisive, just not knowing!

Hugh

For me the initial delight is in the surprise of remembering something I didn't know I knew. I am in
a place, in a situation, as if I had materialized from
cloud or risen out of the ground. There is a glad
recognition of the long lost and the rest follows. Step
by step the wonder of unexpected supply keeps
growing.

Robert Frost

The house in west London is deliciously furnished in generous
American style – chintzes, oil paintings, many rugs. Small
children run through the room from time to time. Hugh
looks tousled and younger than his 39 years. As he talks he
struggles with a stutter.

———————

I first had therapy when I was 19, for eight or nine months. It
was a disaster; I'd been pressurized into it by other people, by
my uncle. This was in the States, of course. He was a psychiatrist
who didn't like to say anything, sat there silent, and physically he
turned me off and eventually the thing terminated when I identified
him with a muskrat in one of my dreams. He was this enormous
muskrat that came down to this pool I was in – I was floating in a
whole sort of subconscious twisted experience, with all sorts of
sexual fears – and I climbed out of this thing and there he was, a
great rat coming down at me! I realized that it was him and that
I'd had enough of it.

I wasn't ready for therapy then. I think you very much have to
be ready for it. You have to choose, you have to decide for
yourself that you want to go somewhere with it. When I started it
again, that's about a year and a half ago, I was absolutely ready.
Yes, that's a big gap, nothing between 19 and 39, unless you count

96

the marital therapy. That wasn't so great, but it helped me to get an impetus – because I decided that having made such a choice, to live, say, rather than do whatever I'd been doing . . . Well, what I was doing was being much more involved with being a writer than with living. This involves all sorts of different postures in which you're trying to turn yourself into something you're not, or you've swallowed a notion of who the writer is, which is something quite different from who *you* are.

And, then, also, I'd heard complaints from various people along the way – I've been divorced twice and was on the verge of it a third time. No, I didn't think of going into therapy then, I had no notion that it would do any good at all. I just carried on with divorces and getting myself deeper and deeper in more and more complicated situations between marriages. The only things that were interesting to me were those that took me right up against the wall – strange people, suicidal people; I wanted to go as far down as I could go.

During those years I was living in the States and teaching at Berkeley. And why I came to Europe was that I was so fussed and frightened by Berkeley, and I'd been given several overdoses of mescalin, which frightened me. At the same time Reagan had been re-elected as governor – and there was no point battering your head against the wall. I wanted to see Asia first; on the way I went to the Himalayas and I got too thin, I lost too much weight and I ended up in France. I was between marriages then.

Then Anna – at that time my wife-to-be – came out to France and she didn't like the countryside. For a writer's wife it's rather dull, if one hasn't chosen France and doesn't speak French, no matter how beautiful it is. To go back to teaching I'd have had to have some more things written; and I didn't want to go to New York. So I took her to see *Mean Streets* and she decided that perhaps London would be better. And I'd been in England only briefly and I felt I needed to know it better.

Well, then when our marriage began to go wrong, we went to see a marital therapist and that made me feel that, oh, I could get a lot . . . and Anna's had a therapist of her own . . .

They felt that I could stand being loosened up and I agreed. I wasn't sick, no. I wasn't sick at all. But there was . . . Well, it depends what sort of family you're from; if your family doesn't have any notion of what life's about . . .

They were very self-driven people. They were involved with winning, getting to the top; you know, succeeding, walking over anyone, rather than enjoying or understanding what life itself is and living it. I was the oldest son and I got plenty of attention, but probably not the right sort. I was brought up by domestics rather than by my mother, who didn't want to have to deal with me in that way. And I was considered the heir to the family empire, which made me a prospective adult rather than a child.

I was ready for the therapy. I think I didn't know, for instance, how to write with emotion or I didn't know any sort of aesthetic that was life-enhancing, I had no access to my own humour, basically – all sorts of things like that were missing from me. I wanted to make my writing different. And I thought, if you hadn't tried this before or if you hadn't developed this side of yourself before, why not do it? And now I have five more sessions and then I finish.

The therapy was arranged on a contractual basis for a certain period of time. I'm on to a very fast type of thing, and, as my therapist says, I was able to take the suggestions offered and run with them. And she was interested in feeding me things – because I'm a poet – in terms of imagery, so she could give me maps or pack things together very tightly and I could get them. I got to her through my marital therapist; she'd been used to working with people of his sort and he thought she was a person who could loosen me up. And I wanted a woman. I much prefer to talk to women, they're much more interesting. And I didn't want, like the last time, having a psychiatrist who was an authority figure.

She's an outlandish woman, big, not very pretty, about five years younger than me perhaps. Very much a flower child. Skirts down to her feet, rings on every finger, different costumes all the time, sort of gypsy thing. She loves the Hopi Indians, their jewels, she has a real respect for primitive peoples. I liked her straight away, yes, yes. Her husband's a TV scriptwriter, she has a great sense of humour. Yes, I'm winding up in five sessions because she's leaving the country. But that's all right, it was on a contractual basis: one year, then look at it again. I didn't have grave problems, I just had to be turned around and shunted off in all sorts of other directions.

The people who go on with therapy for a long time, they're going to sort of unburden themselves, they're doing a whole thorough type of analysis in which they're talking about getting rid of their past, treating the sources in the past that are wrong. I'm not doing that, I'm just using it to go somewhere, using her, really, to go somewhere. She gets me to understand certain concepts that were foreign to me, just says something and tries to get it straight across. Certainly there are certain things that are difficult to understand, and there are one or two things that are hard to decide whether I really want to go in that direction or not. My whole emphasis was on going down to the bottom of things, for instance, which I thought poets should do; diving as deeply as possible into the wreckage, just taking on, like Rilke does . . . making myself kind of transparent. Also trying to make myself feminine, because I come from a family of five boys. I always very much admired women and I wanted something that they have.

The first divorce . . . well, I was sort of kidnapped into marriage, I wasn't strong enough to say no. I was 21 and I was sort of blackmailed into it in a way and couldn't get out of it. I kept trying to run out of that marriage and eventually succeeded after seven years. The second marriage failed for the same reason that this one was failing – I didn't have enough edges, I just couldn't stand on my own feet. And marriage is very different from other relationships, mistresses, whatever; it's a whole different game. I had no sense of boundaries, no edges. Barriers instead of boundaries.

My look was very different eighteen months ago from what you can see it is now. I used to drive people out of the way just with my eyes. I could keep them from ever asking anything, teasing me, anything like that. It wasn't just my marriage; it affected my relations with everybody you could think of. And it affected my writing, because I had no notion of who I was. I'd no notion of who this self was who was writing. I'd been writing an autobiography of what a mistake it was to have become a writer. It was a sort of trap that I'd gotten into – that was my view of it. Instead of, perhaps, just picking up the wrong strand of it or something like that, which is more true. I was writing about this whenever I got stoned. But now I don't feel I've gone into the wrong thing with writing, absolutely not, I don't.

So the first thing with this therapy was to get me some edges, and at the same time I started to know what it was to have my feet under me, which I'd never had. I never even had that sense of, you know, there's my feet, I put them on the ground. Though I can take up any character I want, can play any role I want and choose this or that. I didn't get into any of this in the marital therapy – I was mostly mum during the things that we talked about. I do think my therapist is extremely talented; that's why she's stopping the job – she wants to do something else besides just listening to people. If she were going on with the job, yes, I'd go on with her because she's great and because she sees a lot that still needs to be done for me. She wants the leave-taking to be associated with facing . . . with a number of people who've died during this last year. My father died.

She's so *up*, really, that it's just been pleasure seeing her and being able to change myself. I liked all that and it's too bad it's going to end, but that's all. I think I am open to change, yes, that's what people say about my travel book . . . A lot of writers feel therapy would take everything away from them, and I felt after my first therapy immensely dry, I couldn't write for years after it, all sorts of stuff had been taken from me – nothing left. But I don't think it has to be that sort of drying, horrible experience that a lot of people describe it as.

She's not silent like the psychiatrist in that first experience. She's got all sorts of . . . she seems to know where she wants to leave me and it's a question of tossing things out and seeing whether I could fathom this, while at the same time building up, making it, as she said, so as I don't get pushed around on the bus.

If I brought up something about what had happened, what had gone wrong, she'd say, 'Didn't you fight back? Why didn't you do this? Why didn't you tell them that?' And so on. She'd just try to bring out that, you know, I've got rights in these matters. I used to feel this house had nothing to do with me, it was Anna's house. Now I don't feel that way any more – and if I don't like something, I throw it out.

I do talk about my childhood whenever I can, but she seemed to understand what it was about, what other things were about too, without my needing to go into it very much. She's very, very intuitive – everyone says that about her. We don't talk about dreams that much. Dreams were the only things that interested my first psychiatrist – nothing else – and that was wonderful for me as a writer because that made me a surrealist, in effect, because I realized that all that stuff was me. Probably I wouldn't otherwise have written as a surrealist, but whether that's such a great thing I don't know! Well, it's like playing jazz – I mean, one thing I know I can do is improvise, spontaneously. I'm not sure that thinking isn't better, though!

She feels that dreams are very much one's own creation and you distribute all this stuff among all the actors in the dream. It's the feelings that are revealed through it that she talks about really. To me, all of a dream is fascinating – if I could write like I dream! I have written about a couple of dreams, written quite well on them, but I haven't been able to use them anywhere near as much as I'd like to.

My work's changed. I mean, I come back, say, from seeing her yesterday and I can solve all sorts of problems – what goes where, and with what . . . or anything else. With just even organizing a day. You can make decisions. It's mainly what's happening in my actual life that she's interested in. My father's death or my problems in winning the battle of the home; you know, being able to hold my own end up, give Anna what she needs – some parameters, some walls – and resist her efforts to take over. There's no reason why I shouldn't retreat out there to the studio; I'm not forced to get her shopping any more! It's new boundaries – and the family like it, they like to have me out there in the studio.

It really is true, I had a *prospective* self before, I only wanted to be somebody. I felt that myself was in my writing, not in my life, and I thought I had to make a choice. I absolutely don't think that now. Life is to be lived. All right, Rilke put everything into his work and not his life, but perhaps in the long run he lost. He may still be the greatest poet of this century, but there's a lot of cloying, saccharin, there's a lot of icing on the cake. You might feel threatened as a writer if you had a very Freudian analyst, I think, you might well feel like that.

She had to try to get me around to realizing what it means to be masculine, to play that game, to be able to entertain the prospect of violence and things like that which I find rather repugnant. Now, for instance, I really want to fight! I mean, if there are terrible scenes going on around the house, I want to join in, I want to go and see how do they get themselves into it. Whether I can make it worse or make it better, it all attracts me. It's just getting your feet under you. Once you have your feet under you these things are implied.

You can lose something of it from day to day, I would almost say go backwards, lose this self-confidence, but there's a structure, something like that, which she's trying to keep there. You can reclaim and work your way out after falling flat on your face. I mean, I've been all through this week in a terrible state from being overworked, my whole body hurts from it, and I don't like what my editress is doing to me. Everything just built up – I just wanted, two days ago, wanted to throw everything over, I didn't know how to handle it. After talking to her, it's fine, I can solve all those things.

I feel that she likes me, and I realize through her that other people have been supportive. That's one thing she wanted to have me understand from the very beginning, that people like me – and I couldn't believe that. She wanted me to get out of these things that have been laid on me by, say, efforts to control me by my parents or other people. I get along better with my mother, I think – she notices I'm much happier. I didn't tell her about the therapy at all, she just recognized it. A lot of people have noticed; they say, 'I've never seen you so happy.' It's nice to think you have a stretch of years ahead in which to give yourself a happiness you've not had.

Maybe all this goes faster if you have a sort of maturity. You know, we were talking about William James. Well, there it was, it happened to him all of a sudden, he went up and up and up. All of a sudden you realize what it is to be alive – I remember walking around the streets feeling that, and being able to look at everybody's faces and enjoy all the looks. Well, that was a high and we keep evaporating away from that, but what she did was give me structures to contain the fountain, so I felt in place. Then you've got something with which to confront whatever else is out there. And then she also tried to suggest ways in which I could learn what being a man is about and what winning is about. When I went to Japan, she suggested things like, it's a very masculine culture, that that was the sort of thing I should look at.

I don't think I'll miss the therapy that much, because the whole point of it is to put you somewhere in life, and if you're no longer afraid of divorce or whatever, or losing whatever you're going to lose, you might actually not lose it; or if you do, then it's just what's going to happen. Before, I would have just jumped into the next pair of arms and done it all over again. And I whined a lot and things like that; I nagged about not getting this, not doing that. The things you whine about you may still feel you want – you know, like sex or something – but if you don't get them, you can be amused at not getting them. Probably humour's the only thing you've got which will allow you to handle everything. And I had this insistence on constantly getting into traps, fascinating, beautiful traps, but it's not necessary. You have your strength, you have order and you have your brains. You have this marvellous palette and everything coming at you at once, and you've just got to handle it.

Elizabeth

There is a Latvian proverb: 'You won't make much
headway with another's mind', or something of the
sort. The Latvians are a small people and it surprises
me that they have such rational ideas, that one cannot
get anywhere with someone else's mind. And in psychoanalysis, you live more or less through another's mind.
And that is the danger of psychoanalysis, that one is
dependent on the decisions of others who are not
competent and knowledgeable but who believe that
they know everything and can guide one just because
they are psychoanalysts.

Karin Obholzer: *The Wolf-Man Sixty Years Later*

Surrounded by neatly stacked files and papers, Elizabeth com-
plains that retirement hasn't brought her time to put the garden
in order – she's trying to finish her research book. She's tall and
red-haired and wears slim trousers with a high-necked sweater.
Elizabeth looks back with a kind of humorous disbelief.

———

I first started analysis a long, long time ago in South Africa.
That was in the Forties, before I had to leave and come to live
here. I saw a man first and then a woman; it was for depression,
I'd say. I went to a man for about a year. He'd come out from
Europe; he'd been analysed by Freud. He said he found me a
desperately impoverished person – very little personality, very
little ego, no belief in my existence really, as to what I was or who
I was. Then I got married and went to Cape Town; he went to
America. So I went to a woman for a while, not very long. Both of
them were supportive, they were warm, both of them I felt were
on my side. I was certainly much happier than I'd been before
while I was in analysis with them. The only thing is that perhaps I

didn't change very much, it didn't quite strengthen me as I'd hoped.

Then when I came to England my sister Mary, who's an analyst herself, arranged an interview with a consultant, and he phoned me afterwards and established that there was a vacancy with this other one. I phoned him back and said, 'You know, I'd much rather be with a woman', and he virtually said, 'No, that's nonsense. If you want analysis you don't pussyfoot around.' So I went to this man.

I can't quite recall the first impression. Actually, I had a first impression of kindness, of concern and interest. Which is pretty incredible . . . because it was bad. From the beginning. The first thing that comes to mind was that he did all the talking. I suppose it was him to me in a ratio of about ten to one. I thought I was going in there to discharge and to have someone listening and absorbing everything in a kindly way, instead of which the pattern throughout was that I would be allowed to say something and then it would be used to chastise me for the rest of the time, to say I never did things right, that I had wrong ideas. And his favourite thing was that I had stolen mother's milk and was peddling it as cream! I'm *still* not sure what it means!

The other thing was, no matter what situation we were talking about, he looked for and established the negative. There was never any validation. I can't recall him ever saying, 'You seem to have done well.' It was always turned the other way, that I was claiming credit for other people's work. Everything was always taken back to the fact that I didn't appreciate my mother. Nothing of what I reported my mother had done to me . . . He was always on my mother's side. He'd say my mother was a good woman, I had good parents – they made mistakes but good enough – but I refused to thrive, as I was refusing to thrive now, I refused to take the milk.

I'd talk about current things in my life and it would always be taken back to my ungratefulness, my inability . . . The phrase that comes back is, 'You can't do with and you can't do without. That was how you were from the beginning – you couldn't do with your mother, and you couldn't do without her; you didn't know what to do with the breast, you didn't know how to suck or to really take in nourishment.' Oh, I do remember saying to him once, something about how can one thrive without love, and he said, 'The truth is far more necessary than love.'

There was no friendliness at any point. When I first came he would say, 'Good morning' or 'Good day', or something like that, but then he stopped. And I asked him why he'd stopped, and he said because it was not necessary, he'd taken the decision that there was more communicated by that than there should be. So he'd come to the door, nod, turn away, walk in front of me into his room. I would follow and close the door, and by the time I'd closed the door and had got to the couch he would be sitting sort of waiting for me, absolutely expressionless. And I think at the end of each session, I would turn and look at him from the door, and I think there might have been a sort of imperceptible nod.

I think ordinary, normal friendliness is part of making you feel like a person rather than something to be processed, a robot. It was not so much processed; I think I felt I was someone to be beaten through all that time, to have a lot knocked out of me. I feel that most of the time I was surrounded by a torrent of negative interpretations – sometimes, in my ignorance, I thought I was doing well, but everything was turned on its head. In all the eleven years I cannot remember anything good being said about me or any confirmation of a good deed or good work on my part. The only thing I can credit him for is that he did make me stop losing my temper with my daughter.

Of course, the analysis I'd had in South Africa, it just didn't count, it didn't count at all. His ideas were the true light. I can't bear anyone in any case who believes in any system as an absolute religion and the absolute answer. I was reading Weber on capitalism and the Protestant ethic at the time and I thought, my God, this is exactly it. Weber pointed out that the new Protestantism believed that to go to Heaven you had to be one of the elect, and it didn't matter what you did if you weren't one of the elect already. And I just felt I was never going to work properly because I wasn't one of the elect, I'd never get it right. He *knew* that I wasn't working, wouldn't work. Never, never in all those years did he say anything to encourage me.

One thing is burnt into my mind. He said, 'I've given it a lot of thought' – he spoke kindly – 'and I've come to the conclusion' – quite kindly and I felt something good was going to come – 'and I can only come to one conclusion, that you must have been an impossible child from the word go.' I was born impossible! No one could deal with me, there was no way of making any contact, I was impossible. I threw that up at him time and time again and it was only by about the seventh or eighth year that he seemed to think perhaps he might have made a mistake. But by then it was too late to repair.

He used to say that I would take the good breast and turn it bad. I never knew what it meant at the time and I would ask him and he would say, 'If you won't understand, you won't.' But also he was . . . capricious. I mean, sometimes he would take everything back to childhood and my mother, and at other times I would say I recollected something about my mother and he would say, 'Psychoanalysis is not about the past, it is about the here and now.'

Once when I did cry he said, 'Those were crocodile tears, you don't really mean it', so I went to great lengths not to express anything again. Then once I got angry and he sent me away from the session and said he wasn't going to put up with that sort of tantrum. He said he wasn't going to be an audience for me, he was a creative person; and he said he wasn't going to take undirected emotion, that analysis was a controlled situation. I wish I hadn't come back. But then when my parents died, he criticized me for *not* grieving. They were killed together in a motor accident in South Africa, and I know it was terrible, but they were 80 and neither could have survived without the other. I said that to him – and did I get it! You know when I think back now – he was saying there I was, selfish as ever, lying there, didn't think of my wonderful parents, relieved. I did cry after my parents' death, but I couldn't prove to him it was real grieving.

I *knew* that it was a ghastly relationship – I couldn't discuss it with him. I used to complain that I wasn't allowed to talk, and then he'd say, 'All right, talk then.' The pattern was that there would be silence so that he could prove to me that I wasn't using it. The moment I started to talk he talked over me. It was like a gaoler. I knew all the time that I was in a sort of Nazi situation. I felt then, as I do now, that I was attached to him in the same way that sometimes prisoners are to their gaolers. I'd just read a book about a woman in prison in South Africa and her relationship with the warder and I felt it was like that.

Every time I spoke of breaking, saying I wasn't coming back, two things would happen: he'd go back to being really very kind and sweet, and also he'd make it clear that it wasn't going to be better anywhere else, that unless I'm prepared to work . . . And every time I'd ask him what did he mean by work, how would I know when I was working, he said nothing. Until the end, eleven years later, I had apparently not yet succeeded in starting to work. 'The analysis has not yet begun' was what I always heard.

I know, it does sound . . . You know, I used to go and tell it all to a friend of mine, and she told me a long time afterwards that for ages she didn't believe me. Her acceptance finally came when I told her he'd chastised me for my failure to my daughters because they weren't taking up professional careers. She was amazed that he regarded taking up a professional career as the criterion, as the ultimate. It could have been my father speaking.

He was so absolutely judgemental. Whatever I said, he first looked for what he would consider a negative motive on my part. When I thought I was going to be made redundant at one time because it looked as if our grant was stopping, he said, 'I suppose you will go and live with your daughter in Scotland' – no, he said, 'batten on your daughter'. And when I said, 'No, that's the last thing I'll do', he said, 'Well, that's something.' And then another thing, I was telling him about the surgeon when he first came over here and we knew already my husband had cancer, how he'd told me to shut up and said I was a hysterical woman – and when I told this to him he said, 'Quite right too.'

When I first went to him I was having a relationship with a man and he disapproved of that. He said – he was crazy – do you know, he said either I give up the relationship or the analysis. When I asked him about this much later, his answer was that he did it for me, he thought it was best. I mean, that relationship probably never would have worked out, I was at my lowest at that time, but all the same . . . I suppose over those eleven years I might have met someone else, but I think I felt too self-conscious about what he'd say. Perhaps I wouldn't have formed another relationship anyway, I don't know. But what shook me was that at one point he suddenly implied the opposite, that if I didn't re-marry, my children would be maladjusted.

I did make an attempt at a break about half-way through. He started to talk about I would have to decide whether I wanted to continue, and the day of the break, he said to me, 'I'll be at home tonight, ring me at seven o'clock and tell me whether you decide to come back or not.' I was going off on holiday, I didn't know what to do, and I was dependent on him for making other arrangements for me when I got back . . . So I phoned him up and said I would be coming back. Of course, he'd threatened to get rid of me several times – he'd say he saw no purpose in the analysis – that I wouldn't work or take it seriously. He'd say, '*You* have to change, analysis won't change, I won't change, *you* have to change.' But when I said, '*How* must I change? In what direction?' he said he'll know when I've changed in the right direction. He would *never* give me or show me the direction. He just *knew*; he'd know when I was working. By about the tenth year he still said I hadn't started to work.

I hated him. I don't know whether I hated him from the start; I think so. I've seen him twice, once at the theatre – I refused to turn round – he looked sick, awful; and then a few years later I drove past him, he was crossing the street with a walking-stick. I've never stopped hating him.

I've tried to think about what he may have been really trying to do for me. Perhaps he felt he must sort of get at the truth somehow at all costs, but then after such a long time he must have seen that the way he was going on was unproductive. It is possible that I just irritated him, but being a professional he shouldn't have let it go on for all that long. He should have said, 'Look, we're just not compatible.' I'm prepared to believe that when I came from South Africa I had a sort of paranoia – I've seen it in other South Africans when they first arrive – a tendency to assume that everybody is trying to do you down, that you have to fight. I would have changed along those lines anyway, I would have realized it wasn't the norm over here. But perhaps he reacted against this very strongly. Or perhaps he was attacking a sort of self-idealization – he kept saying, 'I'm not going to collude with you.' People who've got a very low self-esteem have also got a high self-idealization, it's almost as if it's proportionate. He did stamp on some foolish things – I mean, I can remember coming along once, it was a hot summer's day and I had on a summer dress and I think I came mincing in almost, half shy and half seductive, and he put a stop to that. He said, 'You're an adult person with responsibility, none of this sort of behaviour.' I feel he was trying to straighten me out, you know, and I think he may have done that to some extent – stopped my subterfuges and so on.

But he was not enabling . . . There was no ambience in which I could have grown or have developed or really got new insights, other than his negative ones, which I didn't believe in. I didn't accept them; they were too far-fetched. I feel I was sort of shredded. Really, it's as inexplicable to me now as it was at the time. If anyone told it to me, I wouldn't believe it.

What finally decided me to leave was that I had a friend who was dying of cancer. When I heard of it I was very shattered, but there was nothing from him, no sympathy for my friend or for me, just the same controlled, scientific business – 'You have to face up to reality' and things like that. And when I left him, I'd already arranged to see Mrs Weiss, and I went back to him and I said, 'I won't be coming again.' And he said, 'You don't think that after all this time I would just let you go like that?' I said, 'Well, I've made other arrangements actually.' He was silent for a while. Then he said, 'I haven't done very much for you, have I?'

So I went to Mrs Weiss for a while and she was a darling old woman – her attitude to what I told her about him was that she could hardly believe it. She got so angry with him . . . he phoned her about three months after I'd started to go to her, to invite her out, and she decided not to go. And she kept saying, 'You're a grown-up capable woman, you know; what is this?' If I'd ever told him anything about Jean – my senior at work – no matter what it was, *Jean* was right. And you know, it was only after I'd been with Mrs Weiss that I could stand up to Jean and say, 'Look Jean, we must decide who's doing this job.' Before that it had been 'Yes, Jean', 'No, Jean', because he'd kept telling me that *whoever* it was that was in authority was a good, wise, clever person.

Mrs Weiss would say, 'You're a mature, respected person, not a helpless girl. You hold down a job, you work hard – what is there to be ashamed about? Why should you be cringing and hiding yourself all the time?' I know that before, when I was on holiday I used to feel that I was . . . naughty, let off the leash. According to him, whatever I was at, it was anal play or something like that – it was always unclean. And you know, I can remember telling him an erotic fantasy and he said he didn't want to hear, it was childish. Whereas with her I felt that she was sort of lifting me up. *He* pushed me down all the time. But by the time I'd been with her a few times, I felt I could walk straight.

She was a remarkable woman. She came here just before the war – I think she'd been a nurse – and she worked with Anna Freud at the home, you know, that she set up for children. The tragedy about her actually was that she went a bit senile on me – she got lonely and she wanted to read out to me various things that she'd got, her books, letters people had written to her and so on. But she was marvellous, warm. And at the same time I was going to a Transactional Analysis group – it's a kind of group therapy. The leader was a great help to me, he had a sort of trust and belief that you could and would want to make more of your life, a belief in your capacity to do it. And he was constantly making you recognize that the feelings in you were your own and that you had a choice not to feel that way or at least not to let it affect you that way, but not blaming you for your inability to do it in any given manner, just giving you encouragement.

If I try to think what therapy *should* do for you, I believe the most important thing is to support someone to realize they have far more autonomy than they think. To help them to make choices and insofar as they feel that the past intrudes, to reappraise it, but not in a blaming sense. And I think it's terribly important to be able to forgive yourself and your parents and to realize that whatever you did, the decision was the best you could have made at that point, it was for survival, even though it's a disaster and hasn't given you what you wanted. So it's a sort of accepting responsibility for yourself, but not in a judgemental sense. In the past you made survival choices. So if you look at it in that way for yourself and your parents at that time, there's much more of a sense of tolerance and forgiveness, and I think that's the most important thing. You can't forgive yourself until you've forgiven them.

Barbara

He therefore who has learned rightly to be in dread
has learned the most important thing.
Søren Kierkegaard: *The Concept of Dread*

Going by the stuffed crocodile in the hall, we descend to the basement kitchen to be warmed by the Aga. St Anthony of Padua stretches out tranquilly from a niche, collections of pottery jugs and plates line the dresser. Barbara is ravaged and decorative and very direct.

I can't actually say much about him, the analyst, it's sort of risky – one is so careful about that sort of thing, isn't one? I've mentioned your project to him and he said, 'Don't have anything to do with it.' It *was* a therapy situation, you see, for some years, but now it's become a friendship and it's damned difficult. For instance, I said to him about three weeks ago, 'Look, darling, I'm not going to see you any more, goodbye forever', and he says, 'Don't be so stupid', and hangs up the phone. And a friend rings and I have a conversation with her, and then it goes ring ring again, and it's him, exactly as though I hadn't said anything at all.

It was therapy for several years, you see, then it was beginning to spill over, then I stopped the therapy. But I was practically spending more time with him and his family than I was with my own; I was just spreading myself too thin. The relationship just got so close it was completely absurd. I've found it easier to get shot of him than he has to get shot of me.

One is so superstitious. I think in a way he's a witch-doctor, you know, I've got terribly superstitious about the whole business. We've had the most awful coincidences and things, you know how those things happen – synchronicity or whatever it's called. So I got sort of worried about that and everybody said, 'Don't be so stupid. Of course he's not a witch-doctor', all that sort of stuff. The actual therapy – well, I don't know whether it helped. I went to him because we were all of us in disarray and he did help my son, and certainly things have improved now, but it's impossible to know whether it's just that time heals all or whether we'd have been worse off without him, or what.

So I'll talk to you about the Church instead, the Church as a kind of therapist. The confessional. Talking to your therapist, it goes on and on; oh God, I was boring myself to such a degree, darling. But there is in the confessional an added ingredient. For one thing, in the confessional you tell the truth, otherwise there's no point, whereas you can fool about with the shrink – I mean, I played a lot of silly games with mine just to see what he'd do next, all that sort of stuff. In the confessional you tell the truth. And the added ingredient is that if you believe it, you're forgiven. Now the shrink's got no power to forgive your sins.

Forgiving yourself – no, I find that impossible. If you've lost a child, as I have, I think – no matter how – for some reason the guilt is insupportable. You just think, I should have been there, I should have . . . if I hadn't gone out . . . All that sort of stuff. And I think you go mad. I think you go mad in grief. It wasn't till two years after Peter died that I started the therapy.

The Church, well the Church was very, very odd. Some peculiar things happened, coincidences again. After I'd been to the Father for prayers and things. Peter did come out of the coma but totally brain-damaged, so I thought, what's the point of that? And another Catholic said to me, 'Well, you shouldn't ask God for stuff like that, you know.' So what I came away with was not the feeling that there wasn't any God, not even that he was deeply unkind, but that certainly I didn't understand what the bloody hell he was up to; or something like that.

You just have to remember the crucifixion in those circumstances, that's all. I mean, God did not, you know, get himself a job with Guinness and buy himself a mansion in the country and all that stuff. We're terribly, terribly geared now to thinking that life, for us, ought to be rather comfortable and we shouldn't have many setbacks, and I don't know where that idea has come from. It's partly – I'm sure it's partly the adverts on television and that sort of stuff, you know. And the sixties – we were supposed to enjoy ourself and feel no guilt. Life is as tragic as it ever was, but I think we've failed to recognize that, a lot of us have forgotten it and it comes as a short, sharp reminder.

No, I don't believe anything is futile, it all fits into something. That's where the Church is behind me. Even when God is being vilely cruel, it's a sort of cleansing thing. I mean, if, you know, one remembers one's spiritual exercises, one is supposed to be scoured of self. There's the dark night of the soul and all that stuff, and none of us likes it – it's something we've forgotten, I think, we've got to put up with it and it's just something salutary to remember.

After confession, yes, one does go and sin again. But, you know, one then hauls oneself together again and tries not to do it again. It takes a long time – very few of us have immediate conversions, but you just keep working at it. It's like cleaning a house, you know you've tidied up the bloody thing and it's going to get dirty again, but that's no reason not to clean it. I prefer not to have a personal relationship with my confessor. I have occasionally seen priests, you know, just to sort of talk about things, but it's not anything like as valuable as the actual act of confession. It's the impersonal that I find so valuable, because it's God forgiving you, it's not any bloke; God is forgiving you through the medium of the priest. I suppose there are some sins which are so perfectly frightful . . . It's very, very rare though. Myra Hindley – God, she must have said a few Hail Marys, that one. But they say that, you know, God can forgive anything. The parents – I don't think the parents of the children can be expected to forgive her. I think we wouldn't be called upon to do that; I don't quite see how one could. Which is another sin on one's soul, but I don't see it.

Lots of saints have lived practically all their lives in the dark night of the soul and still kept the faith, which I think is extraordinary. Sometimes you have an awareness of the presence of God, you know, you're on jolly good terms and you will see the hem of his garment and the bottom of his feet or something, you sort of know he's there; at other times, nothing, just black, hopeless despair. You've still got to tell yourself that you believe. You still go on talking to him, even if you don't think there's anybody listening. The moments when he is there are such a reward that that sort of keeps you going. Just one little vision of God, I think, is enough for anybody for a lifetime, really, if they can sort of hang in there. The bad times – well, it's like walking away from the fire into a bitter wind: you know the fire's still there somewhere, you know you haven't imagined it, but it doesn't warm you. But the one thing that would really make me angry with God would be that if at the moment of death I saw he wasn't there, then I really would be terribly angry!

Prayer – asking for things, I mean we all do that all the time, but it's never done me much good and that's not what it really is. It's much more – oh, just an awareness that God's there, which is in a way sufficient. Well, it's not sufficient when things are absolutely dreadful, but it does help. Prayer is worship really, more than anything, I think. And the idea of a life after this one, that's something that can help too – it's the whole idea of a second chance.

My family were mostly Catholic, but my parents joined some silly little sect called the Church of Humanity and then they dropped it, so . . . I was about 19 and I had this . . . I thought I was in hell, I thought I was damned; it was a sort of really bad depression. And what I found extraordinary was that it just passed – not dramatically, but it just wasn't there any more. And then I had this feeling of the presence of God, and of course that passed as well, but . . . You see, the point about God is that the devil isn't his equal. The devil is the adversary of St Michael of the Arch-angels, it's sort of lower down. You know, the gates of Hell shall *not* prevail. There's no doubt that God is more powerful than the Devil. They all say that God always answers prayers, it's just that sometimes he says no. 'No, you can't have that and you can't have that.'

God talked to me through my son, Peter. He came back to me

in a dream the other night and he said, 'God wants to know why you're still grieving after all this time. Have you got no faith?' In my dream I thought, well, I've got a few questions I could put to *Him*, just mention *that* when you get back! You know, that wasn't really a religious experience – well, in a way it was ... I am staggered at the extent of suffering that some people are called upon to undergo. It's like being seized upon by an enormous wild animal, and tossed and ripped and rent and flung about. But I've a very peculiar faith, because I go around in despair but hanging on like hell, like, you know, hanging on to the strap in a crowded Underground. I'd never kill myself, I certainly wouldn't go jumping under a train. I just know that you'd pop up on the other side and they'd say, 'Ha, ha, you got that wrong, honey, and you'll go back and you'll do exactly what you didn't do, and you're going to go through this until you've eaten it all up', you know, like spinach. Yes, even with terminal cancer, everybody's got to bloody well stick it out. Awful, isn't it?

I do think the Church has evolved a lot of wise things. Another interesting thing about therapy is that I was in a convent for a time as a postulant and it seemed to me, over all those hundreds of years they had worked out such an excellent, excellent – oh, not psychotherapy precisely ... but the community I was in certainly ran marvellously because of the way the older nuns, the superiors, handled everybody. They seemed to have psychology off to a T, human psychology. They understood – oh, so much, what a muddle we're in with all our relationships. Of course, there were bad-tempered nuns and tiresome nuns, but the sort of rules and the way they lived, it was just so smooth; and I've never laughed so much in all my life, it was a wildly happy sort of atmosphere. And you hear these terrible stories about convents and how ghastly they are – it wasn't my experience at all.

And Caroline's headmistress – she goes to a convent school – I find an incredibly sensible woman. How the Church has got this wisdom – well, it may be God-given or it may be acquired over the years of having to deal with closed communities or just with the flock. And we have rituals for dying and being born – yes, they help; it's like lunch and tea and dinner, it gives a bit of structure to life, do you know? Life goes on and on, but if you've got these things to hang it to – posts here and there – it's not just completely sort of soggy. The actual gravestone for Peter . . . well, it's in a little church in Wales, and the only good thing ecumenicism brought us is that they let me bury Peter there, because it's just near our house, and I've bought all the land from him down to the wall, so there's room for the rest of us. I like it in the graveyard.

All these things, one sort of carries it about. One does turn to it, but I have to tell you it doesn't always help, you know. Actually my therapist, my Mr X, is quite religiously inclined. He was quite good about all that. He's a very peculiar therapist – actually, he's supposed to be a Freudian analyst, but very odd. When I went to him, it was the family I was more worried about than me. I could see myself not relating properly to the children at all and I was saying things to my poor husband like, 'Oh why did God have to take Peter, why couldn't he have taken you' – which is not a nice thing to say, you know. I mean it's mad going round saying things like that. And I think I even did it to the children, I just sort of went completely bonkers. Which seemed to me, you know, to be a suitable case for treatment. There is the time when you have to do that or else take pills or something. Once you really think you're a poached egg.

Depression, I've never really found *anything* for that. I've tried the pills and they made me go blind, and the therapy, well . . . You see, I don't think Mr X is any good at grief. He's good with families who aren't getting along, he's very sensible at pointing out what you're doing wrong. His view is that you sort of project your own lacks and withouts and what nots into other members of the family. That's how he sort of got a hold on me, because if you think you're damaging your children you'll do anything . . .

Do you know what the stupid ape said to me? I found a picture of Peter recently and I showed it to him, and he said, 'Oh, is that John?', and I said, 'No, it's not', and he said, 'Oh, I know, it's Peter.' So I said, 'Yes', and he said, 'When Tibbie died' – this is his bloody cat – 'I was grief-stricken, she lay on my bed and her kidneys had gone and she wet my bed, she died and it was absolutely dreadful, and then I bought Mopsy' – this is his second cat – 'and everything was all right.' And I thought, well . . .! That's what's so odd about him, you see, sometimes he's so stupid and other times he's very, very right.

It's very difficult to discriminate between spiritual malaise and mental malaise and when you need one kind of help and when another kind. I certainly think for guilt, unless it's turned sort of psychotic, you get a greater sense of release coming out of the confessional than you do with getting up from the couch. It's somehow much more positive than going on about your boring old psychic fears. You say, I've just done the most frightful things – I think a shrink often wouldn't agree that it was a frightful thing. I think most human beings know bloody well there's such a thing as sin. The sin against the Holy Ghost is despair. But that's what I've been saying: you can't help having it, but you've still *got* to hang on.

Jeffrey

Each time I opened one of the dreaded doors, I realized that the mechanism of the lock was not as complicated as I had believed, and that, where I dreaded to discover terror, torture and horror, I discovered the little girl in all her moods: unhappy, infatuated and terrified ... What I discovered was a child's fear ... I relived the moments with her, I became her, I felt her fear. When she disappeared I would wake up and begin to clear the newly conquered terrain.

Marie Cardinal: *The Words to Say It*

A mock-Tudor house in a serviceable suburb. At one end of the sitting-room a deflating football, a packet of disposable nappies, chipped bricks, a wooden duck, Dinky cars are neatly herded together. Everyone is upstairs with chicken-pox, Jeffrey explains. He has a solid and candid and scrupulous manner, cautious at first.

===

It's a process I think that does require some warmth, some comfort. If I'd found somebody who was totally blank, cold, I'm not sure I'd have ever got to first base. I've heard Janet – my therapist – say that there are some patients she knows she just won't get on with. We did get on. I wanted some feedback and I did get that. There was a high element of trust in the relationship right from the beginning. I mean, there was a bit of intellectual sparring to start with – you have no background in the field or way of measuring qualifications and you have to make sure who you're dealing with.

I'm an international tax consultant, married with two children under 5, and I work for a large multinational. The history of how it happened was basically that there were sexual problems in the relationship between me and my wife, and she got more and more depressed. Eventually she went to a clinic and they directed her to a psychotherapist. The results of that weren't altogether positive in many ways. I felt under considerable assault – she was talking about leaving me and the children. It wasn't the therapist that was the problem – I'd met him and I didn't feel threatened by him at all – but I felt the therapy was being used against me. My wife would twist it and use it as an assault on me. So I in fact spoke to her therapist and asked him if he could refer me to someone, and I think Janet was someone he'd worked with on a number of cases. That was about two and a half years ago. I started off going once a week, that went up to twice a week after about two months, and at one point I went three times a week just for a short time.

To start with I felt that I was a bit of a fraud, that all I wanted was a shoulder to cry on because I was in a personal difficulty et cetera, et cetera. But in a way, even from the first session, I was fairly well aware that there were fundamental problems that I'd had for years. I knew my reaction to what was going on in the marriage was neurotic, that the degree of depression it induced was way out of line. I was basically depressed enough to become non-functional in many ways. I mean, I was attending work, I was doing things, but I couldn't concentrate; I was surviving on a wing and a prayer. The kids weren't a problem, but the marriage was a disaster area all the time. So, anyway, I started off there, once a week at first.

One of the initial terrors was that it would never be completed, that I'd be hooked into it for ever. And then the pressure in terms of getting time off work – Janet lives in Crouch End and I work in Slough – so I did eight o'clock on a Saturday morning and eight o'clock on a Tuesday night and seven-thirty on a Wednesday morning. It was fantastic of her to work those hours. I think it was part of the development of trust in a way, that she'd put herself out that much for me. She's an extremely frank person – brutally so, some might say – but that suits me. And she's got a great sense of humour. She doesn't claim to be infallible or omniscient; I mean, she will express doubt, she will effectively think out loud in terms of what she's trying to get to, based on what I've told her.

She's also sometimes taken time out to sit down and explain a bit of the theory, and I found that a great help. Because one of the things that, especially at first, used to happen was that I would go away in total confusion, unable to grasp what had been said or whether I was getting to her or anything else. A lot of it resolved itself in time anyway, which I think is part of the treatment; but often if I understood a bit of theory, I could spend time during the week thinking about it and often things would just sort themselves out into it, which was very useful. It gives you a tool kit. I felt I'd come away after two and a half years with a set of tools I could apply to myself using some of the concepts. It does make you look at yourself and understand why you reacted to things in a certain way – though I'm not saying it's infallible or a substitute for professional help.

I was very dependent at first. I'm not sure how long that lasted. It was just that I was extremely depressed and here was someone I could actually talk to about it. I hadn't talked to anyone much before, not really. If I'd been cut off from contact with her I'd have been fairly devastated, though it wasn't a dependency in terms of I can't make it through the weekend, you know. It was frightening at times, the thought of, how do I get off this? It solved itself all right in the end as it happened. There's sometimes a certain tendency to intellectualize things – I think she found that difficult to get through on occasion. But it worked none the less. I do believe it did.

It was a bit of a new world, not totally alien, you know, but I'd never looked at things with this degree of intensity. A few times I broke down and cried, which is something new for me – once when I was driving down a motorway, which is extremely dangerous! Something just suddenly went click. We worked a lot on dreams – having them, recalling them, the frustration of forgetting them. I don't really recall them very much now, but there was an intense period when I had them two or three times a week and they became the main focus of everything. It's like peeling an onion – things floated up in layers; the idea of actually going back to childhood . . . If I look back on it now, there's a pattern. If you read through the dreams chronologically as I actually wrote them down, it's a zigzag line that you can see happening. She would sometimes say she didn't understand a dream, which makes you know that you're not dealing with a charlatan; in any sort of field you work in, you know the level of honest ignorance and uncertainty there is. She's a very unmysterious person. I needed to feel that the person was human and fallible. Sometimes she'd be about to say something and she'd just stop and say, 'No, I don't want to say that yet', and be quite open about it.

We've had some conversations where she was expressing that she had no needs of me – though I didn't, in fact, need that reassurance, but she's said that she does have colleagues who she frankly believes do have needs of their patients and that they're in the wrong business. And that sort of power mystique thing, too – I don't think I would have got on with that. I mean, hostility in therapy I'm sure comes from neurosis, but it does also come from a genuine clash of personalities and I'm not sure that some therapists recognize the one from the other. Of course, I did get hostile to her sometimes, though it was difficult for me because a lot of it was suppressed, sort of intellectualized; the conscious and adult me was keeping fairly strict control over the rest of me. Which became a standing joke! To the extent that it became recognized and admitted it wasn't so much of a problem, because you work round it. There was only one time when I felt like getting up and walking out, which in terms of me was massive hostility, I suppose. But we talked it out in the following session. The other thing is that I desperately need warmth from people, and if she'd been cold, the hostility would have been more of the whipped dog variety, it would have made me introspective, introverted, rather than angry in an external fashion.

The first session, well . . . I went in and basically I explained the background, and she just said, you know, 'How do you feel? What's happening?' And I said that there was this feeling that I was a bit like a sort of proboscis, sucking the life out of something else, parasitic, in my marriage. That I felt empty and useless and all that stuff. And after about fifteen minutes – she'd been silent throughout – she said, 'Why didn't your mother feed you?' It was dramatic. And it sort of went on from there.

I came away from my first session feeling elation, that I'd prised the lid off something, got through to something in me, that here was somebody who actually . . . it wasn't just to do with my marriage, it was my whole life, and I knew it from way back. I felt that suddenly there was some chance of being free, of being whole.

It was a fairly dramatic first session, I was very lucky. After that it was just a lot of bloody hard work. At the time it would seem unsuccessful, it's only looking back on it – you look back six months and think, my God, what it used to be like. The difference that it's in fact made to my life has been quite profound. On the emotional level for the first time I felt a degree of security, an inner self if you like. I feel solid for the first time in my life. Take a simple thing – let's say I'm in the South of France working and I have to rent a car and drive it across a strange territory. That would have terrorized me three years ago – I still would have done it, but it would have terrorized me. Now it can make me uncomfortable – I don't particularly like trying to find my way to somewhere I don't know in a strange town – but I have confidence I can do it and that I'll get there.

I believe now I have something to offer my children. Before I wasn't really convinced of it. I felt I was a sort of phoney, like I was too clever, too tricky, that I'd be found out, everybody would know the truth. You learn, I suppose, to quite like yourself, and the bits you don't like, you learn that they're part of you and that's that; you get a sort of inner peace from them.

I've asked Janet and she says she has absolutely no idea theoretically how it works, and that's one of the reasons I believe in her and know she's an extremely intelligent woman. She doesn't know why it works, but it does. There are the mechanics of it, if you like, discoveries – problems with mother, I cut off when I was about 3, when my brother died; that all came out of the woodwork. And then sort of reaching back to early childhood, though at the time I was never really conscious of doing that on a day-to-day basis; going back there, lifting it all out, growing roots.

Understanding what went wrong, understanding how that has affected your behaviour – it makes a significant difference. But the bit I don't understand is that it has a healing effect. Why it heals I don't know.

I'm not terribly mystical, but there's a mysterious element in there. I think it's founded in the relationship with the therapist, I think that's what it's all about, but I don't know why it works. I think all those elements are there, the relationship, the analytical, the mapping, the understanding yourself, the bringing out what happened in the past. But what catalyses all those elements into healing someone, I don't know.

It's not just that she has a healing personality, though I think that's true and I think that helped. At the beginning, anyway, I saw her differently, I saw a coldness. I can see her much more as she is now. Of course, I was seeing my mother in her at the start. No, it's not that I had a difficult relationship with my mother – I didn't *have* a relationship with her. Not after a certain age, anyway, and that was the root cause of the trouble. Something happened when my brother died when I was 3 and the entire thing fell apart after that.

My mother was probably very depressed. And also I think I blamed myself for my brother's death, I felt I murdered him. There was the feeling of developing a sense of loss, both for him as a brother and for her as a mother – feeling that there was anything to *have* lost, it took me a long time to realize that. You know – my God, what I could have had; actually accessing that, it was very painful. There's a profound bitterness about the years I've spent chasing my own tail because of that early relationship.

Oh, I know in some ways I've survived quite nicely thank you, compared to some people, and I'm still young. But my God, when I was 16 or 18 or 21, things might have been different in such a lot of ways. OK, at first I just thought, well, that's water under the bridge; it's now that one develops a feeling of loss. It's a feeling of loss that I didn't in fact *have* a mother. That was the most difficult thing to come to terms with. She was a shiny steel sphere to me, totally inaccessible; there was no form, no function, no nothing to her. And trying to crack into that . . . One of the things that Janet said was immediately noticeable to her, which wasn't noticeable to me, was the entire *absence* of her, that she didn't seem to exist – which is, you know, bizarre.

Trying to access that, to access my mother, was very, very difficult. Because I was trying . . . you know, like trying to do your homework – why can't I do this, I ought to be able to do it, I'm failing. Then, I suppose, after about the first six months things were getting better. It's a bit like surfing, you just kind of learn to get on the board, stay on the wave as long as you can and just carry on. If you fall off the board, fine, you get back on it and wait for another wave. And you learn not to fight it, but just to arrive with it. And OK, there'll be days or weeks when you really feel you're moving and covering a lot of ground – that's when you're on the board, when you're up on the wave. And then you'd fall off. But what I learnt was that another wave would come along, and you learn patience, you learn just to take your time. There'd be sessions or even whole weeks or a month when you felt you were going round in circles; that was immensely frustrating.

You went in and hadn't had a dream, for instance, and felt like a failure. It is bloody hard work, it's emotionally draining. That you have to keep grinding away, waiting for the wave, that was the hard bit. There was a desperate need at first; I had the feeling of, can it work, can you help me? And at the same time almost wanting it to work *too* much, the feeling that I somehow ought to be able to make this work, I ought to remember these things, I ought to be able to come up with something. Of course you can't go away and make a list – I'm going to do *a*, *b* and *c* tomorrow. And although I trusted her, there was a desperate fear of being mocked and a fear of wasting her time, not being interesting enough. One thing she said to me once was, 'Well, everybody, in fact, wants to be my most interesting patient.'

There was a feeling after the first session that it was almost like an open book. I think she's said since then, 'Yes, you followed the pattern, you fitted the theory quite nicely' – which is great! It's quite reassuring to feel that you've actually fitted the mould. Maybe I've been lucky. Certainly I was motivated – though there were times when I had to be up at six o'clock in the morning to drive across to the far side of north London and then back out to Slough, when I could really have done without it! But I could see, for the first time in my life I could see a chance of freedom. If it had been taken away from me, I would have been distraught. And I have now, I suppose, reached that goal: I'm free of myself. Well, not totally, obviously, but you accept the ragged bits; you know where you're vulnerable, you know about the relationship with the mother that will never be.

The only way I could handle that in therapy was to see another part of myself as a small boy. He became called Child Anthony and he was always outside in the street and wouldn't come in. Learning to care about him – he was a nasty, nasty small boy, he was too clever, he was too fast on his feet, he was too deceitful – learning to like him and have sorrow for him, I think that was the key. Not feeling sorry for yourself, but having some compassion for yourself. Until he eventually came in and sat on her lap and on one occasion even breast-fed from her, and then he became part of me and I can conjure him up as an image now. This kid was terrified and that's why he wouldn't come in. I could only handle him in terms of being a separate entity. I mean, literally, as I've described it to you, I'd talk about Child Anthony as a third person. And the key to ending the three sessions a week time was when he finally came in from the cold and found that he could curl up on a lap. But to talk in those terms at first, you know, the fear of being mocked . . . And even telling you now!

I think one thing that helped was that, I suppose, half-consciously I knew where the problem was, and that can save you a hell of a lot of time. I knew there was a problem with my mother. There'd been my first wife, a very perceptive woman, and I think a lot of what I was had been described to me, very kindly and charitably. Of course, the failure of that marriage had been related to my problem with my mother too; there was a great sense of loss about that, though maybe it wouldn't have worked anyway.

The therapy has made my present marriage survive. My wife has had great problems in therapy and it hasn't been terribly successful for her, and the marriage is still not without problems.

I don't think it would have survived. I suppose my needs are far, far less. And then, if you like, there's a bit more balance now, in so much as I believe now my needs are normal, as opposed to thinking there was something wrong with me for having these needs. I would be able to think, what the hell is wrong with wanting a normal warmth and affection? Is it bizarre? No, it really isn't. I'd come to believe, because I kept being told it, that it was bizarre. But the turning-point of it all was the Child Anthony thing.

I want to backtrack for a moment, because I've just remembered something. The hostility, the intellectualizing at the beginning. I had a need to cut her down, Janet, I mean, to size, knock her down, make her less powerful. Especially because she was a woman and what she'd come to represent – there was a great deal of fear and a need to cut her down. She had a very shrewd idea of what was going on, though. I was afraid of getting too committed.

It was all bloody hard work. And the other thing is that it's expensive. I was lucky, I could afford to do it. I would, I suppose, have done anything to carry on, to find the money. I always felt very lucky and a bit guilty, because there was this vague feeling, you don't really need this, you're wasting this woman's time, it's wrong that the poor have to be mad while the rich can afford therapy. But that passed later.

We spent quite a lot of time talking about the children. This is the sort of counselling aspect of it. I feel far more secure and confident about the kids and I also feel I have something to offer them. At the same time I don't feel, my God, if I do this wrong this child is going to grow up to be a juvenile delinquent; I'm very relaxed with them. There are certain responses I see in a child that can have a profound effect on me and I understand why, because they were things I experienced as a child myself. You can step back and say, 'You've gone over the top on this, this isn't *you*, it's another child, you're exaggerating because you're trying to compensate for something that happened to you.' As long as you're aware – I'm not saying it's perfect – but you do at least have a chance of understanding what's going on.

Towards the end there was a sort of move back down again. I'm moving to Stuttgart in a few weeks anyway, but I think we felt the time was right to stop. It happened of its own accord. I got to a certain point I suppose and then I didn't need it in the same way any more. So it sort of happened naturally as part of the process. And you get pretty good at being your own therapist towards the end. Oh, it was frustrating, it was expensive, it was painful. But I felt that there was a goal to be reached and there was a form of freedom to be reached. Even when I was depressed, I knew for the first time that it could pass. I don't get depression now, not that sort of black and suicidal depression. Even when I knew I wasn't there yet and had a long way to go, it wasn't just hope, it was a real belief that I would get there.

One of Janet's ideas that she's carried on right throughout is that I wasn't empty, I was more *disappointed*. She said, 'You can come across people who are totally empty,' – I can't quite remember, but she did explain it – 'but', she said, 'you weren't like that.' She said, 'Something did go right for you, it may not have been good in many ways, but you had some expectation that was dashed. You didn't just turn off and say, "this will never be".' There was something that I'd always been searching for – I wouldn't have been looking at all if it had never been there.

People in my line of work would be horrified if they knew all this, you know. Oh, if you're in the BBC or the literary world or something, it's OK, but in the City, for instance, if they knew you'd been to a shrink, they'd write you off. But I don't care. I suppose I've got to the point – it's not that everything's fine, it'll never be totally perfect – but I've patched it all together and it's not a very pretty edifice but it's very solid, it's on very good foundations. OK, if I'd had a different childhood and background, it would be an aesthetically pleasing structure – but it works and I knew I was building it and if there are ragged edges, I can sort of understand why they're there and do something about them.

I don't expect to be *happy* exactly, but I don't think I'll have that kind of black depression and despair. I don't have to go around hating myself all the time – just disliking myself some of the time!

It's all right, I don't mind talking to you – it's like giving blood, isn't it? I've got it and I'd like to pass it on.

Harriet

the air and then the earth in the great cold the great
dark the air and the earth abode of stones in the great
cold alas alas in the year of their Lord six hundred
and something the air the earth the sea the earth
abode of stones in the great deeps the great cold on
sea on land and in the air

Samuel Beckett: *Waiting for Godot*

Lined with books and stacked with papers, Harriet's study
looks out over the sea front and smells of spray. She brings in
China tea and scones and seems to find it hard to start talking;
when she does, it is mechanically but with a certain desperation.

It was a long time ago – over twenty years now. I don't know if
you want to know about things that go back that far. In a way
I've sort of forgotten so much – and yet the memories of that
time are stamped on me, permanently stamped in. It sounds
ridiculous, but sometimes I think nothing else that's ever happened
in my life – no, nothing – has affected me quite so much. I don't
know whether I can really get it across to you, why it was so
important.

I was 30 when I started psychoanalysis; for all the usual sorts
of reasons, I suppose. I don't know if my childhood was dramatically bad, but something seems to have messed my brother
and me up. My parents had a very absorbing life, and we had a
string of nannies – I don't know what they were like, I often
wonder. Then when I was 5 and he was 2 we were in a home for
six months because the nanny was ill or something while my
parents were away travelling. I don't think that was too good. And
I was ill a lot – at death's door, apparently, three operations and so

on. Away from school for a year at one point. I still have a sort
of horror of hospitals and dentists and the smell of antiseptic, it
smells of dying to me.

The thing was, my parents seemed to be continually going away
and then one would be left with the nanny and the staff – cook,
housemaids, all that – and there was a feeling of . . . awful
bleakness. I have a sort of memory of walking through the park at
around four o'clock on a dark November day, holding on to the
pram with my brother in it, and I was in disgrace for naughtiness,
I think, as usual, and there were rooks cawing and it was everything
that was dark and desolate. One knew one was eternally naughty
and unforgiven and that they'd never come back.

My mother . . . actually I'm a bit weary of talking about my
mother, I've talked to so many people and blamed her so much. I
have a definite feeling that she's sort of out there somewhere
listening to me blaming her and getting very angry. Oh yes, she's
dead, of course. I expect, in fact I'm sure, I was an awful child
and didn't deserve anything much. But I do remember the first
words I ever said in analysis. I sat on the couch – I couldn't cope
with lying on it yet – and I said, 'My mother seems to hate me and
I don't know why.'

One can't be sure one's remembering things accurately about
childhood. In particular, I can't remember much about it because
I was evacuated to the United States for nearly four years during
the war, that's World War Two, and I sort of forgot everything
about my home and childhood out there. I was very homesick and
there was a kind of blank-out. So I can't be sure of anything that
happened before I was about 11. I know I was very fond of my
parents and, of course, when I got back to England, they'd sort of
gone, they were a couple of strangers. So childhood is only scraps
of memory and I think there were good times as well as bad. What
I can remember is after the war, when I was growing up or grown
up, and that's when the hatred came in.

I do remember one thing she said. It was when my children
used to wake me up in the night, and she said, 'When you were 2,
you used to wake up crying, so I said to you, "You'll damage the
baby if you wake me up and you'll damage me, and if you go on,

I'll put you in the boxroom", and you *never* cried again!' Great!
Implying that's what I should say to my children.

Anyway, the lead-up to analysis. There was college, when I was
occasionally quite depressed, and then rather crazy times living on
my own in London. I was sacked from my job, I was involved
with people in sort of neurotic ways. Then I got married at 24,
had my children, separated at 27. I can't go into all that, it was a
completely neurotic mix-up. Anyway, I was very, very depressed
after the divorce. I mean, what I called depressed then – not
nearly as bad as now, but it seemed pretty bad at the time. I had
the children to bring up on my own and no money. It was much
more unusual to be a single parent in those days, believe me.

Actually, I remember now I'd always wanted to be psychoanalysed. It sounded fascinating. I knew, of course I did, that
there was a hell of a lot wrong with me. I remember saying to
some friends that if I came into a fortune I'd be psychoanalysed.
I remember them sort of groaning – 'Oh, typical of you'. I hadn't
read any psychoanalytical books or anything though. I don't think
I had any idea how to go about being psychoanalysed, or what
were the differences between all the various kinds and so on.
What happened was that I met a woman who'd been in therapy
and she told me to write to the headquarters of psychoanalysis
or whatever it is. It went on from there. I remember her asking
me why on earth I wanted to be psychoanalysed and I said
because I didn't feel life was worth living, and she burst out
laughing!

I know this is a very boring bit, but I must explain exactly
about the beginning of analysis. You see, I went to see someone, I
can't remember his name, who offered me a free treatment –
because I got virtually no maintenance from my ex-husband and I
was very broke. He was quite nice. I told him I felt like someone
swimming and trying to hold up the two children and we were all
starting to sink. But the trouble was he could only see me at
various odd times during the week when it would have been very
difficult to get the children looked after. So we agreed I should
wait until they were both at full-time school. But then my mother
at this time was dying of cancer, they said she had only a year to

live, and she wanted me to promise I'd move out of London to look after my father after she died. As it happened, ironically, it turned out to be the last thing he wanted, to have me and two children living with him, so it never arose.

But I thought I had only one year left in London, so I decided to go back to a consultant and make use of my last year and ask to go to a paid psychoanalyst so that I could choose my own times to fit in with the children. I would pay out of my Post Office savings. But then – I'll explain this in a minute – what actually happened was that as soon as I'd settled in with this analyst, he changed all the appointment times, so I was worse off than if I'd taken up the free place. That was part of all the awful things that happened. And then – I'm sorry to go on with all this – but when I think back, I don't believe the consultant should have let me get involved when I thought I had only one year available. I don't think I knew that it could take ages longer than that. And he said I'd probably get so much better that I'd earn more and work out the finances of it that way. Quite untrue, that was. And he said there weren't any analysts in my home town anyway – well, analysts, therapists, call it what you like, there would have been somebody, I'm sure.

So. Well, I started off with this analyst he recommended. Very nervous. And I thought he was just wonderful from the start. He was about my own age, unmarried, he'd even been at the same university at the same time as me. I think I thought as soon as we'd got the tiresome business of analysis over we'd be sort of together in bliss for ever. Psychoanalysis was a whole new world. I remember I slept and slept during the first few weeks, as though I'd been waiting for this and finally got there and dropped down exhausted. I was with him for three years, first twice a week, then three times. I didn't care about the money. I'd have gone every day if I could – weekends were just agony.

It's funny, there were all those hours and hours and I'm not sure what we did talk about. My mother; I think he did make me see how much was her fault rather than mine, so to speak. Some things stick in my mind. I remember some time fairly early in the analysis I had a sort of nightmare, one of those dreams where everything goes all spooky and weird and out of control, funny faces glaring at you and everything very spooky and menacing; and I was in among all this chaos and I kept calling out, 'Where's the doctor, where's the doctor?' And in the corner he was there, in a white coat. I felt that the dream sort of meant that nothing would ever be so bad again, that he'd always be with me. But that's what he wasn't.

It is quite incredible the feelings you get. I was very, very puzzled as to whether they were *real* or not. I mean, in a way this seems the most totally real person who's ever been in your life, but in another way this is just a paid psychoanalyst who keeps his whole self secret from you. I'm baffled still as to whether this can be a good thing, to go into a state of . . . bemusement, bafflement. It's an enchantment or something. It's because nobody in your whole life has ever listened to you before, ever paid you any attention, and it seems as though this was what you were always waiting for and finally it's come true. There were two lines from a Shakespeare sonnet I used to keep repeating to myself:

> But if the while I think on thee, dear friend,
> All losses are restored, and sorrows end.

All losses are restored. That's what I felt.

I'm not sure if this was just a honeymoon period. I think it was more or less all through the first two years, until everything went wrong in the third year. I remember those last few steps before reaching his front door and ringing the bell. I remember running and that feeling that I just *couldn't* bridge the gap fast enough. Though when I got inside and upstairs I might be quite blank about what to talk about. The talking seemed to be irrelevant really; life was a question of whether I was *with* him or *without* him. The holidays were awful, awful. He'd go off for six weeks in the summer and he said there wasn't any address I could write to. I had the children to look after and the money to earn, and I somehow had to keep going, but I felt I couldn't. I used to count out the days – it would be forty-two or something, and then what seemed like years would pass and I'd count again and it would be . . . thirty-eight or something! I think they should set up some sort of locum for you during the holidays, just a phone number you could ring in an emergency. Perhaps they do that nowadays.

I remember Christmas, wandering round the shop windows trying to decide what I'd like to buy for him – maybe a marvellous silk tie or maybe some incredibly rare expensive bottle of wine. I was quite put down when he said you weren't allowed to buy presents. In a way I hate to remember the way I felt. Often the children had little illnesses, you know, and I'd have to cancel the session, and I practically hated them. I had a funny idea – I felt everywhere I went out, outside in the street, he was watching. Somehow I was *seen* by him everywhere. I couldn't bear the thought that I wasn't. Even now, in a particular district, I won't say which, I feel he can see me. The idea that I was just me, a separate person, out in the street and nobody caring, was somehow unbearable.

At the time I started the analysis I'd just met a man at a party who seemed quite keen on me and he was ringing up a lot and asking me out. But I felt, no, I've got this analyst, he's the only person in my life, there can't be two, so I put a complete stop to it. Also I developed great panics about going out on social occasions – the maddening thing was that I never had this before starting psychoanalysis. So I didn't have any affairs or anything during the analysis, and I remember the analyst attacking me in a frightening way and saying, 'I don't believe it. You're having affairs on the sly and not telling me.' It wasn't true, completely untrue. Then after the breaking off, which is what I'm going to tell you about, I was completely ill and didn't go out with men at all. So it meant years of my life blanked out in that respect, all my thirties.

I know that I couldn't conceive ever parting from him. It used to flash across my mind vaguely sometimes, you're supposed to get better and leave him, but I just dismissed it, it was unthinkable. It would sort itself out somehow. If I brought up the subject, he'd say that I'd reach a point where I didn't need him any more. It seemed about as likely as not needing food or air or something. I suppose . . . I do realize now that I must have been an intolerable sort of millstone hanging round his neck, but then you're really encouraged to give yourself up to the analyst, not to resist. They encourage you and then they punish you for it.

There was a sort of way in which I had to give up *myself* in favour of him. It's hard to explain. For instance, I remember an argument about how long it took to get to Cambridge. I *knew* it took whatever it was, an hour and a half or something. He said it was some different time. He was the psychoanalyst, laying down the law about what my dreams meant and what my thoughts were, so how could he be wrong? It seemed to pose some awful choice, of believing myself or believing someone else. I do realize that this feeling was connected with my mother in some way.

There's a particular incident I'll never forget, I remember it more clearly than anything. I'd been out in the evening to a coffee bar, they were all the go at that time, the Partisan coffee bar it was called; and I was absolutely frozen with shock because I looked up and thought I saw him at another table. Of course, everywhere I went I saw him, everyone looked like him, in the street and everywhere, but I really felt it *was* him at the other table. So the first thing I said to him at the next session was, 'Was it really you at the Partisan coffee bar last night?' He didn't answer. He said we must discuss why I wanted to ask the question and so on. Which I suppose we did, but what we said's totally forgotten. Then when I was putting on my coat to go I said in all seriousness, 'But *was* it you there last night?' And he just opened the door for me and waited for me to go, didn't say anything or look at me, just stared solidly over my head.

I haven't explained the thing about the appointments and getting the children looked after. You know I said that I turned down the free place that was offered me because it would mean leaving the children with babysitters, and then when I thought I'd have to leave London I specifically went to this paying therapy so that I could choose to go while the children were at school. But after I'd been with him quite a short while he told me that in future he was going to have to see me *after* four in the afternoon because he was doing a course during the day. I was totally upset about this. But I was sort of trapped – I couldn't possibly move to another analyst by then. What was so really unfair was that when he told me about this, he said I could probably come after eight in the evening sometimes, when the children were in bed; but, in fact, when I raised that, he just remained absolutely silent or changed the subject. They can do that, you know, and you're quite helpless. So several times a week I had to go to work, then go by bus to fetch the children, take them round to whatever friend would look after them, go on to analysis, go and fetch them home, then housework, supper et cetera. I know it wasn't good for them. The point is that if I'd known, I might as well have accepted the free place. It really took every penny to pay for my sessions, no question of holidays or anything.

I think one of the things we talked mainly about was my mother. Not unusual! I mean, he shifted things around ... I knew that either my mother or myself was quite barmy, and basically I felt it must be me. Without exactly accusing her, he let me see how much of the wrong was on her side. I remember saying that people liked her so much, she was so attractive, and he said, 'But they didn't have to be her daughter.' This was a great help, but then, in a way, it all got swept away during the break-up. Also he was very perceptive about my dishonesties and stratagems and so on. He was very strict with me and I think that was good – a sort of training in honesty.

My mother had somehow given me very deeply the idea that I was a non-loving person, that I was a kind of freak in that respect, different from everybody else. My marriage had given me that idea too. But what I seemed to be getting out of the analysis – and maybe, maybe I still have it – was that I *could* love people. I mean, I loved the analyst, I knew that. The children, of course, but that's sort of different, they're almost part of you. I hugged it all to myself, but I felt that I had this treasure in me. That's why the ending was so ... well, awful isn't even the word. It was some sort of cataclysm.

I think what happened was that in about the third year things went wrong. I mean, when I talk about adoring the analyst and so on, it doesn't mean that I wasn't an awful patient. I resisted him all the time, he said; I argued about everything. And during this third year or so he kept on saying that I was hostile to him, sort of that I hated him. He seemed to keep saying this, whatever various kinds of thing I talked about in the sessions. I think I felt it as a terrible hurt, that there was one person in the world that I *did* love, and he kept implying that I hated him. I know now – I mean, they keep telling you in analysis that you can love and hate the same person, but that's an idea I couldn't have handled. I can't now for that matter.

Certainly there were reasons for me to be resentful. He would never discuss the arrangements by which the children had to be dumped with various minders after school. And then, far from making such a great improvement, as the consultant had implied, I got much worse symptom-wise during the treatment, to the point where I was terribly nervous about travelling or going out any-where. This put such a stopper on life. Of course, that wasn't his fault, but you unreasonably feel it is; you're paying out your last penny and you get worse instead of better.

Oh, I've just remembered a way in which I *did* feel better. It's very intangible, not like getting a better job or getting remarried or something. I'd just dropped the children at school – they went to a private school that my father paid for, and all the other parents had cars and so on and I felt terribly inferior. I was just coming out of the school and some great imposing stockbroker or barrister father was coming in, and my shoe fell off! And instead of feeling desperately humiliated and rushing past, I caught his eye and burst out laughing! It seemed a whole new freedom – perhaps I've still got it, saved it from the wreck. I don't know.

Well, the wreck, yes. I've got to explain about that. I have a helpless feeling that I can't get across what it meant to me. What happened was that he was always telling me how hostile I was, and I was moaning about how he wasn't making me any better. And he said, 'If you feel like that, hasn't it ever occurred to you to take some time off and think the whole analysis over?' I was very taken aback. But in a way I'm a very obedient person as well as being rebellious, and at the next session I said, yes, I'd do that. I felt very sort of exalted. I felt I'd trust him truly for the first time, I'd stop clinging, he'd stay there for me.

I took about two weeks off from analysis. And it was a very

extraordinary time. They use this expression now, to turn something around. I felt myself almost physically stretching and growing and shifting round, like a compass needle, just a degree or two, but away from my badness of heart and towards the good, a change of heart. I wrote a lot – I'd never done that before – poems, bits of stories and so on. I'd let go of him and then rediscovered him and made him real. I wrote to say I *would* like now to go on with the treatment, and on the way back from the letter-box I had this extraordinary feeling inside, a movement inside as though a baby were shifting in the womb. It was September, I think, very golden and beautiful.

Then the next thing was, I got a letter from him saying he was surprised to hear I wanted to recommence my analysis, as I'd broken it off. I hadn't. *I hadn't*, damn it, damn it. *He*'d suggested I take time off to think things over. I remember the letter, reading it in the kitchen, small neat handwriting on blue paper. He said I could come and discuss it. The night before I went to see him I had a dream which proved to sort of come true. There was a person who'd been chopped up into a whole lot of bits lying all over the room, and I was very worried and was asking, 'Where *is* the actual person now they're in bits?'

I can't remember exactly what he said when we met, it's got blanked out – it was that he wouldn't go on seeing me, basically that I was impossible, that I resisted him, a feeling that there was nothing to be done about me. So there I was, chucked into the bloody dustbin. I can't describe the smash-up. I do remember going around and my face was sort of absolutely stiff and I was afraid people would notice. And then I remember going to a public lavatory and trying to open the door with my front-door key. I was in a sort of dream. But what I want to explain is that he stopped seeing me because he stopped, in fact, being an analyst: he gave up all his patients. But he didn't tell me that or give me a recommendation to another analyst or anything like that. I only found out from friends of friends who knew him.

Well, briefly, the rest of it was that I went to another analyst, a woman, for about a year, who was very kind. And you won't believe it, but instead of being angry with him, I had one thought during that time, which was to survive for his sake, to show him that he hadn't destroyed me, somehow like a present to him. After about a year of working at this, I made an appointment and went back to see him. It was to be a sort of final thing, to say that it was all right. And it was unbelievable, he just kept saying over and over again that I'd come to persecute him. I got very panicky and kept saying, 'I'm sorry', and every time I said that he said, 'You're saying that to persecute me', and that made me apologize more than ever. I came out and went to a public phone and rang the woman analyst and told her the whole interview and said, 'Either I've gone mad or he has', something like that; and she said, 'It's all right, I believe you. I do believe you're telling the truth and you're not mad.'

But everything went totally to pieces after that. I'm sorry it's such a sob story. I went quite to pieces. I used to cut great scratches on my arms with scissors, I lost about two stone. I went pretty barmy, I think. What I really feel the great bitterness about was not what happened to me, because in a way I don't think l matter, but that the children should have had that shadow over them, being brought up by someone who'd gone almost mad.

I suppose I sort of recovered. And yet I haven't. I've been to all kinds of shrinks since then and I've been on anti-depressant pills for years. It's sort of like the Wandering Jew or Flying Dutchman or whoever it was, wandering on from place to place. I don't think you recover that much from an actual smashing up of yourself, when everything is turned upside down and in a way you stay sane but underneath things are quite weird and mad. In a way you're always in a dream for ever after. Anyway, there you are, there it is. I'm quite exhausted.

Michael

'That doesn't seem to me so very bad', the psychiatrist
said, with the casual power of delivery attainable only
at the highest, thinnest altitude of wisdom. It was like
golf on the moon; even a chip shot sailed for miles.

John Updike: *Problems and Other Stories*

Michael's flat in Dulwich is next door to a greengrocer. His manner implies a better background to come. Piano, books, typewriter, bicycle, chipped mugs of Nescafé, a frequently ringing telephone; a torrent of talk. Michael's hair is cut short all round except for one long lock hanging down his back.

———————

My first contact with psychoanalysis came ages and ages ago when I was about 8 and I saw a copy of Freud's *Three Essays on the Theory of Sexuality* on my parents' bookshelf. So it did start quite early. Yes, I did look through it and, of course, I didn't understand it because it had all these long words in it, like auto-eroticism and things like that, and I didn't know what on earth those things were. At first I'd thought, ha ha – these are Mummy's and Daddy's sex books, and I locked myself in the bathroom to read it. No diagrams, no pictures; very boring. I didn't learn anything about sex, I was just further mystified.

The reason my parents had analytical books on their shelves is because I come from a very well psychoanalysed family – not to say that they benefited from the treatment, but they'd all undergone the treatment. It wasn't all that long ago really. I'm 26 and my mother had me when she was 21, you see, so I had very young parents and grandparents. So my Dad was actually analysed in the Sixties, it wasn't all that unusual. Both Mum and Dad were analysed, and both my father's parents were analysed, some by very eminent ex-Viennesy analysts.

The way the analytical history started in my family was that my grandfather had severe back problems and his brother, my great-uncle, had gone to Vienna to train during that great pilgrimage during the Thirties of those Anglo-Saxon psychiatrist physicians who wanted analytical training, so he studied with Freud and with Helene Deutsch, you see. I knew him only very tangentially; he died when I was still quite small. Anyway, he was the one who got things started, I think. He recommended to his younger brother, my grandfather, 'You might want to try analysis for your back problems' – and it cured it just like that.

So Mum and Dad were analysed, there was analytical blood floating around in the family. Actually, Dad was very resentful that he had to go into analysis because his father – my grandfather – had pushed him into it in a way. He thought that this was the great panacea for everybody – he assigned all his children to analysts, as it were – and for the first year my Dad didn't go, and he doesn't really talk about his analysis. I think he's a unique, remarkable person, my father – very warm, natural, extremely tender and loving, very unusual. My mother boasts about the fact that he was one of the only fathers of their set who would spend any time with his children. So he played with us quite a bit, and I think a lot of my nurturing qualities come directly from my father rather than my mother, though she has her nurturing tendencies too. She went into analysis because she had a post-partum depression after the birth of my younger sister. No, it's not biochemical – I'm a real hard-line Freudian about that sort of thing, actually. Absolutely, even for physical problems. I'm very interested in the literature that's coming out now on psychoanalysis and cancer, for instance. In fact, I hold the belief that Freud and Freudian therapy can do just about anything, including revolutionizing the world and bringing peace and so forth. That's on the cards for my life agenda!

So there was this analytical blood in the family. Now, neither my brother nor sister have any interest in psychoanalysis. There's something about the first-born, the reason being – this has been bandied about quite a lot – that children of depressed mothers recognize the pain in their parents and become therapists. I remember my mother turning to me during her times of emotional distress. You see, she was a ballet dancer and she had three children in four years, and that was too difficult for her because she couldn't dance during that period. So I remember being very sensitized towards my parents' problems.

I was a very shy boy indeed, extremely shy. I suppose you might call me withdrawn and schizoid, and that's something psychoanalysis has certainly helped me with. So I was very friendly at home and loving and nurturant and so forth, but very shy outside. I used never to eat in people's houses – I mean, if I went to a friend's house. For me, food was very much my mother's food. I started to read Freud at a very early age, I can't remember what, when, and so forth, but I was very interested in the whole thing. And I have one of those photographic memories, so within a year or two of reading this kind of thing I was quoting journal articles off the top of my head; very strange. Around 16, that kind of thing. I read everything I could put my hands on, even things I didn't understand – I forced my way through them. So there was some kind of inner yearning to learn more about mental health.

And, of course, being shy, I was quite introverted, and I became a very good listener and friends would turn to me and, you know, I wouldn't necessarily say anything to them, but I would just listen and they would bring all their problems to me, so I was a sort of miniature therapist before I began, you see. And people said 'You should become a therapist, because you're very easy to talk to.' So I guess that idea sort of stuck in my head and by the time I was 17 I said, 'Right, I'm going to become a psychoanalyst.' It just became a very rigid, entrenched conception, I'm going to become a psycho-analyst.

I started out thinking I should do medicine first, because everybody said, much more prestige, and all those silly things . . . And, in fact, I tried to do medicine and during my first chemistry course I nearly had a mental breakdown because I'm one of the least practical people you can imagine. I can't light the bunsen burner – no test-tube abilities whatsoever. My background is really from music (I had a training as a classical pianist) and from literature. I've abandoned my concert training – the directors of my music school said, 'You'll have to go to Switzerland', all that – and, of course, my classical style has gone to hell, but what I do is accompaniment, I play in restaurants and cocktail lounges, and that's fun. Also inside this body of a would-be psychoanalyst is a composer yearning to break free, so that might happen. One way I've tried to combine things is by doing music therapy in psychiatric hospitals and I find that great fun.

So I hated medicine, chucked it, and did psychology and French literature at Oxford instead. The psychology course was just disgusting; it told me exactly what psychology shouldn't be and the kinds of research the government shouldn't be wasting its money on. I'm very bitter about a lot of training programmes, about a lot of so-called professionals in the field who have no expertise in human relations whatsoever. Sadistic, some of the hospital psychiatrists – sadistic. I feel comfortable using that word. When I get my book out, I'll make a lot of enemies because I pull no punches and I make analogies between these people and Nazi commandants; there's no question about that, cruel, sadistic things are being done and nobody speaks out.

Well, anyway, there I was with this psychoanalytical interest and I went into therapy for the first time because I thought, well, it's a good training experience. I was 17. I was pretty high-functioning, you know, a very high flyer at school, an over-achiever. There were personal reasons for it as well – I had a very false-self type of character, no question about that, very, very unsure of my sense of self, very pompous probably in a lot of ways. I was kicked around a lot at school, dreadful at sports, a little swot. And what had really done me in was a very, very early engagement, being engaged to be married at a ridiculous age – 16 or 17 – it was just silly. I was madly, madly in love, a hugely passionate relationship. And the girl sort of dumped me – not sort of, she *did* dump me. So I was really shaken by that and I made this sort of mock suicide attempt in front of her; she knew it was just a plea for attention. I was very, very hurt, very devastated, because I'd really pledged my life and soul to her.

What happened was that a friend of mine, a social worker, said, 'You should go and see Dr X. He was my analyst; go and see him.'

So I said, 'Right'. And it went on for months. She said, 'Have you rung up Dr X yet?' and I said, 'No, I will do, I will do', and she said, 'Go on and do it.' And I didn't. But I wasn't feeling good at all, burying myself in my work, not having the confidence to enter into another relationship, crying myself to sleep a lot at nights, wondering what the hell I wanted to do with my life, all these kinds of things.

I was at her office one day, this social worker friend, and she said, 'Ah, good, I'm glad you're here. Dr X is on the phone', and she just thrust the phone into my hand and I said, 'Er, er, can I make an appointment to see you?' And he said, 'Fine'; so in retrospect I'm very glad someone gave me the push to do that. I might not have done it otherwise. I mean, I had this idea, this abstract idea – sooner or later I will, for professional reasons. But here I was confronted with being asked to see a therapist for personal reasons. And I soon got over the whole 'going into it for professional reasons' bit. And I'm not ready to start my training as an analyst yet, being 26, but I have analysis for personal reasons. Of course, it will have professional repercussions as well.

I liked this analyst; he was OK, he was a nice man. I stayed with him for three years. But now I wouldn't find him good at all. He was very threatened by me and I didn't recognize then that that's what it was. I went in with sort of blind faith – you know, he's the shrink, he knows what he's doing. But I knew so much about Freud, you see. Being threatening is a lifelong problem I've had to cope with – you know, phallic rivalry, 'Are you more potent than me?' At the first session he had a clipboard in his hand, taking notes, and I thought, it's very efficient of him, but in retrospect I wouldn't go to an analyst who took notes. I have this photographic memory myself, you see, and if I'm listening carefully I'll remember what a person tells me without that. And he challenged me from the very first bit. I said, 'I'm depressed', and he said, 'Prove it. How do you know you're depressed?' And I told him why and he said, 'Are you sure that's depression?' I mean, he was trying to get into my internal world, but he was being combative with me from the very start and in retrospect I think he should have known better.

So then he said, 'What job are you doing?' and I said, 'I'm working as a pianist for the moment, from 4 p.m. to 1 a.m.' And he said, 'Well, you could be depressed, having a job like that.' So here he was, first doubting that I was depressed, then telling me that I was a depressive because I was working at a night job rather than a day job, trying to avoid sunlight and reality . . . There was some truth in it, you know, it's got to be quite depressing being awake all night long in a sort of sozzly bar. So then he said to me, 'Well, you're a psychology student', and I said, 'Yes, I want to be an analyst.' And he said, 'Do you know anything about Freud?' and I said, 'Yes, I've read all his writings' – and I might have said it in an arrogant way, because it piqued him. And he said, 'Oh, yes, you've read all of Freud's writings. How many volumes in his works then?' And I thought, oh God, what a stupid question, and I said, 'Do you want it in the German or the English?' I was quoting from the *Gesammeltewerken* in the standard edition. He said, 'In English, then.' And I said, 'Well, it's twenty-three volumes, twenty-four if you count the index.'

So you know there was rivalry going on from the start, because he couldn't cope with the fact that I was young and knew so much. And even analysts today find me very funny, a lot of them. Some of them say, 'Ah, isn't it nice that this young man has taken such an interest in our field'; others are very threatened that I've made it my business to learn about their profession, you see. I gave a paper recently at a conference and I was introduced as the psychological whiz-kid – and, you know, I suppose I am, having a TV show in the States and so forth – but that's not the way to introduce somebody because I could see daggers were ready to be thrown. And one woman who's only just qualified and done a book on Freud herself came up to me afterwards and said, 'Why are you a whiz-kid and what have you done to deserve that title?' People don't know how to place me because I'm involved too early, I've not gone through the orthodox mill. Ideally, I should be a milquetoasty consultant psychiatrist who then applies for training at the age of 35, goes through an infantilizing training analysis – but anyway, that's by the by.

That first analyst helped me a lot, though, I should say that, I

mean, he did contain me. He did hold me. He did validate my
sense of self-esteem. I was able to talk a lot about my sexual
identity conflicts, you know, am I man enough to be a man or am
I just a little wimpy kid? So we went through a lot of my early
childhood traumas on the sports field and so forth; he was very
good about that sort of thing. We started once a week, very
quickly went to twice a week and then a few months after that
were doing three and then four times a week. I liked it. I mean, he
had a nice office, though in retrospect I'd say there was too much
sunlight – I like dark, little womb-like offices – a bit too daylight,
a little bit too daylight. He'd answer my questions, which I appreciated. I asked him questions about his training, 'How come I've
never heard of you? You're not famous.' I felt a bit more held and
contained and so forth, and it helped me get over the real abandonment depression caused by my girlfriend's abandonment of
me. He gave me more confidence and I think I became less
arrogant as a result – less boastful, much more aware of how I
affected other people. But I think it wasn't a successful analysis –
well, it's difficult to say. It served its purpose at the time. From
an analyst of his generation, it was one of the good analyses.

I did feel frightened and threatened, though, at certain points.
Because I remember having the fantasy that . . . coming to his
house – it was down a hill in a sort of wooded area of town – I
thought, this is a witch's house, witches live inside it; so there
must have been some negative feeling, whereby I was frightened
by him. And on another occasion he escorted me into the waiting-
room and he had a rickety coat-rack and he said, 'Yes, it's a bit
wobbly, isn't it? I bought it and thought it would be sturdy, but
now it looks a bit like a guillotine.' And the next day, walking to
the session I started humming a song and eventually I realized it
was from *The Mikado*, you know, the execution song –

> To sit in solemn silence in a dull, dark dock
> Awaiting the sensation of a short, sharp shock
> From a cheap and chippy chopper on a big black block –

you know that one, it's a song about those men who are going to
have their heads cut off. So I thought, oh my God, I'm singing

this and, you know, the fact that he had mentioned the guillotine quite frightened me and I wondered how safe I really felt with him. He was very good on one occasion, because I had a very frightening hallucination at one point – you know, I was fully aware it was a hallucination, but it was quite scary actually – I thought that . . . It's quite morbid and frightening to talk about, if you won't mind . . . I'll tell you what it was. I had this fear that snakes were coming out of my eye-sockets – very, very disturbing, you see – and I felt very ashamed and embarrassed by that, what the implications might be with the obvious symbolic connotations of snakes. I can't remember precisely what brought it on, but I know he did comfort me a great deal about it when I talked to him and it served to bring things into the open.

If nothing else, it primed me for my second analysis, because it takes practice opening up and talking about your private life, doesn't it, and now I feel so free to talk about it. I can't wait to get into the real nitty-gritty with my third analysis and talk about early infantile feelings of shame and embarrassment and mistrust and that kind of thing – it was a good preparation. It wasn't really about infantile material. Yes, we lay on a couch – sorry, I said *we* were on a couch! He analysed dreams in great detail and taught me how to analyse my own dreams really. I'm a multiple dreamer, you see – like multiple orgasms – I remember several in a night. Now that I'm sort of temporarily de-analysed for a bit I'm not dreaming so frequently, but there was a time when I was re-membering three dreams every night. He taught me that one is connected to the other, the second dream takes up where the first left off, and the third dream where the second one . . . So I learned to read dreams as narrative, you see, from him. I re-member in the first consultation I was very hurt and offended because I brought him a dream and he said, 'Well, I can't listen to it right now because I don't know you well enough – I don't know your language, I don't know what to make of it.' So I felt I was bringing him a gift and, yes, I felt very rejected.

So, in retrospect, were I having an initial consultation with him nowadays, I wouldn't go to him. Because (a) he was taking notes, (b) he challenged my internal world when I said, 'I'm depressed', and (c) he didn't listen to my dream. But, again, I didn't know. I didn't know that one could be a consumer, you see. And I think that most people going to therapy for the first time, even the second time, don't know they have the choice in choosing a therapist. One thing we've been trying to do on this television programme I do in New York is to educate people about the consuming process in therapy.

So he and I agreed to sort of part ways, you know, when I finished my university course. We had a very nice, amicable parting. And curiously enough, his son was graduating at the same time, though I hadn't known it, and I thought, so I'm not his favourite teenage boy, and I wondered, what does his son do and all that kind of thing. Yes, I'd have recommended psychoanalysis to anyone at the time, though I was a bit more cautious then in terms of who I told – now I positively boast about the fact; some people think I'm potty, you know. What I actually got out of the first analysis I don't know, I don't know; certainly I became more empathic, more tolerant of people, more confident as well – confident in a secure internal way, less narcissistically confident where you need to boast and so forth.

I did still have pretty severe bouts of depression, I got very sad at times. I lost my mother when I was $4\frac{1}{2}$ – I mean, she didn't die, but she went into hospital after my sister's birth, you see, from this post-partum depression. That was a pretty severe six months' abandonment, when I went to live with my grandmother; that's the chief issue in my life. And we were not told the truth, we were not told where Mummy was, they said she'd gone on holiday – what does a child make of that? Why is she going on holiday – did I send her away? Why didn't she take me?

Now analyst number two was a bitch in the extreme – well, helpful in a lot of ways, but I'd say on the whole hurtful. I'd changed towns, you see, and I was in my first big hospital job as a psychologist – no, not an analyst or psychiatrist, just working alongside in psychological assessment and so forth. The consultant psychiatrist to whom I was attached said, 'I recommend you to start on some more analysis. It's not required but it would be a good thing', and he recommended me to number two. She was really not nice at all – very sad woman really – divorced, with no prospects of getting another man in her life; I mean, very hard, very bitter, extremely alibidinal, a very, very cold, hard woman.

The funny thing is that she and I had been to a workshop together before I even knew who she was; it was a psychodrama workshop for professionals. Anyway, Doctor Two and I were supposed to be partners in this exercise, it was a touching exercise. The leader said, 'Now close your eyes and put your hands up like this and feel the contours of your partner's body'; so I thought, oh well, I'm game, all right. So she and I were lined up together. I started feeling down her body but her hands were rivetedly fixed to my shoulders and shaking, so I didn't want to overstep my bounds with her – she was obviously nervous – so I shimmied my hands back up her arms to her shoulders and sort of rested them there and I gave her a little squeeze to say, 'It's all right, you don't have to feel up my body if you don't want to.' She got so frightened she left – it was a three-day workshop and she left straight away, this was on the first night. I thought, strange woman.

So when I went round to her the first time, I rang the bell and who should answer the door but Doctor Two, the woman from the psychodrama. Well, I thought, I've seen you before, who are you? And then it instantly dawned on me she was the really fucked-up woman from the psychodrama workshop, who had real problems with her own body and couldn't even touch somebody else's. And she didn't recognize me. And do you know something –I mean I'm embarrassed to say this – but I never mentioned it. I stuck with her for three years and I never mentioned it. I thought, oh no, too late to turn back now.

One day I'd like to write a book called *How to Choose an Analyst* or something like that and describe in detail my two first analyses and the initial consultations, and what I now know was wrong with them, to help educate people to be better consumers during their first consultation. During the first consultation with her I said, 'I'm depressed', because I'd just ended yet another love affair and I was having problems with my senior at work. She said, 'Do you want me to give you some drugs?' I thought, goodness, you're supposed to be an analyst . . . I was trying to like her, though, because my boss had recommended her.

She was very unethical, because she wouldn't set a fee. I said, 'Well, how much am I going to pay you?' She said, 'You're young, you don't make much money, don't worry about it, we'll talk about that another time.' I thought, OK, fine, and no mention of the fee came up for about six months. So this gave rise to fantasies about how she's supporting herself, what does she do for a living, maybe she likes me so much she's not going to charge me . . . Then she slaps through a bill for £900! It came out of the blue and I thought, oh my God. When I've told this to other analysts they've said, 'I don't know any analyst who works that way.' It was just sadistic of her to give such mixed messages. And then the other thing was, she did a lot of consultation in other places and was flying about all the time. Often. And I thought, OK, these are just Doctor Two's weeks abroad, and I got used to it. But it's unconscionable. Here I was suffering from abandonment depression from my childhood and she was playing into my own particular problem by abandoning me on a regular basis.

At that time I hadn't started to write papers – I wanted to, I had sort of 5000 files of notes of this article, that article, you know the syndrome. I mean, now I'm starting to publish a few things, but then I was really bothered. I had a writing block – I'd always been a very skilled writer and nothing was coming out, absolutely nothing. She was quite good on that, and I was able to talk much more freely about my sex life with her, which was good. And she did help me to get in touch with the full nature of my abandonment depression. Many times I felt very good coming away from her, but many times infuriated, very much infuriated.

Her consulting room was dreadful, lights and birds chirping and so forth. We had no fixed time either, we kept doing it on a week-to-week basis – you know, come at eleven on Tuesday, twelve on Wednesday, one on Thursday. Today I'd never put up with that kind of routine, never. 'You're such a fucked-up woman yourself', was what I felt like saying, but I never did; 'How can you be helping me? I'm much more mentally healthy than you are.' But it was too late to back out, I felt trapped in a way, really.

She did say some good things. Once I said – I'm embarrassed to say this to you – I said, 'On the way coming here I was cycling along and I had a dream, a little fleeting fantasy that my eyeball had popped out into the road and got squashed under the tyres of a lorry' – yukky, yukky, stuff – and it was very nice what she said; she said, 'Are you frightened that if you come to me in different pieces, I won't take you in?' And I really liked that.

Once I saw her in one of those big Oxford Street shops – Selfridges, I was in the basement at Selfridges having tea with my parents and Doctor Two came round the corner – she was looking through some bathroom things and I quickly hid, I didn't want to see her. And then, to end it, she abandoned me, she only gave me three months' notice, she went to take a job elsewhere. Yes, it was upsetting, though in a way I was pleased to get it over with. I played a little cat and mouse game with her because I couldn't pay my final bill, which was quite substantial. I felt like saying, 'Right, she's been unethical throughout the treatment, I don't owe her any money', but my father said – you know, my father tries to smooth things over – he said, 'Pay her, keep her quiet' and so forth, and that's that. I just felt so bad surrendering so much money to her – she was charging me a hell of a lot, more at that time than Doctor Three is going to charge me now.

Anyway, that's all sewn up and done for. There were one or two things where she was remarkably helpful and I'm grateful for that – just one or two little things that she said – but you don't pay all that money and give up all those years of your life for one or two little pearls of wisdom. But I'm glad I had Doctor Two – it taught me a lesson. You know, you have to develop standards, you have to know what you don't like before you can find out what you do like. I'm not all that embittered by it because I feel that the knowledge I've learned from two lukewarm analyses is that I'll be able to put this into public education, you see, and ease the pain of my own bad experiences by helping others to learn from it; and that's very satisfying, actually. I'm not bitter, because I try to live my life according to the credo set forth by an American analyst who wrote, 'The goal of a good life is to turn your traumas into triumphs.' It's tough, it can't always be done, but I try whenever possible to operate my life on that basis.

After that, a friend began to pressurize me into having another analysis, she's very intuitive. But I'm away a lot, I'm commuting to the States, so I've met Doctor Three but the way I've left things is that we'll start sessions when I'm in London for good, for ever. And it could count towards training to be a psychoanalyst myself. I met him through this friend and I knew of him because I'd been to his lectures on several occasions, and I'd decided that he and one other were the two analysts I'd finally targeted. There was a lot of internal shopping around, getting to know lots of the British analysts over a several-year period, and I went through the list and settled on these two and finally on Doctor Three. They were the only two people I'd even consider. I think Doctor Three was quite intrigued by me, the whole thing you know, the work I'd done and the TV programme. I mean, let's not fool ourselves that analysts don't have motives for taking certain analysands. I think he'll get an internal sense of pride that he's treating someone who could make a contribution to British mental health.

I think he's the best analyst I've ever found – I'm almost hesitant to refer other people to him, I want him all to myself in a way. What I want from him is an anchor. I can get on without it, I get on very fine without it, but I want it. He's a more skilled analyst than the other two and I'm a more skilled analysand than I was – we can go to the deeper stuff quicker. The first two helped me to the third; for both good and bad reasons they catapulted me to number three.

I've just had the preliminary consultation with Doctor Three. It was wonderful; I enjoyed it, I really did. He was quiet, he listened very carefully – I don't know whether he'd heard of me, I don't think so, and that I liked. I told him about the horror stories of my first two analysts. He politely sniped off analyst number two – they'd trained together. He said, 'I'm shocked that she's done that kind of thing. No analyst I know would handle the bill in such a way.' He said, 'You'll get a regular bill on the first of the month and regular sessions – I'll be here for you.' He said, 'You're a very tenacious man.' He said, 'Anybody else would not have gone back for a third analysis.' But my desire has not yet been satisfied from psychoanalysis, so I'm looking forward to him. I said to him, 'Look, if you don't like me now, let me know straight away because there's no point in us wasting our time if you don't think we're going to be a good match.' And he said, 'I don't see anything in your presentation that suggests that you can't be analysed.'

He answered all my queries to perfect satisfaction. I said, 'Will you promise me that you'll never write about my case?' I said, 'I would like a word of honour from you that you won't write about me' – because he's well known in the field and I'll become increasingly so myself, and eventually everybody's going to know that he's my analyst anyway, so they'll be looking out for details and so forth. So he said, 'That's fine' – he didn't get freaked out by that completely. Because patients can write about their analysts, but not analysts about their patients. And the other thing I said was, 'You must promise not to abandon me', and he said, 'I promise.' And then the other thing was, 'If you feel threatened or rivalrous with me – you know, the male potency kind of thing – that we'll be able to talk it out as gentlemen rather than you acting it out in sadistic ways and so forth.' It was a very gentlemanly consultation. I felt pleased paying him £30 – I'd just had two cheques bounced, but it was all right – yes, I really felt pleased to pay him. I walked out on a cloud. Wonderful.

Jill

On the sly, my fantasies enlarged his house into a
great manor or castle. I endowed his wife with truly
divine qualities, and the metal of his automobile, when
I happened to see it, became an object for furtive
caresses. It was not just metal, it was meta-metal.

Tilmann Moser: *Years of Apprenticeship on the Couch*

We go through her shared south London flat to sit in the
garden, where lily-of-the-valley and bluebells have been
persuaded to grow riotously. Jill is neat in immaculate jeans and
shirt. She talks diffidently, as though what she says is hurting.

Yes, I'm in therapy now and I have been for about two and a
half years – at first once a week and then twice a week. I'm
33. My therapist actually wanted me to see her four times a week,
but on a social worker's salary that's impossible. She felt things
would have moved quite quickly then, because if I lie down in the
session I can quite easily slip into childish thoughts and dreams
and things. She works a lot by dreams.

What used to happen was terrible depressions, so awful that I
could hardly get around, and I took an overdose. I'd been in the
country staying with friends. I think it was seeing my godchild
have all the things I'd never had myself in childhood. Probably it
wasn't a serious attempt, but it did make me realize something
must be done. My doctor had kept me going on tablets for a long
time. Then he died – well, he committed suicide. He was only 35.
It was awful, because I used to go to the surgery all the time and
he was the one person I could talk to. I was in an awful relationship
at the time, a mess, and I talked about that and my depression. I
still feel so bad today that I didn't realize what he was going

155

through himself, I had no idea. After his death I was assigned another doctor in the same practice – because I was going there, you know, and bursting into tears – and he suggested I have some therapy.

I was doing some voluntary work at the time, so before I went into my current therapy I started to have sessions with a woman from that office. I don't think it was therapy at all really, just sort of chatting; she wasn't really trained, she'd done a few odd courses. It was terribly irregular. She lived in Essex and sometimes she'd come up to London and sometimes she wouldn't. And then every time I went she'd be sitting in a different place and the room was always in chaos . . . nothing was set. But perhaps it supported me a bit; I was doing a training course, I managed to keep going. Then she decided to stay out in Essex permanently, after I'd been seeing her for about eighteen months. She said, 'You can come and see me in Essex', but it was impossible. It was when I went into my present therapy that I realized how much she had pushed me around and let me down. I suppose it wasn't her fault. I was pretty crazy still at that time, very depressed, although I was holding a job.

I'd been back to the doctor – the new one, of course – and by now they had a therapist attached to the practice. So I went to see her and that's how it started. I've recently joined a therapy group too – which I hate! – and now that I'm doing that I can have my session with her on the National Health.

In the beginning it was . . . very painful. It was very difficult for me to actually engage with her. It took me six months before I'd lie down on the couch. It was a great resistance, a great mistrust, which I do have anyway – it's part of my problem – but after my experience with that first woman, I had a specially deep distrust. Suddenly saying – well, to me it seemed sudden – that she wasn't coming up to London any more, she was going to stay in Essex. And my mother died when I was 25, so it really is about that, about women letting you down. When I went to Marie, I had that same feeling, that she was going to let me down. Mistrust, fear, that's the basis of it all, isn't it?

Marie works from home. She has a house and she uses the flat at the bottom of the house for her practice, so the room that I go to has been the same since I've been coming, nothing has changed. That is consistent, it's helped tremendously. Terribly important, because so many people who go into therapy have the experience that I had first, you know, that the sessions aren't reliable. Awful things can happen.

I don't think you realize how strong the power of therapy is until you're in it. One can't sometimes grasp . . . it's very difficult to explain what it is, other than that at some level it's a dependency. And now, you see, my therapist has had a baby, I haven't seen her for three weeks, and there are all those feelings again about being rejected and farmed out to the group therapy. Sent away. It's the fear of abandonment, all those old feelings have come up. I *know* she has to be with her baby, but the thing about therapy is that on an intellectual level you can understand, but it's the feeling level that you can't rationalize. I think that's what therapy's about somehow. She *is* going to see me . . . I mean, we came to the agreement that I'd see her until I'd sort of settled into the group and could deal with leaving her and moving on. But I have great resistance to the group at the moment.

Things from the past kept coming up in the therapy, things that I'd blocked off for years. My father died when I was 8 and I was terribly close to him. He suffered from depressions and would hardly talk for months. And his relationship with my mother was very strange. They came from totally different backgrounds. She came from a rather wealthy family, she had nannies and maids, and my father was a sort of working-class accountant from Aberdeen. Very, very different. And they had me quite late -- my mother was 40, it was partly because my father desperately wanted to have a child. And so . . . I mean, after I was born, he really put all his affections into me. So I think I must have picked up at a very early age the rift in their marriage, I mean non-verbally.

And I sort of relived all that in therapy, once I'd really got into being able to lie down and associate freely. All those feelings came out; and his death. And I went to boarding-school -- the year he died my mother sent me off to boarding-school. So I worked through all those things, being sent away, all that. My mother I never really knew, in a way. I was at boarding-school and she was working; she started a shop quite soon after my father died. She'd never worked in her life, but she opened a dress agency. I was at boarding-school till college, so I never lived much at home, never had a feel of home life at all. But I think I took over the role of looking after her, actually. My father used to do all the cooking and things like that and housework, he really used to mother her, and then when he died, I took that over. And yet I don't think I was terribly close to her. I think I cut off when my father died.

You know, I went to see an astrologer once, she's quite well known, and she said, 'Something died in you at the age of 8.' It was years ago and I knew nothing about therapy and she said, 'You must work through the death of your father.' And I said, 'How should I do that?' and she said, 'You should go into therapy or something.' I recorded her on a tape actually – when I played it back it sounded unbelievable, how much she'd picked up. If I'd listened to her and gone into therapy straight away, I think my life would have been very different. But I didn't; I left it for years.

Marie feels like a sort of home and mother that I never had. I've been desperately dependent on her. Awful agonies when she went away on holiday. I mean, even if something was moved in her room, half an inch . . . And about a year before I actually went into the therapy group she thought I was progressing quite quickly and she mentioned something about maybe a group would be good for me, and that sent me into actually almost suicidal despair. I slipped right back. And that was just one little comment. Awful to be a therapist and have all that responsibility – because I do think feelings of suicide come up much more strongly when you're in therapy. This dependency is awful; I wish I knew how one solved it.

I don't know whether I've *really* trusted her yet, I can't say whether I've worked through that. I do trust her more. It's certainly got better – somewhere there's trust around. But when she's gone away on holiday I've got angry with her, refused to turn up . . . I've taken her presents – I went through a phase of taking her flowers from my garden. She would take them without making any interpretation about what it meant until much later. She doesn't say a lot, but she feels quite *real*. She'll do things like, when I went on holiday once, she lent me a book of hers to take on holiday – I think it was sort of to keep her presence with me.

But I don't know anything about her at all – her private life, nothing. I do feel very curious, yes, and perhaps she would tell me if I asked, but somehow I don't want to intrude. Once she took me upstairs to look out at her garden – often we talk about the garden because it seems that there's something there ... something we have in common. And she took me up to see her garden, which meant going up the stairs actually into her house – that felt very strange.

I saw her once where I go swimming – she was actually swimming. And the person that I swim with knows quite a lot about Marie – I mean the sort of fantasies that I have about her – and she was surprised to see that she looked just ordinary! And of course that shattered all my fantasies about this woman being something superhuman. It threw me completely, because at some level I saw her actually just in a swimming costume and ordinary.

I think it's right that they don't tell you about themselves. And I've noticed that as I've sort of moved on in the therapy, we talk more about ordinary things. For instance, I went to Charleston a couple of months ago – yes, the Bells' house – and I was telling Marie she must go. And I photocopied the map of how to get there and then she told me a week or two later that she'd gone. So now we're talking a little bit more, because that would never have happened a year ago.

It'll be interesting to see ... to see whether she shows me the baby or not. I've never ... I mean, yes, I have wanted to know about it, but I've never asked her anything. I know she has other children.

She's telling me a little bit more now, it comes out, without my asking. For instance, because I'm a social worker she rang me up because she wanted help with somebody that was referred to her – she didn't want to get involved because she lived in the same block of flats with this person, so could I help out. I know the relationship with her is good. And yet . . . I still don't think I trust her completely. And I still question about the dependency – you know, is this actually helping now or is it just that I can't leave her?

They do have a lot of power when one's dependent. That first woman I told you about, for instance, she was charging me more than Marie does now and there were fares – if I went out to Essex that meant I would have to pay my train fare on top of that. She'd often say, 'I'm not coming up to London, can you pop down?' I really felt very angry actually and I didn't deal with that anger for a long time.

Sometimes I think depressions are just something chemical, because I can be feeling fine one day and then suicidal the next day. I do still get them, but sometimes – not all the time – I can actually understand where it's coming from and that does help. I mean, they're certainly not the black depressions that I used to get. When I was in the States recently I had one, but that could have been because I was away from her.

Why do I feel a bit better? It's the sixty-four dollar question, isn't it? I wish I could get a definition of it – it's so hard to explain to people. I think for me it was working through some things . . . as an 8-year-old, being sent away to a strange school the same year my father died, it really seemed that the end of the world had come. And I got very dependent on my housemistress – I wouldn't say she sexually assaulted me, but there was a very close relationship there and that affected me an awful lot. And Marie comes down the stairs – it sounds so silly – but she comes down the stairs, into the room where I see her . . . I sort of relived lots of experiences of this housemistress coming downstairs. I think that moved things a lot. Because I actually . . . I relived all the pain of being sent away, and once I managed to talk about that, I think that was some relief. And I think talking about my father . . .

It's not so much, I think, just the support; it's the fact that you can tell your therapist something without the fantasy that they're going to actually disintegrate with the pain. And I've always, for years, sort of kept things in, for fear of really hurting somebody.

And that was something: she survived. I used to test her out an awful lot, but she survived that. Things like – I would tell her something very painful and then I wouldn't turn up the next week, and then when I came back – she was there. But it's very hard to know, isn't it? I'd like to have been out of therapy for a few years, or talk to someone who has been, and see if those depressions come back. And to see how one leaves therapy. It seems that my problem most of my life has been people leaving me.

I suppose I am angry that she's had the baby, but I find it hard to be actually angry with her, which is a lot of my problem anyway. I suppose it's true that depression can be really a sort of suppressed anger – yes, loads of times I've felt angry with her and then got very depressed instead. I've talked about that but not really had it out. Often I go out and drive past her house, just to see if her car's there – ugh! I've gone miles out of my way sometimes, late at night, just to look at her car. Then another thing; I went through a period of always moving her chair back – her chair is always the same and I always used to move it back, as if I didn't want her to come too near me.

I sit up now rather than lying on the couch. I wish I could lie down again – I feel she's sort of getting me ready to leave, that and getting me into the therapy group. I think I'm doing these things to please her, which is just what I did with my mother. I have told her that. A lot of my sessions are silent anyway – well, not the whole session, but half an hour perhaps. Sometimes it's an angry silence. But sometimes it could be a very trusting . . . you know, like a child, that kind of safe silence. She knows me so well, it's frightening sometimes. Often, if she doesn't say anything, I feel she's rejecting me and yet if she does say something, I feel she's being intrusive – one wants them to get it *just* right! She's succeeding much more in doing that now.

It's quite difficult if you're in a relationship in ordinary life, it's very hard to explain to the person you're with about therapy, sometimes it's quite a toll on them. But also I find, the relationship I'm in at the moment, I tend to analyse what's happening all the time and then take it back to Marie – I don't know whether that's healthy really. Relationships are still very difficult for me, but I think therapy's helping there, slowly. And one thing it has made me realize is that I chose to go into social work because I had problems myself – to deal with other people's problems instead of looking at my own. I'm working at the moment with a family where the child's very disturbed and she goes to a therapist, and I've seen how helpful that's been to the child – if one goes very early in life I'm sure it helps. By the time *we* get there! So much to undo, so much you want to keep locked up.

I'd never want to become a therapist myself – I don't think I could sit with that level of stress. And knowing how dependent people become . . . I'd want to reach out too much. It's hard enough sometimes as a social worker to stay objective and not get involved – I don't know how therapists can do it over several years. They still stop at twenty past nine, even if you're streaming with tears – I couldn't do that. And the power that's invested in them! They can't fail you, can they?

Andrew

And I knew that all you wanted was the luxury
Of an intimate disclosure to a stranger.
Let me, therefore, remain the stranger.
But let me tell you, that to approach the stranger
Is to invite the unexpected, release a new force,
Or let the genie out of the bottle.
It is to start a train of events
Beyond your control.

T.S. Eliot: *The Cocktail Party*

Andrew turns off the rock music, leads me past precarious stacks of paperbacks to a neat sitting-room where we share a table with *The Budget Good Food Guide* and a plastic pack of beer cans. Genial phone conversations intervene repeatedly. We adjourn to a room containing a word-processor and socks in many stages of dampness and he talks on carefully, conscientiously.

———————

At the moment I'm a journalist, a very hard-working one, but I've been a teacher, a writer, various things. I'd done a little bit of therapy when I was a student. I'd been in a bit of an anxiety state and the college doctor had counselled me when I was about 21 during a rocky period I was going through. I think it was helpful, yes, although it didn't disabuse me of my idea that therapy was something to be avoided. I thought it was self-indulgence. I mean, I had a theoretical objection to it, which, retrospectively, I think fairly valid – that because I was a socialist I thought that solutions to things happened through political and social changes, and doing therapy seemed to me to be very individualistic.

That was a crude view, which I wouldn't argue for now in the same way at all, and I also... well, I also was frightened of therapy. I suppose it's probably fair to say that the reason I was frightened of it was that I was frightened of my own psyche, of what might be revealed if I went into therapy – things I couldn't handle. Going right back to adolescence, I was uneasy about who I was and so forth. I wanted to be normal, the same as everybody else, and even to admit I had complicated feelings, you see, would be to show I wasn't normal. But I also think there was a healthy aspect to my doubt, which is that ... well, the process of doing therapy can mean a great deal of self-preoccupation and intro-spection and egocentricity, and I think there always has to be a question-mark. I mean, my position is that I benefited from therapy, but I want to explain why I had a resistance to it and I think that in some respects the resistance was to do with my refusal to deal with my problems, but that also there were other things about it than can be defended.

How I got into therapy? Well, I have to go back. I married in 1966, we had two children and round about the early seven-ties we reached a point in our relationship when, I think, we were both very frustrated within it for different reasons or per-haps even the same reasons. And that happened to coincide with an atmosphere or mood or attitude which was prevalent in the circles we moved in at that time – left-wing, feminist and among the men sympathetic to feminism – partly an attitude that not only was the nuclear family something to be looked at very, very critically, but that even to be in a couple was a con-servative, stale thing.

So at a time when there were strains, considerable strains in our relationship anyway, there was an ideology around that encouraged us to think we needn't be monogamous, that it was almost sort of reactionary to be monogamous, that one ought to break these ties and experience one's individuality to the full, have lots of re-lationships with lots of different people. So we embarked almost consciously on a programme of destructing our marriage, our relationship. What that meant in practice was that Serena took a lover and I connived at it and said, 'Yes, this is right and proper', and so forth, while actually being deeply anguished about it. And we became what I suppose you'd call an open marriage and actually pursued this for several years of very, very intensely difficult relationship experiences during most of which myself, my wife and her lover lived together.

I did have relationships myself, yes, but none of them really were of sufficient importance to me in the end to change that basic configuration of us being a threesome. And it was, I mean, it was a nightmare the entire time, actually. But all of that time I kind of felt that what I was doing was somehow politically right and so forth and that I was learning a lot through it; which was true in a way. It was around the late seventies that I had a relationship with Megan, and she'd been doing therapy for quite some time – as a matter of fact several women I knew were doing therapy at the same north London centre – and Megan said, 'You could do it, you really ought to.'

I finally realized that, yes, I should. That this whole situation had been going on for a very long time, that I'd never been happy about it, never been in control of it, never been really self-directing in it – I was reacting to things rather than initiating for most of that time – and it was ghastly and everyone was unhappy the entire time really. It was crazy, you know. And Meg said, 'Do some therapy. Find out what the hell's going on – you know, why the hell you're doing it', and so forth. So I did. Funnily enough, the very first thing therapy did for me was to stop the relationship with Meg, I'm afraid; I felt it was an unhealthy one for me. It was ironic from her point of view since it was she who'd pointed me in the direction of therapy. Horrible really, but the right decision for me, I'm sure.

Incidentally, I had done something called co-counselling before this therapy; that's when people in a group pair up and take it in turns to be therapist to the other. The view we had at that time about co-counselling, you see, was that it was democratic – therapy was considered to be authoritarian. The therapist has the expertise and you're there as a sort of object – he's going to sort you out, tell you what's right and what isn't and so forth. That view was very strongly held by a lot of people and was again, perhaps, part of my resistance to therapy.

Co-counselling was good, it was a release, it helped me think about how I am as a person, how I relate to people, and it made me listen to other people and their anguishes and worries and so forth. However, I must say that in the end I did pack it in for various reasons – I think I realized it wasn't going to be enough. And it was immediately clear from the first session with Jack that he wasn't going to be simply a shoulder to cry on, and in the end that's what co-counselling is actually.

My therapist, Jack, was at that stage the boyfriend of Meg's therapist and my wife's – so it was very incestuous and if therapists report back on their patients, which I'm entirely sure they do, they must have had some very good conversations about us all! I was frightened, I think, at the first session, because I knew this kind of therapy was going to be different – more rigorous and more serious, you know. I didn't lie on a couch, oh no. Sitting face to face. He said that it would be painful, which it frequently was . . . I'm not sure whether I liked him, really! I think it's very amusing about therapists that you never know them, you don't know who they are. But I frequently enjoyed it, by the way. What I enjoyed most was that he was witty – I felt sort of connected to him on the level of humour. I think I felt that I had someone special, someone for myself. I'd kept a diary for many, many years, and still do, where I sort of poured out my miseries, and it was very nice to have an actual person rather than a diary that I could do that with.

After I'd been in therapy only a few months I finally sort of insisted that we split up at home as a threesome. One of the major things that had kept this bizarre situation going all this time was that I didn't want to stop living with the children; in fact, I'd only been doing part-time work, so that we could split the week between us in terms of looking after the kids. When I look back I feel that I was sort of paralysed by problems and questions of identity and so forth, and rather gave up on work, on being active in the world. I now think that was a colossal mistake. It would have been far better for both of us probably if we'd got a child-minder. I lost quite a number of years of work – because these issues seemed more important to sort out, I suppose. The decision about losing the children was an excruciating one that basically floored me for about five years of my life. And I wish I'd done therapy a lot earlier and got back into being fully part of the world much earlier than I did.

So Serena and Bob and the children went off to live in the country, which they still do – except that, interestingly enough, she's split up with Bob. So my therapist had to help me to sever the connection with Serena and, to a degree, with my children. I then had to decide who I was if I wasn't a married person living with children. To some extent what I wanted a therapist for was to deal with sex and my relationships with women, and for the following two years I steered through a number of sexual relationships with the help of Jack. Most of the therapy was about sex, actually.

Inevitably it was also about – well, it went back to my formative relationships with my parents, and the key issue for me always had been the fact that my father was killed in the Second World War when I was round about 2½. So I'd grown up with a very unhappy mother who was desperately sort of traumatized by the memory of a wonderful husband. I went into the consequences of that, in terms of my relationship with her, what she demanded of me, the sense of responsibility I felt for having to replace my father, feelings of responsibility and of anger as well – working out all those issues and seeing how they were playing themselves out in my relationships with women. Great guilt in not living up to what they wanted, hence putting up with the situation of my wife being with someone else, for example. And I wanted very sincerely to have relationships with women that were equal – you know, I've taken feminism on board very seriously.

There really was a very big element of getting things off my chest, there's absolutely no question about that. There are all sorts of sexual fantasies and so forth that, you know, I felt ashamed or worried about, and being able to talk to Jack about those was wonderful – just being accepted, Jack was wonderful about that. And I hadn't had a father to be that kind of person in my life. I used to cry with him; that was . . . that was good, really. I mean I'd done a bit of that already – it had been part of our world that men were supposed to cry. Of course our whole ethos at that time, I think now that it was naïve. We'd had ideological a prioris of one kind or another about how one should or should not feel and behave, you know, which weren't really rooted in an understanding of how people are.

He told me very little about himself – he was much more the observer and the watcher and the listener than the participant. But his sense of humour wasn't too unlike my own, which was nice. I think I did feel understood. Whether he did or didn't understand, he was good at not appearing surprised by the things I said. Not that anything I'd thought or done – speaking in a rational mode – was very terrible, but . . . you know, I've carried an immense amount of guilt around with me and sometimes still do; but things which perhaps weren't so terrible but which I'd attached guilt to, I'd tell him about and he wasn't shocked, which was good.

He even succeeded in making me feel that the two of us together were engaged in a sort of inquiry into sexuality in general – turning something that was ill understood and in many ways an area of anxiety into something that became almost a sort of quest, a voyage of discovery. That was very, very positive indeed, actually. And he did unusual things for a therapist – well, I assume they were – like lending me books, so that I could look at myself as a case, which was very useful at that time for me. And we would take it back to childhood configurations, how women could be threatening, and my feeling responsible for making my mother happy always, that was one of the things that came out straight away.

It was, yes, almost entirely heterosexuality, I'd say. I feel sure that – as with anybody else – there must be somewhere or other some homosexual element in me, but I haven't cued in on it really. During that period in the early Seventies when couples and all the rest of it were very much in question in my particular friendship network, one of the options that was almost obligatory was to be bisexual. And I tried it, you know, and I didn't get anywhere with it, it didn't sort of do anything for me. So the content of my therapy really was about my relationship to women. Though I've often wondered what difference there would have been if I'd had a woman therapist.

After I split up with Serena I saw him twice a week instead of once – that was partly sort of working through the grief of splitting up, with the children especially, which hurt terribly. I see them now, of course, yes. Adam seems to have joined some sort of punk rock band! I think one of the reasons I didn't find a stable relationship for myself during the years of the threesome was that I didn't want to make a decision that would lose me the children. I think I chose almost deliberately inappropriate people, people that I would get into a mutual 'isn't life awful' thing with.

As the therapy went on the thing that happened more and more was what the Californians boringly call, 'I'm OK, you're OK', you know? There was a sense in which I did need to be reminded of the fact that I wasn't such an awful person; there was a sense in which the therapist simply – by confronting some of these sexual guilts and everything – enabled me to give myself a pat on the back. So that I wasn't completely stuck in the past and stuck in a sense of failure about myself, that I could look ahead and like myself a bit. I know that if you go into therapy looking for pats on the back, that's not what you're going to get; it's more about a certain kind of honesty about yourself. But in the course of being honest about things you do sort of realize that maybe you're . . . well, not so bad after all.

There was a change in my political attitudes too, I think. Before, there was a kind of moralism, how things ought to be and how people ought to be. What people call idealism if they approve, but rigidity or dogmatism or whatever if they don't. I see politics much more in terms of a rich and very complicated process than as a series of simple abstractions now. And in personal things I was trying to impose an abstract notion of how relationships should be. But now I feel that the way people are and the way they tend to feel, you know, is something one has to respect and not simply arbitrarily legislate against, either politically on a big scale or emotionally on a small scale. Those things are there and that's what you work with. Don't think I've joined the Tories or the Alliance or something! It does worry me that therapy is only for people who can pay, yes. Absolutely. Then there's the issue of power, relating persons to politics – if I were doing therapy now,

I think that would interest me. My generation refused power to some degree, wrongly so. There was 'small is beautiful', there was a return to domesticity, which in the end doesn't move things forward.

Funnily enough Jack kept questioning me about my feelings for him, for ages and ages. I didn't see why he kept on about it, it didn't seem the point at all. 'Your relationship with me is this or that', he kept saying, and all the time I thought why is he asking me this? But in the end I got to a point where I saw I was dependent on him, that he was someone I saw every week to moan at and complain to. You trot along every week and you think, I must tell him this or that, I must remember to tell Jack and then everything will be all right – so in a sense you're still not being responsible for yourself, you're giving this responsibility to someone else. At the point when I realized that the function of the therapy was to save up all the things I felt miserable or resentful about and then moan to him, you know – at that point I thought, well, actually what's going to do me most good now is to stop it. He didn't really argue with it. I said, 'I think I'm leaning on you in a way that actually is no longer useful. I'd be better now to stand on my own two feet.'

So I stopped it and then I immediately embarked on absolutely, entirely the happiest period of my life. I had a couple of very enjoyable affairs, which I felt far less guilty about than I ever had before – and I'm a person who, I suppose, lived through one of the most promiscuous ages in hundreds of years with such intense guilt that even when I was being promiscuous I wasn't enjoying it.

Funnily enough, I'd been living in a lesbian collective through those years since I split with Serena! I had a lesbian friend and when I'd been suddenly homeless and miserable, she'd said, 'Go on, you can have a room.' I was there for about three years, an odd living situation, and, you know, I couldn't conceive ever living with a woman again, couldn't conceive of it. To have that degree of intimacy and trust seemed totally out of the question. And then I met Jenny, that's nearly six years ago, and I can tell you from the start it was a deliriously happy and sexy relationship. Within about three or four weeks of us sort of getting off with each other Jenny said, 'I'm going to live in Italy for a year, would you like to come?' So I said, 'I'll give it a go', you know. The arrangement was that she would teach in a language school there, and we lived together for a year out there.

There was a feeling of great freedom – I'd been free since Serena left, actually, but I hadn't felt it – but I really did feel free then, and having sort of decided that I didn't need to see Jack any more was part of that sense of freedom. I felt I'd got something from him I could keep. I was wonderfully irresponsible in Italy, too, because basically she was providing for me and I'd always been so responsible. It was absolutely what I needed, it was terrific. At last I felt totally and completely at ease with someone, above all sexually. We're still together. There you are, quite a happy-ending story!

Sarah

I was your infant and child. You were my mother,
and father, and husband, and lover. You were my
wife, and the times when I was a boy, a man, or a
hermaphrodite, you were my brotherly friend. You
were more than all these too. More than doctor,
teacher, and stalwart supporter. You were something
more which must remain silent.

Sarah Ferguson: *A Guard Within*

Dark-skinned and dark-eyed, an elegant and successful
woman in a handsome drawing-room. Her husband lets me
in and the children, somewhere in the flat, are obediently quiet. A
big dog sleeps on the green dralon sofa beside her. A hesitant
voice, a powerful personality.

━━━━━━━━━

It goes back to when I was about 17 and very, very depressed;
my periods hadn't started, I was terrified of growing up. My
father had died when I was 8 and my mother had never quite
wanted to take over as parent – she was dealing with her own grief
and she was a very young widow at 38. I had a very confused start
in therapy, I'm afraid.

My mother's GP referred me to hospital and the consultant
there thought I should have private treatment, as money was no
problem. So I started with a woman therapist when I was 17 and
in a way I was quite in love with her, but she was ill herself, going
through a severe depression, and after a few months she passed
me on to her husband, who was a psychiatrist – I don't think he
was really a therapist. I think she had understood more than he
ever did. I stayed with him until I was 19, but it was pretty
hopeless, all a hell of a mess.

I was phoning him every minute and because of that I sort of got caught up in the marriage breakdown between him and his wife, the woman I'd first seen as therapist. He'd given me the number of his mistress's house and I'd be phoning him there. Later I heard that his first wife had killed herself. He was pretty well at the end of his tether with me. I was on Librium; he'd prescribed it for me. I was really in very bad shape. When I was 19 I took the law into my own hands and went off on a round-the-world trip with my mother – oh, I was supposed to be doing A-levels, but I was terrified of failing and I went off on this trip. I think both of them tried hard and I suppose it was at least someone for me to turn to. But I terminated with him, I think he wanted to be free and move into the country with his new wife. I felt that, really, I was in the way, because I was a pretty heavy commitment.

I was referred to someone else, a psychoanalyst, and – it's very interesting really – I was assigned to someone who absolutely replicated my mother in that she was a woman on her own with a daughter. It was a most disastrous choice. It was a different situation from my family, because we were Eastern – originally from Syria – and there was an extended family with lots of comings and goings, but, still, the nucleus, the mother and daughter thing, was the same.

I went to her five times a week till I was, I think, about 22 or 23. It was much more disastrous than the time with the first two therapists because it went much deeper, everything was stirred up, and yet she couldn't handle any of it. It exacerbated my desperateness, my longings and . . . it really got completely out of hand. I was flinging things around the room and banging the door and running in and out of the consulting room . . . being chaotic, very destructive. Once or twice she even called the police because I was behaving outrageously. But that wasn't really the point of how to deal with it. I believe now that somehow she hadn't faced her own incapacities, her own wish to merge, her own helplessness, in such a way that she could really identify with them and there-fore contain them. She couldn't understand. I think she was frightened by me; sometimes I could see fear in her eyes. And you can't feel safe with someone who is afraid of you.

I think if a patient is behaving outrageously aggressively, the therapist should be looking at her relationship with her own aggression; if she's in touch with her aggression, the patient shouldn't need to act out in that desperate way. And it was all a question of being understood. I was trying to get across a lot about my mother, about how disturbed I was and that she had to do something about it, and also that I was longing for closeness, really, which she was afraid of. I mean, she was always telling me I was attacking the breast, and how destructive . . . But – it didn't mean anything to me. Maybe I was attacking the breast, but that wasn't really the point.

I would chuck the flowers around in her consulting room and then I'd pick it all up. And there was a Chinese ashtray, I remember – I replaced it three times; I remember going to the shop in Baker Street three times. And then I wouldn't leave. I would refuse to go and she had her next patient waiting; it was impossible. A lot of it was about wanting to repair things for her really, but I don't think she actually appreciated how much I wanted to put things back *together* for her. You know, it was that bit that she never got in touch with, that I wanted things to be well for her. But because she always interpreted things as being destructive and aggressive, I just became more destructive and aggressive. Sometimes when it got intolerable and I was quite out of control she would say, 'I can't take it. I'm getting a headache and I'm leaving the room' – which was just awful. And I would be deluging her with letters all the time too.

I always felt sub-human with her. I felt I was this big greedy baby or the destructive sadistic patient. I never felt – oh, sometimes I felt the clever girl – but I never felt really that she treated me as an adult, proper person. Well, I wasn't, I suppose. And even though I was behaving like this stupid big baby she insisted on calling me by my surname. After all, I was only 20 and she insisted on this; I found it quite humiliating. I do think that if she'd sat and said, 'Look, you're behaving absolutely outrageously and I know that you're in trouble and you're hurting, but perhaps it's also something in me that you're responding to' – if she'd just sat and said that once. I did in a way want to make her look at herself as well. There's something there again of being too similar to my mother, that she never sat and looked at herself, at what was *her* part in it.

I felt very accused. I felt it was all my fault, that I was doing it wrong and just couldn't get anything right. I didn't see *then* that it could be anything to do with her. I felt dehumanized. To be fair, she would tell me I was an extremely clever girl, but all the same I knew she had grave doubts that I would ever make it because she thought I was totally loopy.

She said, 'I can't see you in my consulting room any more', and she got me into hospital. I was relieved; I was longing to be in hospital. And she treated me in hospital, though I was never really *in* hospital, I came out for a lot of tutorials, I was all over the place. Then she agreed I should go back and do A-levels, and all that necessitated me being at a polytechnic, which I couldn't have done from hospital. She knew I had to get my exams if I wanted to go to university. She was very good about it, she'd already encouraged me to study, which had given me a little confidence. So she very nicely agreed to see me back in her consulting room again. She thought I was able to keep more in control by then, but it began to get out of hand again.

One day I just pinched my file; in front of her I took the file with all my notes. She made an interpretation about stealing or breasts or attacking . . . I don't know what it was all about. But when I went to Dr White later and told him the story, he said, 'You know, it's very simple really. You just wanted a present.' I think it had been my birthday, but she never got to that. But you see, he had an entirely different way of looking at the same thing.

I feel sad about her. You see, I think if you're understood, you don't need to act out in that violent way. If you're *really* understood, if someone is hearing your anger, then you don't need to. Of course, she might see it all quite differently. Actually, I met her about twenty years later and I did say to her that I'd been revolting, that she'd had to put up with so much. I think she understood it was an apology – I think she was absolutely amazed, too, at how I'd developed, at the professional work I'd done. I don't think she could quite believe it. She had the humility to say that Dr White was absolutely right for me. She said, 'The last thing I did for you was the best thing.' She chose him for me.

Things had started to get out of hand with violence again, and she said to me, 'Will you promise not to touch anything in my room?' On the one hand she thought I was totally loopy, but on the other hand she thought I was sane enough to promise. Well, I thought about it and I said, 'No I can't promise that, I just can't do it.' So she said, 'Well, that's fair enough. I think you are saying really that you want someone else, that we've reached the end.'

I was devastated, absolutely devastated. I screamed at her; I said, 'I'm not telling you that at all.' Yes, I think I felt I'd destroyed her. But she said, 'I'll think about this. I can't go on having you here myself and I'll find someone else for you.' And she found White. I kept phoning her, but she said, 'You have to believe that somehow the person I have found is in my view better than me' – which I think was right. I don't think I'd seen him at that point.

Yes, after that it's a success story – yes. I suppose it was good of him to take a patient with such a history of acting out – but then he likes anything that's loopy. He doesn't like your straight neurotics. And he made it quite clear, he said, 'I'm not having any destructiveness. I won't tolerate messing up of my room; I'll just call someone to take you into the next room.' And so in some way it was safe. It wasn't any longer the question of therapist as vulnerable woman alone, as my mother had been. The message he was putting across was that I couldn't destroy him. He said, 'Your previous analyst may have needed you, but I've got many satisfactions in my life and you know you're just piddling, I don't need you' – and that was a reassurance actually. Because, somehow, coupled with all that, there was a real caring and interest. Though he didn't always give me fifty minutes – he was totally arbitrary, he'd say 'I've got to go and do my chores today', or whatever – yet I felt I had total access to him in a sense and that if I needed him he was there.

He has got the two sides. I mean, you can say he's arrogant, he's impossible, he's a difficult man, he's absolutely loopy and yet he is very caring as well. And he's also in some way in touch with his own helplessness and incapacity. I stayed with him for about six years, but it wasn't a conventional analysis in any way. It was awful at times. Often I felt he couldn't be bothered, sometimes my session lasted five minutes if he felt I was impossible or he wasn't in the mood; it would just be, 'Piss off, I've had enough of you.' But really, I didn't mind because I felt that, overall, he was in charge. He'd see my mother if it was necessary and say, 'Order her a piano', or, 'She needs this now', or, 'She must do that now'; he was in control of my life. He always said that with other patients he was different if they needed him to be. Maybe he was, I don't know. And then, perhaps, sometimes he'd give me two hours or he'd let me come back twice in a day. He was there. I know some people would have hated it, naturally, but I didn't.

No, I didn't chuck the ashtrays about with him. Perhaps now and then I might not have wanted to leave, but he always made provision for that. If he saw I was really troubled, he'd let me stay in another room and have coffee brought in to me. If he really felt you were hurting, he would allow it. It was no threat to him. But if he felt you were piddling about, he would just say, 'Oh fuck off', you know. But he wasn't destructive really. I felt he understood. I felt he could look after me. And then he would always . . . at one time, for instance, I thought I couldn't get into London University and would be in Sussex during the week, and he said, 'It doesn't matter'; he said he'd see me Friday, Saturday, Sunday, Monday, so that the analysis could continue.

He really managed my whole environment; my mother, for example . . . The door of her flat was always open and it was like a railway station, people in and out, you didn't know who was going to be there – that's my mother, she's totally manic. And he said, 'You know, you've got to stop your house being like a railway station. You've got to shut the door sometimes.' Things like that.

He never hid or pretended to be what he wasn't. And he always shared his incapacities with you, but not in a way to make you feel them a burden. And he was always giving me presents – papers to read, books, gifts. Once I said, 'That's a lovely little fat blue bird', and he said, 'Take it'. And I said, 'No, I'm not saying it because I want it.' And he said, 'I hate the person who gave it to me, it's more you than me, you take it!' And he demanded presents from me. You know – 'Christmas is coming, I want a silver ashtray' and 'I want this' and 'I want that'; sort of like a kid, but it was fun. That was one of the things I liked about him – he could be ruthless and mean and horrible, but there was a spontaneity and generosity. I was safe with him. He was all right with me, he never sort of took advantage or exploited. I think I was having a father for the first time. I was his best daughter. He always says I'm the best analysis he ever conducted, and I think I probably am one of them. I don't know. He wasn't afraid of holding and hugging you when you were in pain. He said, who else would do it without any eroticism? – and it's true, for me there wasn't any eroticism. I didn't feel threatened by him infringing any boundaries. And if you were in pain . . . often I would phone him and he would say, 'You're in pain', and he was . . . there.

I worked through a lot of the feelings I'd had about the woman analyst with him. Things improved a lot. I did my A-levels, I did very well, then I went on to college, I got my degree. Also he arranged that I should marry. Yes, in a way he did. He thought, you know, I was an Eastern girl, I must get married. He chucked out a lot of my unsuitable people. He'd say, 'That chap, don't bother with that one . . .' So in a way he selected the person he thought the most suitable. I mean, it was going that way and he encouraged it; if he'd said no, I would have ended it.

Then the time came when he decided my marriage should end, that it was curtailing me and I should get out. And I think then I decided, really, that if I was not going to let him run my whole life, I had to get out and break away. I was getting on for 30 by then. I didn't divorce; I'm still married to my husband. And just before I ended the analysis I had a miscarriage. I thought that somehow – I might have been quite wrong – that I couldn't have a child with him around. That somehow it would arouse too much envy, it was something he'd never had himself.

I knew there was a ruthlessness in him. I'd heard about things with other people and other situations. It was impossible not to be sort of taken over, so that was the point when I ended. Somehow I almost felt he was going to destroy the thing he had created. He said, 'I created you, I took you off the scrap heap.' I didn't mind. It was true.

Philip

I have always preferred to accuse myself rather than
the universe; not out of good nature; but to remain
my own master.

Jean-Paul Sartre: *Words*

In a housing estate on the outskirts of a northern city Philip
shares an immaculately tidy flat with Charlie, a very old cat
indeed. On the walls his collection of prints, on the table photo-
graphs of his grandchildren. Tall and beaky and tenacious, he
talks against a stinging dusty wind as we go out to look for his
favourite vegetarian restaurant.

Well, I suppose you could say that it was when I was about
18 that I more or less fell to pieces. Every day, I mean *every*
day, became a nightmare. I thought I was going insane, I was
suicidal, I had a constant feeling of unreality. Panic, dread, feelings of being trapped, weakness, restlessness – you name it. It's
lasted for most of my life. It was a bit better at times later on,
when I was married and working at my own business.

My mother was a very violent person; full, absolutely full up
with hatred, very unhappy. My parents kept a shop in London.
My father was fairly easy-going, quite kind in a way, but when he
hit me, big weals came up, I can tell you; my mother said he had
iron hands. Yes, I was very unhappy indeed as a child. It was a
tremendously unhappy family – violent rows, hatred and bitterness. It affected my sister, too, though in a different way. My
mother's fury and implacable hatred had to be experienced to be
believed! At $4\frac{1}{2}$ I was sent off to boarding school – the older
boys there bullied me. I was no good at school. I left at 14 and did
various jobs.

It wasn't so much my childhood years that went wrong though. I know it was much, much earlier; I had LSD treatment and it convinced me of that. I don't know about other people, but that's how it was in my case. It was very early, in babyhood, and it all connects up with my anorexia and compulsive stuffing. I don't know what it could have been that went wrong when I was an infant, whether my mother had some incapacity or something, but I do know from my inner experience that she couldn't feed me. I know there must have been a battle between my mother and myself all the time during feeding. I think the unhappiness in later childhood was only the nails in the coffin.

As a teenager I had dreadful symptoms, guilt and despair, I was drained of energy, there was an awful feeling of absolute pointlessness. I felt nothing I did was genuine, nothing was the real me. It was absolutely crippling. And then, later on, I had this anorexia and bulimia – eating difficulties – I don't know if you've heard of that? Once, later on, when I was in my 20s, I decided it was the end and I went into the lab and got a dose of cyanide all ready and I was going to take it, but just at that moment someone came in!

Well, I went to my GP – this was when I was around 18, and he referred me to hospital. I've always refused drugs; they're awful, they cut you off from everything. The hospital referred me to a doctor for talking therapy and for two years I saw him once or twice a week for a quarter of an hour at a time. He was a nice chap really, a very warm personality. But I gave it up. I always gave up because I thought the dependence was so wrong.

I knew I needed real psychoanalysis, but, of course, I couldn't afford to pay much, so I went for an interview with a woman analyst at a clinic, so as to be put on the waiting list for treatment at the cheap rate by a student analyst. All I remember is she had a cigarette drooping from the corner of her mouth. This was in my early twenties, before I was married. But I never heard from them! Never heard a thing to this day!

There were times when things were not quite so bad, while I was in business and married and bringing up my children. I ran a cosmetics firm, but I had to give up because I got absolutely crippled by depression. My wife and I parted company fifteen years ago, when I was 50 that is, and I think I'm just getting free of the bitterness about it, the resentment and my general unforgivingness. I think I am, I hope I am.

You want to know about the earlier years. Well, there were various things. I tried five sessions of hypnotherapy with quite a well known hypnotist, but it didn't work. He said I wasn't cooperating with him by allowing him to talk to my subconscious! I had two years as a private patient having Freudian analysis – oh, that was *hopeless*. He had *no* idea. Completely dim. He was a horrible type, that doctor . . . sarcastic, mocking. He used to carry out some ridiculous thing he called reality tests. I got very annoyed with him, I was really angry. I got so upset, I was weeping, I really lost control of myself. I said I was leaving and then *he* got upset! I wonder who was the dependent one!

Much later, when things were quite bad again, I was referred to another hospital. I went a few times and they offered me an appointment every six months with a young psychiatrist – but it just wouldn't have been enough. I was desperate at the time for help with things that were coming up spontaneously in my mind. Once I tried a kind of group thing, co-counselling; interesting but useless, that was; it set me back. I think there's a great tendency in those groups to make a tacit agreement to avoid anything that's really disturbing. I learned a lot more, in fact, from working with other volunteers at a home for disabled children.

The main period of therapy I've had was ten years with a lay analyst, which included LSD therapy. I saw an article about it that he wrote and it seemed to make sense to me, what I read – getting right back to the roots of my troubles. That analyst was a nice fellow, I'd say the best of the people I've consulted. I still keep in touch with him sometimes. I know he'd been quite deeply psychoanalysed himself. This man believed the genesis of almost every neurosis was between the baby and the mother's breast. I'm not sure about this as ultimate truth, but, yes, I do think it's very, very important.

I wouldn't recommend LSD therapy, though. Terrible tensions come up, you can't imagine. Sometimes I'd be shot right off the couch and find myself huddled against the wall, you know. And I ground my teeth so hard that the analyst was afraid I'd break them. But in spite of all that it doesn't actually break down your defences, as the analyst thought; the repressions just get tougher at the same time and you have the whole conflict over again, only worse. LSD holds out a promise of a cure, but then in the end nothing is resolved really. Of course, it's fantastic in showing what the problems are – anyone who's sceptical about Freudian stuff or imagines that they really know themselves should have a session or two. But I think it's dangerous.

When I was under LSD I went right back to the experiences of my birth, to the womb even. That's absolutely true. It was horrific, dreadfully painful, the head-crushing. That might be a basic cause of depression, you know, the mother holding on with tight muscles. The LSD treatment can make you worse though. I think the outbreak of anorexia I had was due to it. I tried to deal with that by using a yoga technique of fasting. Then there was a miserable complaint, Reynaud's Disease, icy cold hands and feet – that was certainly due to it.

I *did* gain from my experiences in that analysis all the same, but the main gain has been from what I've managed to do by myself. It was terribly difficult to give up the treatment with him – with any of them! But I know now I was right to do it. I liked him, I trusted him, yes; and I travelled a long way nearly every day to see him for all those years. I remember he said to me once, 'You're *not* failing, you're just re-experiencing your early failure.' This was really a sort of revelation to me later on, when I was dealing with such a crippling sense of failure over most things.

The depression got awfully bad again soon after I'd moved out here, and I had more bouts of bulimia, that's food bingeing. You can't imagine what that's like. You're totally obsessed with where the next food's coming from. Unless you're out of the reach of food, in a meeting or something, you just eat *constantly*. You can put on a stone in a couple of days. I'd go up the motorway and I'd know every motorway café and what you could get there, and I'd go to every one and have a complete meal. You can see yourself doing this and yet it's just impossible to stop. It's as desperate as heroin addiction, you know, you're always unsatisfied. And then there was the opposite, not being able to eat. I've only recently got free of it all. I live mostly on vegetables now.

It's a dreadful toss-up who you get as a therapist, you know. More people should shop around a bit until they get someone to their liking, I think, and not swallow the usual claptrap about defences causing them to break off treatment. Psychoanalysts used to put this to me when I knew in my bones they were off beam – and sometimes dim and even unkind. I think now I wasted a lot of time and often should have broken off earlier. But it was a struggle whenever I did make a break from one, a real heartache. I used to get *so* dependent, much too dependent, I couldn't do without them.

I'm not bitter any more really. I see a kinder face; I look in the mirror and I don't see a brute any more. All the same, in general, I don't have much time for the fraternity of psychiatrists and analysts and all the rest. I think most of them are just pathetic – you hear them on the radio and so on – pathetic, awful. Not all, but the majority. I suppose if a friend or relative of mine was in very bad trouble, I *would* advise them to go into some sort of therapy – but very reluctantly. I mean, it's not simple, the whole thing. All sorts of things go into it – what the person wants out of the therapy, what the therapist is like in himself or herself. There are people who get helped in every school of psychotherapy, working from different principles. To really help, I think the therapist must be experienced, he must have a loving nature, he must have been psychoanalysed deeply. Love from the therapist is very important; they won't get anywhere unless they've got that at least to offer. Love in the religious sense, I mean.

Well, I wouldn't say my roamings through the psychiatric jungle were *all* failure. Often there's been support, somewhere to go and, of course, I've picked up a lot of insights. I know the *nature* of my problem, but that just isn't enough for me. It has to be eradicated. I'm much less dependent now than I was. While you're in therapy with these psycho-gurus, of course, you think they're absolutely omnipotent. But it's completely illusory!

My difficulties went very deep, very deep indeed, and psychiatrists in general have only had limited experiences in analysis themselves and so they don't really know what you're talking about. The unconscious protects itself and the more awful your experiences have been, the more repressed they are. I had terribly strong defences, I still have. What I found out from the analysis and the LSD was a rage at the breast of terrifying proportions and dreadful implications. I'm still trying to work at taking it to pieces.

I learned about the causes of my troubles, but digging them out can be dangerous, in some ways it can make you worse. It's that primitive rage that causes depression, at any rate with me – there's guilt and shame and also a terrible fear of retaliation. You have to realize that you love someone, you depend on them, and then, quite definitely and deliberately, you kill them. Yes, I mean that. It wasn't suggested by the analyst, not at all, it just sort of comes to the surface gradually if you allow it to. Then you're entirely alone in the world and the reason you get so blooming tired and weak, you see, is that repressions of these things are held down by enormous energy. When you undo them, you feel it's a sort of death. But there's been a shift of energy going on with me all the time. Over the years I'm slowly getting better. Yesterday was awful though, it was like a physical attack – I felt worthless, I felt I had no right to live. And I just don't know why. It's curious, there doesn't seem to be any particular reason. But there *is* one and eventually I'll find it.

Oh yes, of course analysis can help, I don't deny it. I'd say it can be useful for bringing sort of body-mind problems to light, but it can't do more than that, it can't do anything about the spiritual. A lot of psychoanalysts believe it can make you whole, but I just don't believe that. On the other hand the Eastern philosophies claim to bring about nirvana, but they don't really understand about Western neuroses. That's naïve.

Analysis helped me with psychosomatic difficulties – anorexia, difficulty in breathing, back pain, exhaustion, things like that. And it helped with very bad sexual difficulties, which I know were caused by sex abuse, which started very early; my parents had a succession of teenage maids and very few of them wouldn't

'play'! It's too much to cope with at that age and it plays havoc
later on. Then analysis did help over projecting feelings onto my
children which really belonged to my mother or father or sister.
And I used to have a sort of contempt for my fellow-men, it
cured me of that. But psychoanalysis can only take you so far;
there's a spiritual dimension as well. At the best it frees you a bit
to pursue the spiritual search.

I've read quite a bit about yoga and Buddhism and trans-
cendental meditation. I've looked at quite a lot of spiritual paths
and cults. And I've sort of come to the conclusion that you can't
jump straight onto the God bandwagon by sidetracking your
neuroses. People latch onto all sorts of things to comfort themselves. Yes, of course I *believe* in God – don't you? – but that
doesn't mean I've *found* God. But I'm not committed to any of
those spiritual paths. I prefer to carry out my search in my own
independent way. You can't expect to get into spiritual meditation
and just cut through all the deep conflicts and traumas from your
past. I know it does have dangers, this self-analysis, you can lose
your sense of objectivity; it can help to be under someone's guidance. In the past I've desperately wanted to turn to people, but I
don't feel the need any more. I'd rather go it alone and take a
chance on the consequences.

I'm finding out about it still, all the time. You don't reach these
things in five minutes – your whole system, body and mind, has
to sort of make a gradual change and adjust to it. The earlier these
bad things happened, the harder it is to get at them. Your whole
body and self, your own psyche, can get smashed apart when
you're still a baby, you know. You get long periods of desolation
and despair but you have to go on with the attempt.

I practise Hatha yoga for half an hour and then I do my own
meditation morning and evening – no, not just relaxing – specifically observing myself, trying to see what the unconscious brings
up. It does help. Things do still come up, very much so. I continue
with the work every day as far as I can. The terrible rages, the
traumas, terrifying stuff. It's sometimes difficult to keep yourself
apart from it, but this is the exercise. It *was* my early life that
caused me to be what I am – and yet I don't regret anything.

Really, I don't. I've gained quite a lot from therapy and especially from self-analysis, and I think I'm reconciled to what's happened. Well, perhaps that's not quite true, not quite reconciled. If I have a real regret, it's that I wasn't a kinder father to my children. I did try.

But . . . I haven't forgiven my mother; no, not yet. I'm having this struggle every single day – how on earth can I love this person? I had such hatred for her for years and years and years. She locked me out of the house, you know, things like that. But I'm absolutely sure people come to understand what they did, after death.

I'm not a Christian, but I think forgiveness is the central thing. Somehow it has to be worked for. There has to be a search, you can never give up. I don't have a television; I know I've got a task to do and I don't want it interfered with. I wouldn't like to die yet because I haven't finished my task; it's not physical pain and that sort of thing I'm afraid of. Of *course* people survive death; they have souls, don't they?

I've done a lot to be ashamed of and I'd like to be forgiven. I've done terrible things within my own mind – it doesn't make any difference that I've not actually acted them. Whether it's me that's bad, that's sinful – that I don't know yet. I'm finding out. I'm working every day.

Ruth

Thoughts were things, to be collected, collated, analysed, shelved, or resolved. Fragmentary ideas, apparently unrelated, were often found to be part of a special layer or stratum of thought and memory, therefore to belong together; these were sometimes skilfully pieced together like the exquisite Greek tear-jars and iridescent glass bowls and vases that gleamed in the dusk from the shelves of the cabinet that faced me where I stretched, propped up on the couch in the room in Berggasse 19, Wien IX.

HD: *Tribute to Freud*

Ruth's is a large, light, top-floor flat furnished in creams and whites, with a view over rooftops and trees. She is a handsome woman, a little nervous; she's not sure, she says, that what she's got to say will be of any interest. Then she talks for long and with total absorption.

═══════════

I'm 50 now, so I was a baby, fifteen, sixteen months, when we came over from Vienna. I think my identity problem goes right back a long way. People say, 'What was your first language?', and I think it has to have been German because that was what I heard, but I never had a chance really to consolidate what before I was surrounded by English. And I think probably the English values that I learned in school, against a very Middle European, non-English-language background, must have caused a few conflicts. There were crossed signals.

My brother and sister were much older and it was altogether a very powerful family. There was no place for me. You know, there was I, the little thing, and they were all sort of talking nineteen to the dozen up there and I had to say, 'Hey, listen to me, you know I've also got something to say', and it was, you know, 'Quiet, worm!' That kind of thing. And my perception of my mother was that she was always too busy to have any time for me – 'Can't you see that it's not your time, can't you see that something else has to be done, why are you interrupting?' She was only in the kitchen. I think my brother Jake brought me up much more than my father – my father travelled a great deal, particularly after the war. When I look back . . . The problem of immigration, settling, survival – as long as the children have food and a roof over their heads, why should they have any problems? But there were other problems around.

I don't think anybody took my difficulties seriously, which was a cause of pain; and also my schooling, from the age of about 15. I mean, I was amazed to have got into a good school like that, but I went steadily downhill. I couldn't cope, I couldn't concentrate. It presented an educational ideal which I didn't feel I could live up to, which I think was also my father's educational ideal – he was a very, very successful, travelled man. And I had very brilliant school friends – it was so much to live up to.

My mother had a particular view of how a girl should be, and she was very negative and very destructive of me from the age of about 10 or 12: every time I would go out – 'How can you dress like this? Why aren't you like that? Why aren't you more coquette?' And there was I, the fat child, being force-fed by my mother, and every time I said, 'Help me, I can't lose weight', she'd just say, 'Well, you don't need to eat', which is very subversive, very destructive. On the one hand she'd say 'I have to cook for the others', but, you know, 'Find your own way through'; no support.

My father, on the other hand, was never there, I couldn't look to him. And by the time I was 12 my brother and sister were in their twenties, at university, all set to be successful. I felt rather as if I were an only child. I was 18½ when my father died. Yes, of course I was upset, I still am, I can't tell you. That summer I was taking my A-levels. I was at a crammer's. I was going to take my Oxbridge exams, but I wasn't up to it and I knew that. I'm lousy at exams, terrified of putting anything down on paper. I failed the entrance exam. My mother kept saying, 'Take it again', but I just couldn't. There was something in me that knew I had to work, that I'd find any kind of identity I had through my work. My mother would say, for instance, 'Every girl wants to get married', but I said, 'No, I don't necessarily, that's not my priority.' I knew work *was*. I've never married.

It was after my father died. I went to my G P, who had been marvellous and still is, and he'd listened to all the problems. He sent me to somebody, some kind of therapist. I went a couple of times and I was too frightened to go again, because I did this without my mother knowing; I couldn't pay for it, it cost three and a half guineas! An incredible amount. My mother said later that she'd had awful problems as a girl herself; there was her mother-in-law and my grandfather, who was an absolute bully . . . My mother's a woman of enormous anxiety. I think I may have presented a threat to her, actually doing what she might have fantasized wanting to do – get jobs, be independent, go into analysis. She came from a sort of archetypal, rich, middle-class Jewish family – self-made, you know, real *nouveau riche*.

I always felt that my father had a much more benign view, he'd sort of come in and radiate calm, very powerful. It was an incredible loss when he died. I couldn't talk about it to my brother and sister. One of the things that I resent terribly about that whole period, you know, is the fact that it was totally divisive instead of cohesive; there was no way that each of us could share the loss, come any closer to each other. Grief doesn't always unite people.

Well, I went into publishing as I'd always wanted to. I worked in America and here. There were terrific problems at home. A few times I went back to this same analyst, but again, I couldn't afford it and I let it go – I wasn't sort of motivated. Then what happened was that I suddenly fell ill – a raging temperature, no cause that anyone could discover. It was actually a cry for help, an attention-getting device. You know, some people slit their wrists . . . My GP said, 'When you're better, I want you to promise me you're going into therapy.' That's how it happened.

I went back to the same man, yes, it never occurred to me to go to anyone else. I paid for it myself out of my own earnings. I was

around 25. I was altogether such a terrified person – I mean, I
didn't actually sleep with anyone until I was 24. I was totally
neurotic, insecure, the daughter of a successful family, supposed
to be perfect – and there I was, a total mess. So I went back to
him and it was terribly hard to pay, but I did extra freelance
work. It was very funny – I was in broadcasting at the time and I
was going off to Harley Street, either early, you know, or in the
lunch-hour, didn't want to talk about it; until one day out of the
door came somebody who was working in the same office. I
subsequently discovered three other people I knew were going to
analysts in that house!

So . . . I stayed with him for about seven or eight years. In
some ways it was difficult because although I liked him and to
some extent trusted him, I found it very difficult to get sort of
emotionally involved. I was very angry – with my mother, with
my father for dying; there was anger and fear and practical problems about work and about identity; but I couldn't transfer any of
it towards him, I had to keep him intact. There was this fear of
destroying him. Particularly at first, because for years he was a
very silent analyst. Until later on he started talking and then one
couldn't shut him up! I'd say – by this time we were on very good
terms – I'd say, 'Shut up, I want to say something!'

I'd got into analysis because – thank God – I'd realized at that
point that I could find some way through my problems. But the
thing I would say about people going into analysis is that you
should be really driven to it – it's no joke. You go in with a cry for
help, and thank God it was so obvious to me then that that's what
I'd always wanted. I'd always been very introspective; everybody'd
said, 'You're very self-centred, you're only concerned with yourself.' But I was always very perceptive about other people too. I
have a very, very quick judgement of people, which I try to curb,
but I'm usually right. If I don't go by that, then I'm in trouble.
I've always had that, but analysis helped me to back it up with
more tolerance, I think, and sense of reality.

The most important thing Dr X, I'll call him, did for me
during those years was that I was able to work, to hold down a job
and feel that I could grow in it, that I had a place in it, that I had

skills which didn't have to compete with any other member of the family. Because I had a problem of where could I go? They were greater achievers in every branch of every art – so where was there room for the little one? There was an expression in the family – 'Wait, wait, your time will come'; well, in a sense I'm still waiting.

He helped me with being able to work and to take credit for my achievements. I mean, I used to do research for television and I was terrified of putting my name up there, and he said, 'You did the work, you should get the credit.' I would hide behind what I'd done, I couldn't speak out for myself. I began to have a much better sense of myself. But there is the fact, which I'll explain, that it all collapsed again in the reality of when I set up my own business. So since it's taken me really until last year to finish, that time with him was only the beginning. But thank God he was there and he was on my side. He was the only person . . . The great importance, I think, for people in therapy is that, if you have the relationship that you should try to make with the thera-pist, you have him on your side. Whether he criticizes or not, it's critical from the point of *with* you, like a good friend should be, but it doesn't come with all the baggage of parents or siblings, and there's no axe to grind.

He *was* very silent, but I didn't feel he was cold, no. I knew he wasn't. And also, because he wasn't married at the time, it was very funny, I kept bumping into people who'd gone out with him! Once I came out of the waiting-room and there was a girlfriend of mine, and I said, 'What are you doing here?', and, you know, she was a bit embarrassed because she'd obviously come to have lunch with him. One gets so inquisitive! It's like having a crush on a teacher, you want to know everything about them. But I did have difficulty in having a sort of complete trust where I could give everything to him. I mean, another friend of mine who went to him, her feelings were terribly strong, terribly emotional.

I think one of the greatest achievements was that he enabled me to have the strength to move out from my mother's house. I was 26, still living at home; I couldn't get away, she wouldn't allow me to. For the first year after my father died I had to share a room with her, and I'll never forgive the rest of the family for what they put me through – every time I said 'I can't take it any more', it was, 'Can't you see, she has to be looked after, think of her grief.' What I blame her for was that she took away *my* mourning. That's one of the recurrent things that I brought up in my analysis; she took away my mourning, I couldn't have my way of mourning for my father. Because whatever I would say about my relationship with my father, she went one better – he was her man. But he was *my* father. I think maybe I've begun to dissolve it now, all these years later.

I moved upstairs to a sort of flat in her house and every time I'd come home the door would open and she'd come out, and I knew within five minutes the phone would ring; 'Well, are you coming down to dinner?' I'd say, 'No, I've got guests'; 'What, you've got guests?' You know, total possessiveness. I *couldn't* move – well, psychologically I couldn't, and then I couldn't deal with the combined strength of the family saying, 'Why are you doing this? How could you move away?' She threatened a heart attack – oh, the whole bit. You see, I was the useful homebody, I was the spinster daughter there to look after mother. I was having relationships with men, but terribly bad relationships with people who were totally unsuitable, who I liked more than they liked me – well, I imagine a lot of people *did* like me, but I couldn't believe that they did . . . and my mother constantly reinforcing the fact that no wonder they didn't – 'You're fat, you're this, you're that, you're not nice, you don't smile, you don't wear your hair this way.' So the analysis for me was the counter-balance.

Then when I did move out, it was to West Hampstead, it was a multiracial house – I had a very nice flat, it cost me seven quid – and there was a mixed marriage in the basement, very nice. And once I was ill and my mother came to visit me, and she came up and she'd seen the black man, the West Indian; and it was all tears and 'Oh that it should come to this!' Guilt, guilt – she is a marvellous guilt-merchant. So again, the purpose of the analysis for me was for the analyst to show what she was trying to do.

Well, then I went and worked in Canada. I'd decided I'd finished the analysis. Then, when I came back, I joined a concert agency, but I had a problem with the director there and I found things extremely difficult, so I went back to the analyst for several more years and it was very supportive. My relationships with men were getting better, I think, but I was miles away from being able to feel secure enough to want to get married or even think about it. Nobody could understand why I didn't marry, they said it must be my fault, it was the way I treated people. I don't know that marriage is the answer to things. What I do want is a good relationship and the relationship I have now with Mark is very good – though he'll be going back to Malaysia and I'll be back on my own. But I'd certainly rather be on my own than in a bad marriage. Because on a scale of one to ten, about eight and a half of my life now is very desirable.

I did eventually wind up my analysis. I wanted to set up my own business and I felt I needed my energy to deal with that. I still had terrible problems with my mother, but I felt very much that I'd come to the end of what I could get from the analyst. There was an emotional barrier that I never quite got through. But he got me to the point of being able to function professionally and he got me to the point of independence from my family. And I was able to feel that, you know, I did have something to offer and was a worthwhile person. You know, he thinks I'm the cat's whiskers and he tells everyone that too!

Well, then came the disaster. I'd set up my own business, starting from scratch, and I'd achieved some very good results, but there were a lot of difficulties and I decided I was going to give it up and wind it down. Then what happened was this classic thing, I think, of someone who is redundant, out of work: the loss of identity, the guilt, all the things I'd read about people in that position. It took me two years to get another job. I got more and more depressed as I wound up the business, it was like discarding children, throwing them to the wolves. I had no money, I had no job, there was all this self-hatred.

There was one incident . . . well, I'd put on weight again, and my mother phoned me and said she was preparing Friday night dinner and what should she make. And she said she was going to make pancakes, and I said, '*Please* don't, because you know I'll want to eat them.' And I got there – and I'd had this discussion and said, 'Please don't' – and she'd made a whole *mound* of pancakes. I was so angry that I found I'd picked up a knife, I think I was almost about to kill her. This absolutely typical example of how she would work against me, seeming to feed me, no support, why couldn't she support me once in her fucking life. I was so appalled at that sort of total anger in me that I was terrified, I said, 'Hold everything, I need help again.'

So I went back to Doctor X and told him this, and he said, 'Well, look, you know, our relationship's become more of a friendship now', and he felt he'd really got to the end of what he could do, and that since I had a problem with my mother, I should to go a woman. So he sent me to this woman who I think must have been about 80 then – a wizened old thing, but brilliant. I said to her, 'I'm not really about to start another analysis, I'm sick of that. I want a relationship where I can talk. I don't want you to start analysing me in a Freudian way; I've had it. I'm not going to have you sitting back there just saying, "Yes, yes, yes".' And she was wonderful.

She came from a generation and a background that my mother came from, except that she'd gone to a university and she was a doctor. There she was around 80, about my mother's age, and every single thing my mother would say about Vienna in the Twenties – one didn't do this, one didn't do that – there was this woman saying, one *can* do this, and one can still be a nice, reasonable, upright Jewish middle-class person, and one could have an independent life, and go to university; so I had these two images of what one could be – my mother saying, you know, one must be married and have children and be a pillar of society . . .

There was one time when I listened to what my mother was saying and I had the insight that she was envious, that it was pure jealousy; she was saying and doing things that, if I were objective, could only be interpreted that way. She can say the most devastating things and then if I get upset, she'll say, 'Why do you take it so seriously?' I'll say, 'Because you actually said it, you may not hear it but you did.' But you know, my mother *is* a wonderful person really, but she's wasted her capabilities out of vanity. She was only 49, after all, when my father died and she's done nothing since.

Anyway, there was this Viennese analyst and she was wonderful, really. I think she got all my anger out. It was more sadness that came out in the first analysis. I used to be in tears so much and it was awful going back to the office in tears. I had difficulty in dreaming. I often couldn't remember dreams, but I found that the pattern of my dreaming was that when I'd taken an internal decision, I would then dream the reinforcement of the decision I'd taken; so I knew that at each point when I had a very vivid dream, I'd had a breakthrough.

I had a recurring Hitler dream. I'd be fleeing from some sort of Hitler figure along hotel corridors or something like that. You see, there's something here that my second analysis helped to deal with. I was left behind in Vienna with my grandmother while the rest of the family had got out. The *Anschluss* came; my father and mother were in Belgium, Sheila and Jake got out because they had passports and met up with my grandfather in Switzerland, and I was a baby on my mother's passport. I was left as a Gestapo hostage; they wanted my father back. Then all sorts of things happened; my uncle came from America, somebody stepped in to save me and bribed my Nazi nurse to take me by train to Antwerp. You see . . . we don't know what effect separation has on children. There was some perception that I was abandoned and if I ever get close to somebody, I think they're going to flee. So all this was very much part of the second analysis, going back to these very early things.

Also we worked very hard on the whole Oedipal problem – she felt if I could somehow restructure my very early relationships to my parents, that if I could have a better relationship with my mother, it would actually release my father. You see, I never felt I had either my mother or my father for myself – so how could I in later life have anything, have anybody? I think in the first analysis I was enabled to make a very good relationship with my bosses, so in effect I have the good father. With her, I had the good mother.

I stopped seeing her about six months ago – and I'd only expected to stay for a couple of years! Every time I wanted to stop, she said, 'No, not quite yet.' But why should analysis be quicker really? Your problems didn't arrive in one or two years, they took years to build up. What you're trying to do is get out of the head into the gut; you can talk till you're blue in the face, but until you've got that sort of gut feeling . . . and that takes time, you can't force it.

I think both the analysts I had were absolutely remarkable people; first of all as human beings – I had total trust in them as responsible individuals – and then I think intellectually they were very, very fine. And I've heard of too many cases where, because it's somehow been the wrong person maybe, it hasn't worked and people have been damaged. I do know some analysts socially now and not in a million years would I give any kind of trust to them. I was very lucky. And also, the other thing was I never felt I was going to be bound to them forever. With the second one I said I wanted to stop, but there was part of me that knew that she also would stop when it was right. A lot of people have said to me, 'What you will find is that the greatest progress you've made is after you've finished', and I think that's true.

I think there's an order to things, I think we're here to try to do as much as we have the opportunity to do, and if we can't do it, then take action. There were these things stopping me and the person to deal with that was called a therapist.

About three years ago . . . well, my father was buried in America and I'd been to the grave a couple of times, but it hadn't meant anything to me. In a sense it's like he's on a business trip and just hasn't come back. But I felt that I wanted to make that relationship with him dead, with that plot, with that name-plate. So I went to the grave . . . Oh, I had a great deal of difficulty – this is the strength of my wretched relatives in America – in going there on my own. I said, 'I've travelled around the world on my own, I can find his grave in the New Jersey graveyard, tell me where it is.' I went there alone and I said the Buddhist prayer over his grave – because I've got very interested in Buddhism – and this was very important to me. It was marvellous because I'd sort of faced it.

Antoinette

I do not want to give away my solitude; it is only that,
if it were a little less in mid-air, if it got into good
hands, it would lose its morbid undertones entirely
(which will have to happen sooner or later in any
case), and I could achieve at least some kind of continuity in it, instead of being chivvied amid the din of
shouting from pillar to post with it like a dog with a
stolen bone.

Rainer Maria Rilke: *Letters*

Antoinette is dark, thin, beautiful and wears a straight grey
dress with a long string of amber beads. A precariously
quiet space is cleared in the north London house; somewhere
upstairs teenage life explodes. She speaks hesitantly and with
tentative gestures.

———————

It goes back a long way, nearly thirty years I suppose, to when I
was taking finals. At school I'd been legendary for exam panic. I
went up to London from Oxford to my grandmother's, and my
father was over from Brussels, and I said I wasn't going back,
that there was no way I could face the exams. The pressure had
got worse as the field had got weeded out and only the cleverer
and cleverer were left in, and my panic increased accordingly. I
knew I'd fail. My father consulted with my mother and he said I
must go back to Oxford and he'd come with me – he stayed for
about a month. It was in the course of that that I think I said, I
kept saying, 'I don't feel real.' So maybe that was the start . . .
Though I'm sure I was depressed very much earlier than that –
probably from quite a small child. My father was worried; he
thought that was more serious than anything I'd said before.

I did get through finals, yes, with him there. I mean, I had letters from doctors and from my tutors to the examiners, and so on, saying I wasn't all that stupid; in the end I did get through them. I was given 'purple hearts' by the doctor. So I got through and I went off to Spain for several months on the theory that I was going to be an international interpreter – yes, in those days I spoke a lot of languages, having been brought up internationally, so to speak. Anyway, I was terrifically depressed in Spain, that's for sure. I kept feeling there was nothing more, the exams were over, what else was there?

I eventually came back to London and I think somebody told me that this thing about not feeling real was quite serious. My aunt was a doctor, and my father had talked to her and had been to see somebody she knew at the Maudsley or something, so I went to see this guy and I remember that the only thing I could find to say to him was . . . He said, 'What's your problem?' and I said, 'I don't know, but my mother says I'm snippy.' Well, it means sort of sharp, scratchy, unpleasant. And that's all I can remember I ever had to say, 'My mother says I'm snippy.'

He said there were various ways of treating people and the way to treat me was through analysis and he'd find me an analyst. I didn't really like him because he made me feel I did have grounds for feeling sorry for myself, which is something I do *and* don't like feeling. All this time I was certainly going on feeling depressed and feeling not real. And one thing at least I would say for analysis is that for all the many forms of depression I've had afterwards, that feeling of not being real has never actually come back. I can remember people saying, 'You don't feel real? You're so definite, you're so kind of *there*' – and being really surprised. I suppose I have versions of it, but I don't have that feeling that nobody is walking along *this* street at *this* moment. No doubt it'll come back now I've had to tell you about it! Oh sorry, I'm being snippy.

I expect I'm always snippy, except that when I'm less depressed, I'm less snippy. One of the reasons nowadays I go to the doctor for antidepressants and so on is that I always feel that no-body . . . that everything will *go* because I get to be so unpleasant. I feel that all the good things that happen, happen when I've just started taking some course or other of antidepressants and so become nice.

So I was sent to this analyst lady. She was Welsh and I think she'd probably been analysed by Ernest Jones – anyway, she once sent me to a dentist who'd been Ernest Jones' dentist. He wasn't very good. So I started off, five times a week. My father paid. I'd got my first job then, in publishing. Twice a week I had to go before work, and I was always very late and she would say that was because I wasn't paying for it. She didn't approve of the fact that I didn't pay for it myself. In a sense I think she was right, I think it was part of the excessively patriarchal way I was brought up.

She was all right, I suppose – quite nice, quite ordinary. I was quite glad, I think, that she wasn't Viennese and didn't have an accent – probably because my mother has a foreign accent – and didn't cover me with sentiment. The good side of her seemed to be rather like this aunt of mine, who was a very English kind of woman doctor, sort of straight, spinsterish.

I've forgotten an awful lot. I do remember her being very shocked at my not having read Freud – she seemed to feel I'd failed to take an interest, which was probably true. She was very practical – one of the things I was remembering on the way here was the way she always went on about Bee Nilson's cookery books; every day I'd talk about everything, so I'd talk about the horrors of cooking and she'd say if I got this Bee Nilson cookery book . . . Yes, I did try it and it wasn't a lot of help. But she was like that. I remember her being very sort of definite about how *Gigi* was a good movie and how I was unable to explain to her that however good or bad in some sense, it wasn't going to be all right for me because I had a different view of what movies should be. I can remember having this argument and somehow not being able to say, being afraid of being intellectually snobbish or fastidious.

And there were other arguments, so silly. I remember one about mini-skirts – that she couldn't believe that if you wore skirts that short it wasn't because you didn't want men to have a certain view of you. And then about lipstick – that I tried to explain that none of my friends, my sort of people, did wear lipstick, but she never gave up on the idea that I didn't wear it because I wanted to look like a little girl. I suppose there may have been things going on, psychological changes and all that through-out the analysis, but all that remains in my mind now is arguments like that and a sense of not being able to get through to her the sort of person I actually was.

I went in saying that it's very easy to explain what's wrong with me. That I have this older half-brother who was very jealous of me because my parents were infinitely nicer to me than they were to him, and a younger sister of whom I was initially extremely jealous, who then turned out not to be all right. Autistic. So my theory was – and I still believe it to some extent – that I was jealous of her and then she was found to be damaged and sent away from home, and it was too much of a fulfilment – and that then because my brother was jealous of me, the same thing would happen to me. So I was always trying to get my parents to be nicer to him and always scared of the consequences of people's envy. I'd sort of worked that out on my own anyway and I talked about that. But it's funny, I have no memory of any account of either my mother or my father in relation to me at all.

My memory of it was that it was a day-to-day thing, not making such a mess of things on a day-to-day basis, and sort of being in the world and not alienating everybody. I mean my mother tre-mendously forcefully said when I was about 15, she said, 'You know, nobody likes you.' That sort of thing. I certainly came out of it feeling, I'm doing better at everyday life, and that's what I wanted. I don't think I remembered submerged things from childhood, though. And I didn't dream, I still don't feel much interest in dreams. It was very *ordinary*, it was about getting through the day. I know flying came into it. For the first time in about ten years I went on a plane; I went to America. And I was able to break off with this fellow I'd been with since Oxford, which I'd always felt I should do. Then, when I did marry John, I think the idea was that that was one of the improvements, that I'd never have been able to . . . so it was in all six or seven years, I suppose, right through my twenties. And then a bit later I went back for a year, when my mother had cancer.

I know I still got depressed – I can remember, for instance, having phases of being terrified of being somewhere where the window was wide open, that I'd jump out of it. And I remember asking a friend to come and sit with me at weekends sometimes because I was frightened of being so depressed, or at least I felt overwhelmed by the feeling of what I might do. I don't think I talked about it to people much, though. The theme of it in the analysis was why I was so scared of being overwhelmed by my feelings – flying was supposed to be to do with that – and it was related to my autistic sister, that she was out of control. I still go into depression very suddenly sometimes and then suddenly out of it. The feeling when it comes is just devastating, but then one conversation about something else can make it go. The time when I was married to John was, I suppose, my least unhappy time. I'm sometimes depressed now in a way that makes me wonder why I don't kill myself, that the children would be better without me. In a sort of way I was always hoping, one day, to be liked. Now I've completely given up the idea!

Yes, I know I've always seemed to be very fortunate in a way, but that made it worse. The thoughts always went in this order: I'm quite intelligent, I'm quite nice-looking, I've got money – and I'm miserable. So that compounded it, made it all worse. Of course, I've always been lucky in working in interesting jobs, I did appreciate that; it was Friday nights that the depression would start.

But about the drink thing, that's what I want to tell you about, because I'm still furious about it. I was going to the analyst at three different times of day – before work in the morning, at ten to six in the evening, and at six-thirty in the evening. When I went early in the morning, I was very bleary and didn't do very well and, anyway, most of the time was spent discussing why I was so late, which never really improved. She was fairly untalkative in the morning. Going at ten to six was the best. But when I went at half past six she was always quite excited with me, quite talkative and sometimes quite flushed. Occasionally, she'd behave strangely and the most I could think was that it was the asthma drug that did it – she did have slight asthma. I'd often nerve myself, the following morning I'd nerve myself terrifically to say, 'You seemed a bit strange last night, was anything wrong?' And then we'd have this thing about, what is it about me that always thinks other people behave strangely? It was always supposed to be *me*, not her. I remember telling a friend at work about it and she said was I sure it wasn't drink – and I thought of course it wasn't, how could it possibly be? I'd never sort of seen people being drunk, I mean, people weren't like that in Brussels in those days.

It didn't really get that bad, I suppose. I remember her ringing me up once after I'd finished the analysis and John answering the phone and thinking it was my grandmother's German house-keeper, who was always a bit excited on the telephone. But, in fact, it was my analyst asking John and me to supper – it was odd, it wasn't appropriate to her way of doing things and she sounded so over-excited. Then there was a time towards the end of the analysis when she'd apparently broken both wrists, she'd obviously just fallen down. But still I didn't realize. It was quite a long time after that an analyst friend told me about her drink problem.

The last time I saw her she kept asking me the same questions over and over again, and I would say, 'But I just told you that'; and there were silly questions like, 'Is John coming to fetch you?' and her speech was slurred, and it was just . . . I was just outraged and furious. I said, 'What's the matter with you?' Nothing, of course, the usual. I remember leaving – John did come to fetch me – and I remember being in an absolute fury. I had some friends who were analysts and I went to see one, to talk to him about it, and he was sort of bland. He fixed me up to go and see a senior analyst – I wanted to talk, I was so enraged with this behaviour and with the lack of explanation. He said to me, 'She's had some difficulties', and I know I felt that wasn't enough; I was full of this rage. What I suppose I think now should have been done is that at some point – given how carefully they monitor everything – somebody should have stepped in with all her patients and done something about it.

It's partly a question of this mystique they set up; I mean, you wouldn't mind so much otherwise. Everything is denied and thrown back onto the patient. Analysts choose to take this excessively neutral path, when you'd actually like them to be less neutral – and then they spring things on you. For instance, when I broke up with the man I was with before John, I can remember my analyst telling me he was schizoid and I remember being very angry with that, saying it was unfair to tell me that and what was I supposed to make of it, was I meant to tell him, why tell me at all? And then when John and I were about to divorce, he told me his analyst wanted to see me. And *she* told me John had some big thing wrong with his character – I can't think now how she put it – I suppose something like what they call a personality disorder, and that he would never get better and that I should keep away from him. I suppose she thought she was being helpful, but again I thought, what am I supposed to do with this? Am I supposed to tell him or not tell him, and on what basis is she telling me? I never told him, actually. But it would be all right, you see, if they didn't make such a fetish of their rules.

Perhaps it wasn't or doesn't seem to be so bad, that last session I had with the analyst. It had been pretty similar on all the other Wednesdays when I'd gone at half past six. But, you see, if you go to an analyst because you want to talk to someone level-headed, because you have such an excitable mother, you have a big invest-ment in their being level-headed. Also, you go to sort out – which is also to me tremendously important – which of your perceptions is right and which is not. I mean, to some extent that's the most you can hope for, and it all just threw me completely out. I was so mystified. If I'd ever had the sensible thought that this was drink, I'd have been able to deal with it. My reaction does seem dis-proportionate, I know. But also I was pretty young – 21 or 22 when I started with her.

For some reason or other I decided to try analysis again. This was while I was still married to John. Partly I think I felt it was unhelpful to him to have me being . . . snippy. Also I suppose I resented the fact that his problems were now supposed to be so important; his analyst used to do things like ring him up at the weekend to make sure he was all right, which I thought was unfair. It was sort of competitive – which one of us was the more needy? – because somehow with men, they always make me feel that they're more entitled to behave the way they do because they do it out of feeling, whereas I do it out of *méchanceté* or something. Anyway, I said that this time I wanted to go to a man and I wanted him to have a sense of humour.

So I went to this man. I went a few times and then I just got up and said, 'I'm not paying to listen to this.' And never went back. He'd put me down all the time for thinking I knew it all, telling him what was wrong with me instead of free-associating, which was never my strong point. There was a big thing about his car, which was outside, and sort of had psychoanalyst written all over it – it was a huge estate car and it had a big sheet of opaque plastic stuff covering God knows what, and I always wanted to know what it was covering. *He* wanted to know why *I* wanted to know what it was covering; and I'd say, 'It's there and it's obvious that anybody would want to know . . .' Anyway. I just thought, stuff this. Perhaps I just wanted to do to him what had been done to me. In all the six or seven years with the first analyst I'd never dared look round at her from the couch. With him I just broke the spell by getting up and saying, 'I'm not paying to listen to this.'

It's not that I'm a total foe of every kind of therapy now. The elder of my boys, Joe, is going once a week. I wouldn't like to get on that couch again, though. I think I got more help from the social worker at the guidance clinic than from anyone else; she sorted me out in dealing with the boys in a way no one else has. The feeling that one's fucked up one's kids, given how much the rest of one's life is fucked up, is pretty crucial. I do still feel . . . sometimes I feel that there's something that *could* unblock me, if I knew what it was. But partly I'd be scared about the fact that whatever I'm told I am, I immediately become it. It's somehow the awful effect of my mother on me – that anyone who says anything about my life, I start doing it or believing it.

I do think that a lot of people would benefit from the step of thinking there was something wrong with *them*, rather than always wrong with the world; that would be a terrific breakthrough for them. But on the other hand I think there are a lot of people who are too much hooked into the whole therapy thing. I suppose if my best friend was in a terrible state, I'd say 'Go into some kind of therapy' – not into analysis, though. I'd say 'Avoid the claptrap, the power game, the sort of blank screen game.' I'd never have the patience again to lie there blank-screening away, as it were.

After all, you do have a certain knowledge of yourself – obviously you don't have the same capacity to see yourself as the analyst does – but you do have a capacity to see yourself, and they override it, they undermine it. My sense of myself is tremendously important to me, and if I'm enclosed somewhere with someone and no verification, then I'm at this person's mercy. Then the only thing I can do if he's not going to agree with me is absent myself, disagree in secret – but then the whole thing's wrecked. All right, some people don't have this experience of having to choose between two realities – but maybe they're more accommodating.

Have you – I wondered whether while you've been doing this project you've heard of anybody absolutely brilliantly good? Because . . . given how difficult I find so many things, I do wonder whether I could still find someone to sort me out, get me out of the enormous number of difficulties I let myself in for. But I don't know.

Patrick

The first expression of salvation is continuity.
Søren Kierkegaard: *The Concept of Dread*

He shares a modest house on the fringes of London with a friendly group of lodgers who help pay off the mortgage. We sit round the kitchen table and Patrick talks clearly and candidly in a gentle Irish brogue.

━━━━━━━━━

I've been a primary school teacher for about fifteen years, and before that I was doing research in Classics, that was my field. I was born and brought up in Ireland, I went to university there and got a studentship to travel abroad, which I took to London – and, in fact, that was the beginning of my search for therapy, one of the main reasons for choosing London. I came to the idea originally through the confessional, which seems illogical really, because one would think that the usual view would be that God deals with all these problems and solves them if you have faith and prayer. But, in fact, I had a very enlightened confessor when I was at university, and he suggested I should perhaps see a psychiatrist. When the confessional interferes in areas, like the sexual area, where you feel, well, that's your own private morality, then you feel, you know, that that's not the place for it. No, I'm not a practising Catholic any more.

I saw a psychiatrist in Dublin a few times, then, when I got the studentship, he advised me to get some therapy in London. I tried various ways. In fact, I even went in off the street to a psychoanalytic centre, but was turned down by them – I had no letter of introduction or anything. Eventually I went to the student counsellor and she put me in touch with a psychoanalyst.

At that time one of the main things was depressions – I had very severe depressions, which prevented me from really getting on with my research. And there was this conflict about the Church and my Irish Catholic background. Particularly its view of sexuality, because I was discovering that I was homosexual at that time and that was so much opposed to the whole morality of the Church. I found I just couldn't tolerate the attitude, the narrow sort of morality, particularly in confessions . . . And, of course, all my family still believed – oh, very deeply, yes. I found myself totally at odds in my whole sexual orientation and my whole view of life. And so, in a way, coming to England was a way of getting away from all that, of being private.

Because you couldn't have a life of your own in Ireland! You live a collective life. But you can be lonely. We had a little village shop, so our life was shared with everyone from around. But it could be painful, very painful, because as an individual you're ignored, in a sense. I felt completely isolated and cut off from the rest of the family. I got scholarships all the way through my education, which was a great help – there wasn't that much secondary education available in those days in Ireland. But I was destined for the priesthood. The family thing, you know – the eldest son inherits the farm, the second son becomes a priest.

It was an isolated village and it was very primitive when I was brought up, we had no running water or electricity, that sort of thing. And so to get out of that and come here was like breaking away from something very strong and backward-pulling. University was hard, because I had been sheltered, in a way, coming from a small village and then a boarding-school. Oh yes, seminary boarding-school – horrific place. That's a whole book in itself, really! I amaze my friends and acquaintances with stories of that. It had a lay side, but really the main aim was to cultivate vocations to the priesthood; it was always obvious to you that this was what you ought to do, it was the best thing you could be.

I always expected to be a priest. Oh yes, I think I would have been if I hadn't had what I would call my sexual problems. And my decision not to was very difficult, because my mother particularly wanted me to be a priest – I think she always thought one day I would! I can remember from a very early age wanting to be a priest, but then ... In my own mind it was that if you were good enough, if you were pure enough and had no sexual problems, you would then become a priest. My own view was very strict and rigid, that you had to be totally pure. We all had hangups about sexuality from the Church hierarchy and teaching. Although there may be something in the Irish psyche itself, I think, because there are clues to it even in the pagan Irish literature – that conflict between the body and the soul.

I was still a student at the beginning of my psychoanalysis, mainly working in the library or in the Reading Room of the British Museum. And I felt that was very solitary, very lonely. I was reading microfilm, which was very isolating – the old microfilm readers, great big machines, and you're in a dark room, transcribing page after page of Greek. I think even at that point I was thinking that if I had therapy, I would then be able to become a priest, it was at the back of my mind. Therapy to sort me out and then religion afterwards.

I've had two analyses. So with this first one I was lying on a couch and she was sitting behind me – I found that very difficult. It was painful, all of that analysis, right the way through. She seemed to be someone way above, someone very remote from me. There was also the thing, which I didn't say anything about to her, that she was very archetypally English, very much the Oxford-accent type and I felt very inferior in the presence of certain English people; I shouldn't have done but I did.

I had no knowledge of therapy of any sort and it didn't conform to my idea of what therapy was going to be about. I expected ... I don't know really. I expected it to be more positive, at least that I would have positive feelings about what was happening, but I had very negative feelings. She was very silent, but *I* was silent often. The analysis seemed to be very much based on a very primitive infanthood experience. It really circled about that – my feelings of dependency on my mother at a very early age. And all the problems there were about not being looked after properly. I felt this type of analysis a great shock to my system to start with, particularly when I was confronted by ... She would interpret things on a very physical level, the breast-feeding, and I found that shocking! Strange! I found it very hard to accept and I would shut up and not say anything for a while after she had done one of her interpretations like that.

She was very objective, everything had to come from me and I found that very difficult. And I felt caught up immediately in old problems because of the situation, being in a very dependent situation. It was immediately into my relationship with my mother. Particularly what was painful was that I had a great problem in keeping a connection with the analyst – say, over a break and even over the weekend. I was going three times a week and by the time Monday came again, it was as if I had to start it all over again. I found it very difficult because I was in a very needy and very childlike dependence on the analyst. And so I felt the break always broke a kind of relationship or whatever it was. I suppose that by the time my third session of the week came, I felt some relief and there *was* something there. I went into a depression nearly every weekend. It was as if it was a true re-creation of childhood, but *only* a re-creation, with no progress beyond that, no significant change.

She got ill for a long period at one stage, and that was *awful* for me, it was really awful. I developed a sort of psychosomatic state: I had palpitations, you know, I felt as if I was going to die. I was very, very dependent on her.

I could feel two levels going on, because I could say on one level that she, in herself, was likeable, but that got caught up in the relationship which I could feel as soon as I went on the couch, as it were – a totally negative thing. I knew it was connected with my mother, it was obvious, she made helpful interpretations about that. But when I remained silent for practically a whole session, which I often did, to me that was totally useless. But I didn't say anything! I think she nodded off a couple of times, I know she did, which, I mean, was to be expected – it was boring for her. But for me it wasn't, because I was full of all sorts of feelings, dreadful angry feelings, inside. What was blocking them was the kind of relationship I had with her and the relationship I obviously had with my mother.

It reached a pitch at one point where I felt I would commit suicide or something, that kind of feeling. It wasn't actually literally like that, because there was enough of my Catholic faith left to say I wouldn't. But I was due for a break to go to Ireland for a couple of weeks' holiday and I dreaded the thought of this coming up because I hadn't been speaking in analysis for long periods – and it was just dreadful and I was getting nowhere, a terrible block. And I couldn't break out of that. So I suddenly started drawing, at home. In a way she didn't go into very much interpreting the drawings, but for me it was a breakthrough because I felt I had broken through a block, and particularly an emotional block in myself even about drawing, because I'd had that even as a child. And this liberated a lot of energy in me and a lot of life, and broke through it. It probably helped the analysis, though it didn't seem part of the analysis in one sense. I would have thought she'd have wanted to say more about the drawings; that was one of the criticisms I would have had later on – I wouldn't have dared criticize her for that then.

The negative feelings never came out – no. No. I couldn't . . . . That was part of my whole problem, that was part of my relationship with my mother – there was no way, all outward communication was blocked off. I think my analyst probably pointed this out, but even pointing it out didn't break it. Probably that was why when it finished, it didn't finish, if you know what I mean. Because I was never able to be angry with her, it still remained as a problem.

I went to her for five years. I decided to go into teaching – that was a big change in my life. The idea of the priesthood had gone completely. And I didn't finish my PhD; partly I hadn't worked enough, but also it was a bigger thing than I realized when I started it. I still have all the material round; whether I'll ever do it I don't know. Teaching was a big decision in my life – I still don't know in a sense where it came from or why I went into it. I feel there were other reasons, deep reasons. I survived the first year in teaching, primary teaching, and being in analysis helped me through it and solved a lot of things for me. Now that was a dreadful year! Horrific! Because I faced everything from my own past. In Ireland it was just dreadful, we had a sadistic teacher who was fearful for me. But yet I felt that I had achieved something in my analysis which I could communicate and I felt it was through teaching children I would communicate it. So obviously I felt I'd gained something.

Sexual problems, too, had evened out in a sense. First of all I'd accepted myself as being homosexual, which was a big thing, particularly because it went against my whole family, whole Catholic background, all that sort of thing; but also I had formed an ongoing relationship, which was a big step in my life. And it enabled me also to kind of bring that down to earth and so it wasn't any longer a kind of compulsive impulse, it was more day-to-day and within an ongoing relationship. That was happening during the time I was in analysis.

The other thing that was happening, you see, that was connected with everything, was that I was writing. I'd started when I was in Dublin – writing in Irish. And when I came to England that was a major thing in giving me a sense of myself and my identity. During the time I was supposed to be studying my Greek I was actually writing and also reading Irish at the British Museum. I loved Irish. My mother understood it, but we didn't speak it at home, it wasn't my native tongue.

So there were a lot of gains from analysis, yes, certainly. The drawings were the great thing, outwardly, that came out of the first analysis. And I could look back and see that it had changed me and enabled me to live in the world around me, which I hadn't been able to. Looking back, I used to feel life was unreal, you know, that I could put my hands through things, that sort of thing. That went. Mind you, some of that might have happened to some extent because I would have had to get a job, I would have had to settle down, but I do feel that the analysis helped me to sort out all the problems. And yet the experience of being in it was terrible, painful. I feel it re-created too closely, without alleviating it – over long periods at any rate – just that initial experience of life.

The depressions didn't go. Now, I'd been depressed, though I didn't know it as depression, since I was a child and used to have continual bouts of this, which would recur and recur and recur. And they were very severe when they happened, but there was no enlightenment in analysis as to what exactly they were. Now that's changed. But the first analysis didn't solve it.

We seemed to agree about the right time to end it and we worked towards that. Though I've been rereading in my notebooks my feelings about it and I certainly hadn't reached a stage of feeling secure in what I'd gained, I know that. And I was too prone to being depressed, which seemed to me to undo the analysis. Because you lose everything when you're depressed. I used to think of that game Snakes and Ladders, and coming down that big snake to the beginning. There's no connection between one depression and the next, you learn nothing from surviving each one – they're isolated, empty, totally blank.

It was about two years after this that I came to feel that I needed more analysis. I had entered a new relationship, and the teaching was difficult and there were the depressions. I contacted my first analyst, but she didn't have any room for further sessions. Then I was referred to someone – actually that was awful! She said she needed to gain some professional satisfaction from her work, so no question! I was hurt, yes. Then I went to the next referral and immediately that began to be positive.

I felt she was a warmer person – I think I was taken by her smile. I mean, it was a small thing, but she actually smiled – now my first analyst was very, very remote. Then in the second analysis I had a choice of whether I'd use a chair or a couch; now, that to me was the big change. It gave me, I suppose, a certain feeling that I was in control to some extent of what went on, that I wasn't in a subservient or passive position. And the other big thing that was different was that she initiated the talking if I didn't. In my first analysis I was a clinic patient, that meant that I had only a nominal fee; it was as though, well, it didn't really matter if I didn't talk, I'm only paying – ten shillings, I think it was. But this time I was paying and I could feel as every minute ticked away that was another fifty pence, sort of thing!

I was living a very positive life, I really felt good. I felt that what I had done in the first analysis was to clear the very, very first period of my life, infanthood really, and I was now in the next stage, childhood and growing up, you know. And yet to the analyst I gave the impression that I wasn't getting anything out of it. I think that's the only way I could be, particularly with women. No, it never occurred to me to ask for a man analyst! I accepted what I was given, it was as if I must be grateful for what I was offered. I didn't know anything about *choosing* analysts, they were like priests or something to me. To me it was as if all analysts were women – that is totally opposite from what I hear from other people I know. But I certainly could only relate negatively to women at any depth. That analysis was very supportive really, but I didn't let on how much I was getting out of it, I kept it to myself. I stayed with her going on six years, though.

We went back to some of the figures in my childhood, such as my teacher and a man who abused me sexually. But also looking at my current life. I was teaching in primary school. I didn't choose secondary teaching because . . . I had no sense of achievement in what I'd done; underneath I felt it was a sham, that I wasn't what I was supposed to be. It was the same with my Irish writing: I had a book published, I won prizes for it, and yet I felt I was a sham. I didn't want people to find out that I couldn't really speak Irish that well or at least compared with people who were native speakers. It all felt false. My real self was somewhere away from . . . it was something that couldn't cope . . . This was connected with depression, because, you know, when the depression comes, everything is chucked, it's gone. You have to start building from square one again. So I suppose you can't lay claim to anything, because you know that it can be taken away so easily through depressions.

It has been painful teaching young children. Because given my natural inclination, I would go into a quiet corner and do nothing or read or listen to music, that sort of thing. That's connected very much with my life at home as a child growing up in a shop. Which was dreadful! And I loathed it, I still loathe it, this position of being behind the counter with the customer coming in . . . Oh! Oh, it was awful, awful. And it is very similar to that being in the classroom. Demands are made on you the whole time – being grabbed, being called for, being demanded. And I've lived with feeling I hated teaching for most of the time I've been in it! And yet I've gone on doing it so far.

Anyway, that was all going on during the time I was in the second analysis. I was going four times a week most of the time – that, too, was a thing that made a very positive development. Because in the first analysis I had this break over the weekend, I felt disconnected each time, bitty, and that corresponded too much to the way depressions come. So during the second analysis she said, 'Well, I think you ought to come an extra day.' I saw her on Saturday mornings and that was really wonderful, really created a great feeling of being connected all the time.

There was one central thing that happened, which wasn't actually connected with analysis but was part of what we talked about, a part of my feelings of depression. My parents both died, within six months of each other. I felt when my father died that my depression came from him and went with him in some way. I didn't realize – you know, with the eyes of childhood you don't – but discussing it, it seems that he was a depressive himself. Now, I didn't think of that. But it was quite obvious when I looked back and saw that I had taken it partly from him. I was very much in fear and awe of him. He was a very forbidding sort of man, didn't encourage us to relate to him and didn't really talk to us; I hardly talked to him ever. So I feel that depression was connected with him, but also that in some way it went with him. It was as if the depression was certainly connected with feelings about my parents' deaths, even *before* it happened.

I mean, certainly when my mother died . . . She died first and I felt, well, the loss is something that I've experienced already. Because all my episodes of depression previous to that were like mourning, were a mourning. She was always, you see . . . The shop came first; it was her life, her being. My experience – not my memory – but my experience through working with it in my first analysis was that I was allowed to cry, was neglected, even though it didn't seem to be. The priorities were the shop first – and then there were the other kids, I mean, there was ten of us living in the house, six children and my grandparents and my parents. And my mother had to cope with all of that.

I feel in teaching I've put myself in my mother's role and that it's time to give it up. Putting myself into a classroom of infants, where I find it difficult to cope anyway because I'm not naturally inclined towards children or towards mothering or towards teaching even – it's like acting out a role I'm not adapted for but must do. But on the other hand I did feel more positive about teaching a unified approach to things, not split up into subjects. I felt that what I had to give was at that level.

That was more or less the trend of the five or six years with her. The same themes kept coming back, which was good, and reinterpreting them all the time – my mother, the teacher, all the figures from childhood and up to adolescence, the teaching, my relationship with her and other significant relationships in my present life as well. My first analysis I left feeling high, it was too inflated in a way; the second ending, I didn't, I felt it was quite right and I felt it had worked. And the big testing thing for me was that I wasn't depressed any more. And I can only say that this is connected with two things, one of them my parents' death, but also . . . in a way it's almost as if I had done my worst to the analysis, by feeling bad about it over that length of time, and yet it didn't come out like that – it was actually very positive. And I had to admit that whatever I did to it, in myself or in the sessions, that it actually was positive. It survived, in a way.

But I don't know if my analyst realized this! I'd kept on nagging at her and saying, 'You know, this is not doing me any good, I'm not getting anywhere' – concealing from her outwardly anything that might show that I was getting something out of it. Maybe if I had been able to have been outwardly angry and really act out all the very destructive feelings which I did have, it wouldn't have taken so long to come to a conclusion in both analyses. Any physical aggression, that would have been unheard of for me, or even to say anything, to be angry outwardly. No, I sulked! It was eleven years of a sulk, really!

And it was only that which eventually . . . it was like saying, 'My God, I've had enough of this! This has gone on too long. I've got my life to live outside, you know, quite independent of all this. I don't need this any more.' And that was the feeling I left with.

If I were to criticize it, I'd say there was something in me which wanted, because of my background maybe . . . the more immaterial side of life. You could say that might have been wrong for me because of the kind of problems I had; I did need something to bring me down to earth, to the bodily side of things. But I did feel a little . . . if I could have expressed it then in analysis, which I obviously didn't, I felt they couldn't understand another side of my life. I think I expected them to be more interested in my dreams – I'd been writing those down even before I went into analysis. And the side of life which had to do with emotions within artistic things seemed a closed book to them too. I used to have very deep, intense experiences with opera and I was writing poetry; all that side. But I think maybe I was partly to blame, because I didn't want to bring it to them because it would get spoiled. I felt very loath to talk about, say, religion. Yes, I do still believe in God, but I suppose differently, more through my experiences within art and music as something, you know, really deeply, deeply fundamental that can be worshipped; but I haven't found the need to take part in, say, Masses and things like that. I certainly don't feel the guilt that there always was about it – I mean, guilt was the permanent condition of my life.

I couldn't say at all that analysis hasn't fundamentally changed me. It certainly was a healing experience, a painful but healing experience. I got more and more insight, and built up a kind of repertoire of insights into my own being, really. There was no great revelation, they happened in a very small piecemeal way all the way through, like a computer, you know, they sort of change the information inside.

The relationship itself, particularly the second one – I felt very contained in it. It might have felt restricting at times, something to rebel against, something to hate, but it was contained; that felt wonderful. It was almost like a celibate set-up, you know, the room was very bare. There was a kind of permanence, and yet slight variations within that which kept a great sense of something ongoing, day after day, year after year; containment within that room and within that relationship. In the first analysis there were breaks and illnesses on her part, but the second one was terribly continuous. There was something very private, removed, not secret but certainly contained in a quiet area. And that in itself I know worked for me. It was like a devotion, like a religious thing, a discipline of being there with somebody in that space for that length of time – it worked. Reliability was the big thing, I mean it must have been so different to anything I had experienced, that that in itself, I think, would have worked for me.

But there was my cruelty . . . I realize I had – particularly directed towards women – a cruel, sadistic side, which was more denying them than actively doing something . . . refusing to give anything. If you give it away to the analyst, you lose it – I felt that all the time, from very early on. I kept lots to myself, lots to myself. Oh, I did tell her at the end how good it had been. I've written the occasional card too. But I think it was a realization of that cruel side of me which enabled me to stop going and to feel I had changed. And, at the same time, losing the depression has been the most wonderful thing. I've felt I was remade and really so fortunate – because I know how awful depression was. Losing it seems to be connected with losing writing and that is in a way sad, but I don't miss it; before, there was a compulsion to write. That depression was the worst thing in my life.

I feel that in a way, in the end, after both these analyses, I feel that the thing that helped me, that worked for me was actually surviving that sort of relationship with two women that to me were powerful women in a powerful position. And yet I survived it; it was as if whatever negative thing that came, I was in the end able to cope with it.

Further Reading

M. Cardinal, *The Words to Say It*, London, Picador, 1984

H. F. Ellenberger, *The Discovery of the Unconscious*, New York, Basic Books, 1970

S. Ferguson, *A Guard Within*, London, Chatto & Windus, 1973

HD, *Tribute to Freud*, London, Carcanet, 1985

N. Herman, *My Kleinian Home*, London, Quartet Books, 1985

J. Malcolm, *Psychoanalysis: The Impossible Profession*, New York, Vintage Books, 1982

T. Moser, *Years of Apprenticeship on the Couch*, New York, Urizen Books, 1977

K. Obholzer, *The Wolf-Man Sixty Years Later*, New York, Continuum, 1982

FOR THE BEST IN PAPERBACKS, LOOK FOR THE

In every corner of the world, on every subject under the sun, Penguin represents quality and variety – the very best in publishing today.

For complete information about books available from Penguin – including Pelicans, Puffins, Peregrines and Penguin Classics – and how to order them, write to us at the appropriate address below. Please note that for copyright reasons the selection of books varies from country to country.

In the United Kingdom: Please write to *Dept E.P., Penguin Books Ltd, Harmondsworth, Middlesex, UB7 0DA*

If you have any difficulty in obtaining a title, please send your order with the correct money, plus ten per cent for postage and packaging, to *PO Box No 11, West Drayton, Middlesex*

In the United States: Please write to *Dept BA, Penguin, 299 Murray Hill Parkway, East Rutherford, New Jersey 07073*

In Canada: Please write to *Penguin Books Canada Ltd, 2801 John Street, Markham, Ontario L3R 1B4*

In Australia: Please write to the *Marketing Department, Penguin Books Australia Ltd, P.O. Box 257, Ringwood, Victoria 3134*

In New Zealand: Please write to the *Marketing Department, Penguin Books (NZ) Ltd, Private Bag, Takapuna, Auckland 9*

In India: Please write to *Penguin Overseas Ltd, 706 Eros Apartments, 56 Nehru Place, New Delhi, 110019*

In Holland: Please write to *Penguin Books Nederland B.V., Postbus 195, NL–1380AD Weesp, Netherlands*

In Germany: Please write to *Penguin Books Ltd, Friedrichstrasse 10–12, D–6000 Frankfurt Main 1, Federal Republic of Germany*

In Spain: Please write to *Longman Penguin España, Calle San Nicolas 15, E–28013 Madrid, Spain*

In France: Please write to *Penguin Books Ltd, 39 Rue de Montmorency, F-75003, Paris, France*

In Japan: Please write to *Longman Penguin Japan Co Ltd, Yamaguchi Building, 2–12–9 Kanda Jimbocho, Chiyoda-Ku, Tokyo 101, Japan*

FOR THE BEST IN PAPERBACKS, LOOK FOR THE 🐧

A CHOICE OF PENGUINS AND PELICANS

The Informed Heart   Bruno Bettelheim

Bettelheim draws on his experience in concentration camps to illuminate the dangers inherent in all mass societies in this profound and moving masterpiece.

God and the New Physics   Paul Davies

Can science, now come of age, offer a surer path to God than religion? This 'very interesting' (*New Scientist*) book suggests it can.

Modernism   Malcolm Bradbury and James McFarlane (eds.)

A brilliant collection of essays dealing with all aspects of literature and culture for the period 1890–1930 – from Apollinaire and Brecht to Yeats and Zola.

Rise to Globalism   Stephen E. Ambrose

A clear, up-to-date and well-researched history of American foreign policy since 1938, Volume 8 of the Pelican History of the United States.

The Waning of the Middle Ages   Johan Huizinga

A magnificent study of life, thought and art in 14th and 15th century France and the Netherlands, long established as a classic.

The Penguin Dictionary of Psychology   Arthur S. Reber

Over 17,000 terms from psychology, psychiatry and related fields are given clear, concise and modern definitions.

FOR THE BEST IN PAPERBACKS, LOOK FOR THE 🐧

A CHOICE OF PENGUINS AND PELICANS

Metamagical Themas   Douglas R. Hofstadter

A new mind-bending bestseller by the author of *Gödel, Escher, Bach*.

The Body   Anthony Smith

A completely updated edition of the well-known book by the author of *The Mind*. The clear and comprehensive text deals with everything from sex to the skeleton, sleep to the senses.

How to Lie with Statistics   Darrell Huff

A classic introduction to the ways statistics can be used to prove *anything*, the book is both informative and 'wildly funny' – *Evening News*

The Penguin Dictionary of Computers   Anthony Chandor and others

An invaluable glossary of over 300 words, from 'aberration' to 'zoom' by way of 'crippled lead-frog tests' and 'output bus drivers'.

The Cosmic Code   Heinz R. Pagels

Tracing the historical development of quantum physics, the author describes the baffling and seemingly lawless world of leptons, hadrons, gluons and quarks and provides a lucid and exciting guide for the layman to the world of infinitesimal particles.

The Blind Watchmaker   Richard Dawkins

'Richard Dawkins has updated evolution' – *The Times* 'An enchantingly witty and persuasive neo-Darwinist attack on the anti-evolutionists, pleasurably intelligible to the scientifically illiterate' – Hermione Lee in Books of the Year, *Observer*

Asimov's New Guide to Science   Isaac Asimov

A fully updated edition of a classic work – far and away the best one-volume survey of all the physical and biological sciences.

Relativity for the Layman   James A. Coleman

Of this book Albert Einstein said: 'Gives a really clear idea of the problem, especially the development of our knowledge concerning the propagation of light and the difficulties which arose from the apparently inevitable introduction of the ether.'

The Double Helix   James D. Watson

Watson's vivid and outspoken account of how he and Crick discovered the structure of DNA (and won themselves a Nobel Prize) – one of the greatest scientific achievements of the century.

Ever Since Darwin   Stephen Jay Gould

'Stephen Gould's writing is elegant, erudite, witty, coherent and forceful' – Richard Dawkins in *Nature*

Mathematical Magic Show   Martin Gardner

A further mind-bending collection of puzzles, games and diversions by the undisputed master of recreational mathematics.

Silent Spring   Rachel Carson

The brilliant book which provided the impetus for the ecological movement – and has retained its supreme power to this day.